Honorable Business

Honorable Business

A Framework for Business
in a Just and Humane Society

JAMES R. OTTESON

OXFORD
UNIVERSITY PRESS

OXFORD
UNIVERSITY PRESS

Oxford University Press is a department of the University of Oxford. It furthers
the University's objective of excellence in research, scholarship, and education
by publishing worldwide. Oxford is a registered trade mark of Oxford University
Press in the UK and certain other countries.

Published in the United States of America by Oxford University Press
198 Madison Avenue, New York, NY 10016, United States of America.

Library of Congress Cataloging-in-Publication
Data Names: Otteson, James R., author.
Title: Honorable business : a framework for business in
a just and humane society / James R. Otteson.
Description: New York, NY : Oxford University Press, [2019] |
Includes bibliographical references and index. Identifiers: LCCN 2018028611|
ISBN 9780190914219 (pbk.) | ISBN 9780190914202 (hardcover) |
ISBN 9780190914226 (updf) | ISBN 9780190914233 (epub)
Subjects: LCSH: Business ethics. | Social responsibility of business.
Classification: LCC HF5387 .O874 2019 | DDC 658.4/08—dc23
LC record available at https://lccn.loc.gov/2018028611

To Katie

CONTENTS

ACKNOWLEDGMENTS

This book had its origins a decade ago when I first taught a course called "Capitalism and Morality" at Yeshiva University in New York. It was thinking about how to frame such a course, especially for such exceptional students as those I had at Yeshiva, that led me to begin thinking seriously about the political, economic, moral, and other institutions that could enable a eudaimonic, or genuinely flourishing, life. I developed several other courses on related topics at Yeshiva, and my students patiently provided an outstanding environment for me to explore and sharpen my ideas. I express my deep gratitude to those students, whom I shall never forget.

When I came to Wake Forest University's School of Business in 2013, I adapted my "Capitalism and Morality" course to the students in and goals of a business school, eventually resulting in a new course called "Why Business?," subtitled "Exploring the Role of Business in a Just and Humane Society." I put together an edited collection of the main readings I used in the course, which Encounter Books published under the title of *What Adam Smith Knew* (2014)—for which I thank Encounter. Over several iterations of the "Why Business?" course, and through many discussions and conversations with my Wake Forest colleagues and students, I further developed the ideas that ultimately came to fruition in this book.[1] I thank my students and colleagues in Wake Forest's School of Business for giving me the opportunity to work on these ideas, as well as Wake Forest's Eudaimonia Institute for its quiet and encouraging space in which to work. I thank Page West, who convinced me to come to Wake Forest; Adam Hyde and Matthew Phillips, who generously taught "Why Business?" with me and, through discussions too numerous to count, helped me develop and refine

---

[1] My "Why Business?" course was awarded a 2017 Aspen Institute "Ideas Worth Teaching" national award. I thank the Aspen Institute for this honor.

my ideas; and John Allison, who has not only provided advice and counsel throughout my time at Wake Forest but whose career has been an example of honorable business.

I have also benefited from numerous other people with whom I have discussed various ideas in this book. They include Rajshree Agarwal, Jonathan Anomaly, Neera Badhwar, Cecil Bohanan, Jason Brennan, Art Carden, Adina Dabu, Douglas J. Den Uyl, Benjamin Graves, Noah Greenfield, Keith Hankins, John Hasnas, Max Hocutt, Rashid Janjua, Jason Jewell, Cathleen Johnson, Ori Kanefsky, Mark LeBar, Deirdre McCloskey, Phillip Muñoz, Andrew Naman, Rob Nash, Maria Pia Paganelli, Douglas B. Rasmussen, Richard Richards, Gregory Robson, William Ruger, Daniel Russell, David Schmidtz, Michelle Steward, Chris Surprenant, Andrew Taylor, John Thrasher, Michelle Vachris, Bas van der Vossen, Page West, Daniel Winchester, and Matthew Wols. I extend my sincere thanks to them all. I thank in particular David Rose, both for the many discussions and for encouraging me to think that these ideas might be worth turning into a book.

I thank also David Pervin of Oxford University Press for his patience and advice and for shepherding this book through to production. Thanks also goes to OUP's two excellent anonymous reviewers of a previous draft of the manuscript. I have silently incorporated many of their suggestions—including regarding the book's title!—and the manuscript is greatly improved for their efforts. I also thank Richard Isomaki for his excellent copyediting of the manuscript. Of course neither they, nor any of the other people I have mentioned, bear responsibility for any remaining errors in this book; only I do.

I would also like to thank my late father, James R. Otteson Sr., and my late father-in-law, Dennis E. LeJeune, both of whom gave me much-needed encouragement and advice, and both of whom showed me what honorable business was. I miss them dearly.

Finally, I thank my family for their love, support, and inspiration throughout. To my beloved Katharine, Victoria, James, Joseph, and George, you were in this, as in all things, my sine qua non.

Honorable Business

Introduction

Many people believe that business activity is morally suspicious. This view is reflected in the common notion that businesses, or businesspeople, should "give back" to society. Note that people say that business should give *back*, not that it should *give*. Typically when someone tells you that you need to give something back, it is because you stole it. Is that what people who think business needs to give back believe—that what it has, it stole? Or perhaps that what businesspeople have they got through fraudulent, exploitive, or other morally dubious ways? Or perhaps that what they have came through special favors, special advantages, or sheer luck, and hence they do not truly deserve what they have or are not really entitled to it?

Are people, then, *right* to be suspicious of business? Perhaps people believe that businesspeople are motivated only to serve their own interests, and because such self-interested behavior is less than virtuous, business itself is therefore less than virtuous. But compare business to medicine. Both are professions. Both have specialties and subspecialties, both require technical knowledge and long training, and in both cases if one is successful, one might make a lot of money. Yet consider: no one says to the medical professional, "Now that you have made your money, you need to *give back* to society." So why do people say that to the business professional? Perhaps it is because people think that while the medical professional aims to help others, the business professional aims only to help himself. That may seem initially plausible, but of course the medical professional does not work for free. The doctor, after all, wants to get paid too—and often handsomely! And business professionals, for their part, frequently give to charitable causes; indeed, almost all businesses do. So why are they viewed so differently?

The recurring stories of business malfeasance do not exactly help business's reputation or people's perceptions of it. We hear stories about Enron and Bernie Madoff, and we think: *I knew it—businesspeople defraud and exploit people to line their own pockets!* Then we hear stories about businesses lobbying for special regulatory favors, government subsidies and bailouts, government protection from

1

competition, legally mandated price ceilings or floors, and sweetheart government contracts and grants; we hear about exploitation of natural resources, pollution, and dumping, the burning of fossil fuels, carbon emissions, and climate change; we hear about unconscionably high prices for life-saving medicines or medical devices; we hear about hedge funds making money by doing things most people do not even understand; we see economic bubbles build and then burst; and we see the stock market rise and fall—with some people seemingly making money all the same. In all this, and more, we think: *There must be something nefarious going on.* Our minds connect the dots. When we look at a big picture and see a set of data points, we instinctively see patterns, and more often than not negative events stick in our minds more than positive.[1] It is easy—indeed, all too easy—for us to conclude: *Business cannot be trusted.*

All of this inclines many of us to think that business is indeed a morally suspicious activity, that it must be carefully watched, regulated, and overseen, and perhaps even that it must take steps to atone for its sins. It must "give back" to society to make up for what it has done, or for exploiting opportunities society has provided for it to enrich itself.

I would like to make a suggestion. If it is true that business is inherently morally suspicious, that in its essence business involves behaviors we reject, or should reject, as morally unacceptable, then the proper response is *not* merely to ask it to give back. In that case, the proper response is instead to *prohibit it altogether.* For, consider: we do not say to the thief, "Go ahead and keep stealing, as long as you give some of what you stole to charity." We do not say to the murderer, "It's all right as long as at least some of the people you murder are bad." Instead, we say to both of them: Stop! Stop stealing, stop killing. If an activity is wrong, we should stop doing it—period. My suggestion, then, is that we should have the courage of our convictions: if, after all due consideration, we conclude that business is indeed inherently morally suspicious, we should stop doing it.

Are we prepared to demand that? I think we should not prohibit business, but I can justify that only if business is not inherently bad, if there is some way of conducting and engaging in business that is in fact inherently valuable. I would need to make the case that although there are bad actors and bad actions in business—as there are in all walks of human life—nevertheless there is a way of conducting business that is honorable and creates genuine value. That indeed is what I hope in this book to convince you of. Indeed, I will argue that the essence of business is the creation of value, that honorable business is the source of the prosperity we enjoy in the world today, and that the only hope people have

---

[1] Neuroscientist Rick Hanson (2013) says that our brains are like "Velcro for the bad" and "Teflon for the good." See also Zak 2014 for how and why our minds see stories in data.

for improving our material conditions in life is with the prosperity created by honorable business. Even more than that, I will argue that honorable business exhibits a deeply moral way to treat individuals. It is driven not by greed, fear, or lying, but by mutual respect. Honorable business is neither morally suspicious nor even merely neutral: it is a positive creator of both material and moral value.

Starting the Argument

How will I make that case? I begin with the premise that prosperity is good and that improving the material conditions of human life is good. Now, is money all that matters in life? No, of course not. But what wealth can do is enable the things that do matter in life. If I am poor, if I am wondering whether I can eat today or whether my children can eat today, I am not thinking about improving society or stewarding the environment or access to higher education or writing my book on the summum bonum of human life or realizing my authentic self. A poor person does not have the luxury to think about such things, however important they are to a life well and fully lived. What wealth can do, then, is begin to address the more immediate and basic needs of human life—food, clothing, shelter—which allows people to turn their attention to other, "higher" things that help complete a fulfilling life. Millennia ago, the ancient Greek philosopher Aristotle (384–322 BC) argued that the ultimate goal of human life is *eudaimonia*, often translated as "happiness"—but "happiness" not in the shallow sense of momentary contentment but in the deep sense of the cognizance that one's life is worthy to have been lived. A eudaimonic life is one that serves not only a purpose but a high purpose; not merely subsisting but flourishing. Generating wealth does not equate to a eudaimonic life, but it can enable one. It can enable the kind of life at the end of which one can look back with justified pride.

So the first premise of my case will be that wealth is a necessary prerequisite to a eudaimonic life. But that implies that we need institutional structures—political institutions and economic policies—that enable wealth production. Thus the second step in the argument is to figure out what those institutions are. I will argue that both theory and empirical evidence suggest that a properly functioning market economy is part of the set of political-economic institutions that enables *growing, generalized prosperity*—prosperity, that is, not only for a few, or for some at the expense of others, but increasingly for everyone (if not to the same degree). Such an economy enables what Edmund Phelps (2013) called "mass flourishing." Moreover, the key to generating that prosperity will turn out to be *honorable business*. Now, I have not yet defined what "honorable business" is, but I can offer an early operational definition: honorable business is business that contributes to growing, generalized prosperity in a properly functioning market economy. How? By *creating value for others*. So the prime directive of business will be the creation of value for others, and honorable business will be the embracing and internalizing of a professional identity as a businessperson who sees her business purpose as the creation of value for others. Dishonorable business, by contrast, will be the seeking to improve one's own condition *at the expense of others*, instead of seeking to improve one's own condition *by improving the condition of others*. Acting in one's self-interest is not inherently immoral or bad; rather, acting in one's self-interest *at others' expense* is immoral and bad. Pursuing one's self-interest by seeking to create value for others is not only acceptable, it is morally praiseworthy. In this way, and in this way only, we get better together. *That* is honorable business.

You may have noticed that I have also not yet defined what a "properly functioning market economy" is. I can give it, too, a functional definition: a *properly functioning market economy* is one that is part of the institutions necessary to sustain a just and humane society. But what is a "just and humane society"? Although all of us might support a just and humane society, we will have differing accounts of what such a society is, and thus we might have different ideas about what the proper market economy would be that would be part of such a society. So I will have to give substantive accounts of both terms. My argument will be that a just and humane society is one in which people have the opportunity to construct eudaimonic lives for themselves, in which people have increasingly many of their basic needs met so that they can turn their attention to the higher purposes that are constitutive of eudaimonia. I will argue that business can and should play a significant role in enabling such lives, both directly, by supplying ever more of the needs people have, and also indirectly, by encouraging proper moral relations among people.

My argument, then, will be that honorable business conducted within the context of a properly functioning market economy is in fact morally praiseworthy. It is not inherently suspicious, and it does not require atonement. Its moral value arises not only because of the benefit it provides to others in creating value for them, but also in the moral respect I will argue it accords to all human beings in virtue of their status as full and free moral agents equal in dignity to all others.

Understanding honorable business in this way will enable us to develop a code of ethics for business. It might surprise one—or, then again, perhaps not—to discover that there is no generally accepted code of ethics for business. Although nearly every business school offers courses in "business ethics," typically such classes offer a review of cases in which businesspeople or firms acted badly or destructively, without developing an overall theory of the purpose of business, including its moral purpose. A preponderance of those writing in the academic field of business ethics seem, in fact, to be suspicious of business. Reading through the literature, one gets the sense that many believe business to be an unseemly and possibly maleficent activity, something that can at any moment loose destruction and misery on the world. Many of the academics who contribute to the field have been trained in philosophy, which is a dual-edged sword: on the one hand, it means their analyses tend to be carefully constructed, sensitive to fine distinctions, and informed by a deep understanding of moral theory; on the other hand, they tend to have had little training in economics and little direct engagement with business itself, and so their conclusions can often ring hollow—not because there is no merit in their arguments but because it is hard to take seriously critics whose perspective has been formed almost entirely externally and from afar. Businesspeople might thus be forgiven for not giving much credence to most writing in business ethics. One can imagine businesspeople thinking: *If you don't know what I actually do, if you don't know why I do what I do, and if you don't know the actual (not theoretical) constraints and challenges I face, why should I listen to your criticisms?* This situation can thus give rise to a mutual suspicion between business ethics academics and the businesspeople whose activities they aim to guide. For the typical business ethics academic, the work is like standing outside a bordello trying to tell the patrons how to behave once they're inside. For the typical businessperson, the academics' work is analogous to an extended criticism of modern medical practice—from Christian Scientists.[2]

In this book, I attempt to construct a view of business ethics that is sensitive both to philosophy and to business, that treats both fields with respect and appreciation for their good-faith contributions, and that therefore can enable a more engaged and fruitful conversation. Business has much to learn from philosophy, and philosophy has much to learn from business. One goal of this book is to discuss business ethics in a way that both groups would accept and recognize as speaking to their central concerns, aims, and purposes—even if they end up disagreeing with my substantive claims.

I will argue that the proper purpose of business, as well as its role in a just and humane society, entails in fact a few rules that all businesspeople should follow regardless of their industry or field. If, as I will argue, the proper purpose of business is to provide value to others, then this conception will help us to navigate the inevitable difficulties that arise in business. Should we pay our employees more? Should we lower our prices? Should we make that deal, partner with that organization, accept those terms, enter that market, accept that offer? I will argue that the code of business ethics we will develop, informed by the ultimate purpose I argue business should serve, can give us guidance when we face these, and innumerable other, hard questions in business. It may not always tell us

---

[2] For a recent example of this, see Conn 2018.

exactly what we should do, but it will often tell us what we should *not* do; and in any case, it will give us parameters within which to make our decisions. Human life is complex and, to a large degree, unpredictable, so no set of principles will mechanically tell us exactly how we should behave in all circumstances. That is why a framework for business ethics should aim to give us principles of behavior, rather than mere (mechanical) rules. But done right, business ethics should enable us to act in good conscience and good faith, confident in the knowledge that, while we will inevitably make mistakes, nevertheless we are doing, or have done, the best we could—both for ourselves and for others—under the conditions of diversity, pluralism, risk, uncertainty, and scarcity that characterize the human condition.

Plan of the Work

A survey of the field of business ethics reveals little consensus about what it is or what it should do. Business ethics classes have no single accepted methodology, have little overlap in content, aims, or structure, and are often idiosyncratic in their materials. Some of this is to be expected: in many fields there is variation in people's ideas about what their introductory or foundational ideas and goals should be, what skills they should impart or technical knowledge they should convey, and what the seminal texts and who the seminal figures are. Still, there is widespread agreement about what should be in an introductory calculus class, for example, as there is in biology, economics, chemistry, and so on. Why not business ethics? One goal of this book is to propose a unifying theme for the field by providing a framework for understanding what it means to be ethical when conducting and engaging in business.

One might then expect that I would begin, as many other works discussing business ethics do, by laying out the contours of major ethical theories—deontology, utilitarianism, virtue ethics, and so on—and then proceeding to show how those theories would adjudicate dilemmas that arise, or have arisen, in business. There is value in understanding what those theories of morality hold; yet this book nevertheless proceeds in another way.[3] We instead begin with what should be the goal of business and then work backward from that goal to determine how one should behave to achieve that goal. Thus the argument of this book is based on a hypothetical argument: If we assume that x is the goal of business, then how should we behave, and what institutions should we have that enable us, to achieve x? The argument will indicate not only the proper behavior

---

[3] See Hasnas 2013.

of individual businesspersons, but also the political and economic institutions, as well as the cultural and social norms, required to support and encourage such behavior.

Thus this book is not a textbook for business ethics, and, although it will discuss numerous particular examples, it is not a set of case studies. It is meant instead to be a prolegomenon to such a textbook—that is, it aims to set out the foundational principles that a textbook could presume and then illustrate, build upon, and apply. Writing such a textbook would be the next step in my larger project, but this book is instead closer to an extended thought experiment, working out the logic of what business, and businesspeople, should do—and not do—given the goal they should have.

The book's first chapter addresses the central importance of asking the *why* of everything we propose to do, not only the *how*. This is as true in business as in any other walks of life. The necessity of asking "Why?" issues from the fact that human beings are essentially *purposive* creatures, that is, creatures who create and pursue ends, goals, and purposes. The final or ultimate goal of human life is, as Aristotle argued, eudaimonia—"happiness," "well-being," or "flourishing." If that is our ultimate end, then all our activities will have to be deliberately ordered to help us achieve it. That includes business and the political and economic institutions in which business operates. I argue that business should contribute to and reflect our pursuit of eudaimonia. Chapter 1 closes with a list of questions that this conception of human purposiveness suggests remain to be investigated, which will point the path forward for the rest of the book.

The second chapter investigates the explanation Adam Smith gave in his justly famous 1776 book *The Wealth of Nations* for why some places are wealthier than others. We discuss the conception of "justice," as opposed to "beneficence," that Smith offered in his earlier, 1759, book *The Theory of Moral Sentiments*, as well as Smith's economizer, local knowledge, and invisible hand arguments from his *Wealth of Nations* that form the basis of his political economy. We look at the duties of government implied by Smithian political economy, including both what he argues government should do and what it should not do. We also look at some empirical evidence to answer the question of whether Smith's predictions on behalf of his recommendations have come true in the intervening centuries. (Hint: Smith was remarkably prescient.)

Chapter 3 argues that the purpose of business is to create value. It then proposes a code of business ethics that will capture the duties of the individual businessperson, as well as articulate a conception of honorable business that allows business to achieve its main purpose of the creation of value. This code enables the individual to navigate the dilemmas that inevitably arise in business, which are in important respects not dissimilar to dilemmas that arise in other walks of human life. It also allows us to offer a conception of professionalism that connects to business's purpose.

Chapter 4 raises the question of how markets and morality go together, and how our conception of honorable business might deal with some of the leading objections critics have raised to markets and business. We look at and offer initial responses to several worries, including inequality, unfairness, externalities, low worker pay and price gouging, manipulation of consumer choice, and profiteering.

The fifth chapter completes the argument of honorable business and the moral purpose of business by specifying a "hierarchy of moral value" linking the individual businessperson's activities to the purpose of a firm within a properly functioning market economy that is a part of a just and humane society. If we have done so correctly, the individual businessperson should be able to give an account of his daily professional activities that connects them all the way up the chain of moral purpose to the kind of society in which we all want to live. This chapter also looks at the unprecedented increase in material prosperity that the world has experienced since approximately 1800 and connects that prosperity to the hierarchy of moral value I defend. I also explore the extent to which our argument connects to the main historical ethical theories of deontology, utilitarianism, and virtue ethics.

The sixth chapter looks at several obstacles businesses face in the achievement of their proper goal. These include Karl Marx's notions of "alienation," lying, and exploitation; and asymmetries of knowledge and so-called rational ignorance. This chapter outlines how businesses should deal with such worries and address them in good faith. It will also articulate a claim about the proper scope of business's moral obligations, which will go some way toward helping businesses focus not only on what they can do but on what they should do.

The seventh and eighth chapters look more carefully at a series of worries people have about, and objections people raise to, markets and business more generally. These include the inequality to which markets can lead, the seeming unfairness of some of the outcomes of business activity, the instability and displacement inherent in the "creative destruction" (in Joseph Schumpeter's famous phrase) of markets, commodification, and exploitation of natural resources. We also explore the proper regulatory role of government in markets.

The ninth and final chapter brings the threads of the previous chapters together to develop a picture of honorable business. It will first argue that there is such a thing as honorable business, and it will articulate its core elements. It will also describe what dishonorable business is. The argument will suggest that honorable business not only provides material prosperity but also enables and encourages proper moral relations among people, relations based on the mutual respect that our inherent dignity requires. Seen in the proper light, this conception of honorable business could actually be a moral calling.

What Kind of Book Is This?

Let me conclude this introduction with a note about the nature of this book and its intended audience. The reader will soon observe that this book spends considerable time discussing historical figures like Aristotle and Adam Smith, that its argument is informed by philosophical considerations, and that much of it proceeds at a fairly high level of analysis instead of focusing on specific examples of businesses or business cases. In these ways, this book differs from much of the writing about business ethics one can find elsewhere.

Given that, a few words are required about why this book would be constructed in this way. I return to this question several times throughout the book, but let me here indicate what I take to be some of the benefits of the conception of honorable business I will defend in this book. First, for business professors and students, it can give a coherent meaning and purpose not only for what business ethics classes should be about but also for why people should go into business in the first place. Done honorably, business creates value and conduces, ultimately, to a just and humane society. In its own distinctive way, honorable business can contribute to generating the benefit—creating the value—that can enable eudaimonic lives. That is a purpose that means something and that can and should inspire business students.

This conception of honorable business also focuses the attention of not just business students but businesspeople on the central ethical mandate that one is entitled to find ways to improve one's own situation—but only if at the same time one improves the situation of others. Value creation must be, and in its essence is, mutual. So when a businessperson is confronted with a dilemma, the first question should be: would this create value for *both* of us? If the answer is no, then one should not do it, even if one could oneself benefit; if the answer is yes, then it is a possibility one should explore.

This conception of honorable business will also provide a way to understand why wealth has increased so spectacularly worldwide over the last couple of centuries—my answer: because more and more people engaged in more and more honorable business and declined to engage in dishonorable business—and connects that explanation to today's businessperson's daily activities. In this way we can link the activities of the businessperson to the highest social aims of society and the highest personal aims of individual eudaimonia. The honorable businessperson adopts a professional code that requires all her actions to be in the service of these high and noble ends. And because her professional activities all proceed on the requirement of mutuality, of respecting each party's "opt-out option" or the right to say "No, thank you" and go elsewhere if he chooses, then this conception of business has the considerable additional benefit of encouraging *proper moral relations among people*: we must respect others and their choices even when we do not agree with their choices. This respects their dignity as equal moral agents to us, at the same time that it provides the prosperity to allow more people to construct for themselves lives of meaning and purpose. That is the creation of real value, both economic and moral, and it is the essence of honorable business. In this way, honorable business might be not only a *profession*, but a *vocation*; not only an *activity*, but indeed perhaps a *moral calling*.

This book is intended, then, for business ethics professors and students, and also for business professionals or prospective business professionals. The historical and philosophical content of the book reflects my belief that in order to make credible decisions about what one ought to do in business one must have a sense of the larger political and moral context in which those decisions are made. That requires philosophical reasoning, and—perhaps betraying my own training as a historian of philosophy—I believe it also requires an examination of the great political economists whose ideas have formed the basis of our institutions and whose arguments and objections continue to inform our thinking today. To have confidence in the concrete decisions we make, we need to be able to advert to a conception of the proper aims and goals we should have, which itself depends on understanding their proper political, moral, and cultural contexts. So we start with the higher-level analysis of what that context and those goals should be and then proceed from there to see how they apply to the actual circumstances in which we find ourselves.

One might object that it does not help a baseball player who wants to catch a fly ball to give him a lecture about Newton's laws of motion. One does not need to be a physicist to be a baseball player.[4] True enough. But business activity is not only, or should not only, be about how to accomplish one's own immediate goals. Business forms a large part of our social and institutional order, and it has been the subject of a large discussion about the propriety of its aims and purposes and about the means it has availed itself of to accomplish those aims and purposes. That means that ethical concerns are an integral part of business activity. Business decisions are not made in a moral vacuum; they have moral implications, even if we were to pretend not to notice or be concerned about them. So although one might not literally ask the highest-level questions each time one makes a business decision, I believe we do need to understand what these highest-level questions are and to have developed an understanding of

---

[4] I thank Jason Brennan for articulating this worry.

how our daily activities can connect to and be informed by them. This enables us to have confidence in our practical reasoning, and it can provide parameters within which our day-to-day decisions can and should be made.

Thus this book is not intended to be the final word on these issues, but only the first word (or first many words). It lays out the foundational principles that should, or so I believe, frame the discussion of more concrete examples. In this way I hope it can help put business ethics professors in a position to hit the ground running, as it were, in their courses, by articulating an economic and moral framework for understanding what honorable business is, and then allowing professors to show how this framework applies—or fails to apply—to specific issues they will cover in their classes. This further explains why so much time is spent laying out and exploring the "philosophical" aspects of business ethics, and comparatively less time and space applying the principles to specific cases. Professors who teach business ethics will doubtless have their own ideas about specific cases that students should consider; the goal here is rather to provide a framework to think about cases than to limit the cases discussed.

This book is also intended, however, for people who are not business students and who do not teach business ethics, but whose lives are affected by the practice of business. Suppose you are a humanities student or professor, or someone who has not yet had the opportunity to study the nature of markets and business but is concerned about whether they are or can be conducted honorably. Chances are that your life is connected in some way or other to business, and so perhaps you wonder what arguments there are on behalf of markets and business and how they can respond to recurring objections and worries, some of which you might share. In that case, an exploration of what might constitute honorable business, how it might create value in the world, and how it might address enduring worries might interest you as well.

A relatively small but growing field of study at colleges and universities is philosophy, politics, and economics, or PPE. The motivation behind combining these fields is the belief that if one wants to develop informed opinions on what kinds of political-economic institutions, laws, and regulations we should have, one has to be able to assess competing claims and proposals by drawing on the tools of all of these disciplines. The argument of this book draws on a similar PPE-style reasoning, but it applies its own version of this reasoning specifically to the practice of business. The argument of the book will be that there is such a thing as honorable business, as well as dishonorable business, and that knowing the difference—and understanding why the difference is what it is—not only is required for making good business decisions but is a necessary part of developing a conception of business's proper place in a just and humane society. To accomplish that, we will have to draw on philosophy, politics, and economics, as well as a bit of history and psychology. The hope is that this will enable us to be not only better businesspeople but better citizens.

1

The Purpose of Business

Introduction

When considering embarking on any project, the most important question to be answered first is "Why?" *How* to do it, which of course is vitally important as well, should be answered only after we have some understanding of the purpose the project serves. But the "Why?" question actually has several facets. We need to know the purpose of the project itself, but we also need to know what *our* purposes are. More specifically, we need to know what our values in life are, including our moral values, and how they rank in importance to us. This can give us a proper ranking or hierarchy of purpose: once we know what is most important, what is second most important, and so on, we can then begin to organize our lives so that we give ourselves the best chance to achieve our values according to their order of importance. At that point we can assess whatever the project is we are considering: Does it fit with our overall hierarchy of value? If so, then we can integrate it into the schedule of purposes that organizes our daily activities.

As important as asking "Why?" is, this is easier said than done. Consider all the values you might have in life: love, friendship, and family; virtue, esteem, and status; money and work; liberty, peace, and security; benefiting others, serving your community, and pursuing your passions; and even things like paying your bills, traveling, and getting (or staying) fit. We also, if we are to be honest, often have less admirable values—things like getting even with someone who wronged us, knocking others down a peg or two, and so on. And we will have innumerable other ends that are peculiar to our own individual lives and stations, to our own goals and ambitions. Trying to specify a rank ordering of these values, ends, and goals is extremely difficult, not least because many of them change over time. The ancient Greek philosopher Aristotle (384–322 BC) argued that a *rationally ordered moral life* is one that (1) has a schedule of value that is both consistent and morally justifiable, and (2) organizes all its activities in terms of this schedule.[1] Aristotle thought that human beings, alone among creatures on earth, have a capacity of reason that enables them not only to delib-erate about and choose their ends in life but also to construct a plan for achieving their ends. We act *rationally* if our activities in fact lead us toward accomplishing our goals, *irrationally* if our activities take us away from our goals. This means we need to have near-term, or proximate, goals, things we wish to accomplish today; intermediate goals, things we wish to accomplish this week, month, or year; long-term goals, things we wish to accomplish in five, ten, or twenty years; and, finally, an ultimate goal, the final thing for the sake of which we did every-thing else. If we integrate all of this properly, according to Aristotle, we have a rationally ordered life.

There is one more step, however. If we have a rationally ordered life, how do we know if it is a rationally ordered *moral* life? This kind of life, which is what Aristotle thought all humans should seek, depends on whether the goals we seek are not just internally consistent but also moral. In particular, is the final, ulti-mate goal we seek, the end that orders all the others, one that is itself morally worthy? Aristotle offered this as his suggestion of the proper ultimate end of human existence: *eudaimonia.* That word is hard to translate, so the Greek word has been adopted whole in English. It is often rendered as "happiness," but we must be careful: by "happiness" people often mean something like contentment or pleasure. By contrast, eudaimonia results from a life well and fully lived. As an ultimate end, it would be the goal of being able, at the end of one's life, to look back on what one did and conclude that that was a life *worth* having been lived; a life that used all of one's skills, abilities, and opportunities to serve ends that one believes were genuinely worthy. But eudaimonia also functions to inform our proximate and intermediate ends. It is not a momentary or passing state of pleasure; indeed, it can often require sacrifice and pain—which is one reason it can be misleading to translate it as "happiness." Think of it instead as dedicating one's limited resources of time, talent, and treasure to purposes that are challeng-ing yet inspiring—taking on the hard tasks that, if you accomplish them, you can have justifiable pride in what you have done.

In the course of our lives, as we make decisions and take actions, we can develop, according to Aristotle, *phronesis*, or practical judgment.[2] This is a crucial aspect of human nature. We develop judgment about what actions, behaviors, and choices are likely to contribute to our goals, and which not; and we develop judgment about the goals themselves—when we need to revise them, reorder them, or, sometimes, abandon some of them altogether. But judgment does

---

[1] See Aristotle 2000. See also Hartman 2008.
[2] See Russell 2009.

not operate by mechanical rules. There is no formula, no manual or handbook, that you can consult to know whether you should do this now or not. You need instead to think about all the particular features of your circumstances, including your schedules of value and purpose, and apply good judgment. But how does judgment become *good* judgment? On the Aristotelian view, two things are required: autonomy and accountability. We need, first of all, the liberty to make decisions for ourselves. If others are making decisions for us, we do not exercise our own judgment. But judgment is a skill. Like other skills—playing the piano, driving a car in traffic, public speaking, shooting a free throw, and so on—it requires practice. Lots of practice. That is why we need "autonomy": to develop our judgment, we have to use it, and to use it we must therefore have the liberty to make decisions for ourselves.

But autonomy is only one side of the equation: we also need accountability. This means we must get feedback from our decisions, and this feedback must have some purchase on us—it must please us when it is good feedback, and it must pain us when it is bad. There is no other way to develop good judgment. Think of learning to play the piano. If your teacher never gave you feedback, you would not know whether you had done well—so you would not know what you needed to do to improve. The other part of developing good judgment is, therefore, *accountability,* which is being held responsible for what you do, and being willing to accept the consequences, good or bad, of your decisions. When you receive good feedback from having chosen well, you get positive reinforcement, which gives you an incentive to do more of that. When you receive bad feedback from having chosen poorly, you get negative reinforcement, which encourages you not to do that again. As we have over the course of our lifetimes thousands of experiences like this, about both small and large decisions we make, we gradually improve our judgment. And as our judgment gets better and better, we stand an ever better chance of figuring out a proper path to a eudaimonic life.

Business and Purpose

What does all this have to do with business ethics? And why should a business-person today care about what an ancient Greek philosopher said? Fair questions.[3] The first answer is that Aristotle was right about eudaimonia.[4] More particularly, Aristotle was right about the crucial necessity of having and understanding a

---

[3] For a classic statement of the worry that philosophy has little to say to businesspeople, which constitutes, by implication, a criticism of the approach in this book, see Stark 1993.

[4] See Otteson 2006; LeBar 2013; Badhwar 2014; Mansfield 2016; and Den Uyl and Rasmussen 2017.

hierarchy of purpose to leading a virtuous life—including in business. But I would like to make a further suggestion that I believe could provide a framework within which business ethics might find some coherence and even some applicability to actual business decision-making, but without either alienating businesspeople or endangering the value that business can provide.

When internal problems arise in any organization, often they are related to a confusion or a disagreement about what the purpose and mission of the organization is. A successful organization is one that starts with a clear conception of its purpose, and an embracing by all its members of this purpose and the mission it entails. This is true not only for clubs, groups, and firms, but also for professions. And business is a profession. Many other professions, like law and medicine, for example, have statements of purpose and codes of ethics. Business does not, which is part of the problem. It is a problem not only because it might give critics a prima facie reason to distrust business (how, one might ask, could we expect businesspeople to behave ethically if they have no ethical code?) but also because business students—future businesspeople—receive little guidance about what constitutes ethical behavior in business.

In order to know what it means to be a professional, and what constitutes professional conduct, we have to know what the purpose is of the activity we are engaging in. And to be worthy of engagement, that activity's purpose must itself be worthwhile. Once we have a purpose, a purpose that is worthwhile, we can set that as our goal; we can then reverse-engineer our activities so that what we do on a daily basis conduces toward achieving that worthy goal. Recall what we said about how to construct a rationally ordered moral life for an individual, regardless of one's profession. There should be a hierarchy of purpose: our daily activities serve proximate goals, those goals serve intermediate goals, and those intermediate goals themselves serve ultimate goals. For Aristotle, the ultimate goal is eudaimonia. The Aristotelian idea is that once one has figured out what eudaimonia would constitute for one, one then works backward to see what are the intermediate and then proximate goals one should strive to attain, and then one orders one's daily activities so that they stand a chance of serving the goals all the way up to eudaimonia.

Now apply this reasoning to business. Here too there should be a hierarchy of moral purpose. The ultimate goal of business in general should be understood in the context of the social institutions that conduce to the kind of society we all should endorse. Once we understand what kind of society that is, this should provide guidelines for specific economic and political institutions, which in turn should set guidelines for industries and firms, which itself should set guidelines for the behavior of individual businesspeople. If the ultimate goal for an individual is eudaimonia, what should be the goal of society? I will argue for something I hope is uncontroversial: a *just and humane society*. A just and humane society will depend on specific political, economic, cultural, moral, and other institutions. Included among those institutions, I will argue, is a *properly functioning market economy*. What makes a market economy "properly functioning"? Among other things, it not only enables but encourages business activity that is consistent with, and indeed contributes to, a just and humane society. Business is only one aspect of human society, so it cannot be expected to achieve all things;[5] but its nature and its essential activity provides the key to understanding in what way it can contribute to a just and humane society. And what is that nature and essential activity? Business is creation and exchange with the purpose of generating benefit. Put differently, its purpose is the *creation of value*. If business's purpose is to create value, then it will have to engage in activities that benefit all parties to its activities, which means that its activity must be limited to creation and exchange that is positive-sum. And that means that each individual businessperson must, in his professional capacity, engage only in transactions that are mutually beneficial. There are indefinitely many ways that value can be created, which means that there is an open frontier of possibility for businesspeople, but it is constrained by the requirement that its activity creates value for all parties to its exchanges. Because we usually do not know in advance what business activities will actually constitute the creation of value, the test we apply is this: do others wish to voluntarily engage in exchange with us? If they do, that suggests that our activity is valuable not only to us but to them as well. And that implies that our activity is indeed creating value.

I suggest we call such value-creating business activity "honorable business." The honorable businessperson engages only in exchanges that create value, that are mutually voluntary and thus mutually beneficial, and that thus generate prosperity that conduces to a just and humane society. Dishonorable business, by contrast, is activity that does not create value, or that benefits one person or group at the expense of another.

This hierarchy of moral value in business leaves considerable latitude for creativity and entrepreneurship and does not presume to know in advance (and thus limit in advance) in what activities creative people may decide to engage. But it does give parameters that limit and channel that creative entrepreneurship to mutually voluntary, mutually beneficial creation of value. And it provides another test: if others do not voluntarily wish to engage, transact, or partner with you, you should reconsider what you are doing—because you and your interests are not all that matter; other people, and their interests, matter too.

---

[5] Van der Vossen 2015 makes a similar point in the context of justice and academic professionalism.

Whatever walk of life you go into, you will deal with business. Whether you work for a company (or many different companies over your lifetime), whether you start your own company (or companies), whether you go into the nonprofit or charitable world, or into education or government—in any of these activities you will be dealing in one way or another with business. That means that you will have to figure out how your business activity, or business-related activity, fits into your rationally ordered moral life, just as you would any other activity in which you engage. Business is a part of our lives—indeed, a very large part—so if we want to lead a life worth living, we have to figure out what role business should play in it.

All of this means that we need to understand what the purpose of business is. What is—or, perhaps, what *should* be—the purpose of business? Before we can address this question, a bit more background is required.

Most discussions of what is called "business ethics" proceed by first laying out several competing theories of ethics—like utilitarianism and deontology—and then using them to adjudicate specific cases of difficult business decisions. Utilitarianism is a species of a larger category of moral theory called "consequentialism." Consequentialist moral theories suggest that we should try to imagine the likely consequences of an action or decision we are considering, and ask whether they are on balance good or bad. Utilitarianism specifically asks us to look at the utility—variously defined as benefit, pleasure, or preference-satisfaction—likely to be gained; to estimate the disutility—cost, pain, or preference-sacrifice—likely to be required; to compare the two, subtracting the disutility from the utility; and, finally, to do whatever leads to the greatest net increase in utility. By contrast, rather than looking at likely consequences of our actions or decisions, deontology asks us to consult the relevant rules and see whether what we are considering is consistent with them, forbidden by them, or required by them. What are the relevant rules? Here different deontological theories differ, but an example is the Ten Commandments. They are not the Ten Suggestions. They do not ask us to consider whether, say, a particular act of theft might lead to an overall increase in utility; they say instead, "Thou shalt not steal"—regardless of the consequences.

Once laying out the various aspects of these, and perhaps other, moral theories, many business ethics books and courses then present readers or students with a series of examples, hypotheticals, and actual cases, and ask: "What would a utilitarian do?" and "What would a deontologist do?" This can be a useful exercise, but the thoughtful reader or student inevitably asks: "Now that we know what such theories would tell us to do, which should we follow?" This is a hard question, maybe *the* hard question, but a survey of business ethics books, textbooks, and course syllabuses reveals little consensus. Note, moreover, that the question of what a business is for—what its purpose is—is either absent from the conversation or only vaguely implied, leaving it to the reader or student to figure out. This can lead to both confusion and uncertainty regarding not only the ultimate value of this exercise but also its applicability to the actual situations businesspeople, or future businesspeople, are likely to face. We might all agree that what Enron and Bernie Madoff did was bad, and, after learning about utilitarianism and deontology, we might be able to explain why what they did would be condemned on either theory. But for the day-to-day decisions businesspeople make (Should I take this job, or that one? Should I hire this person or fire that one? Should I increase our company's health benefits or pay higher salaries? Should I partner with this person or this company, or not?), it is not clear how the exercises in many business ethics books and courses can provide concrete guidance.

I suggest that a better way to proceed is to take Aristotle's advice and first ask what the proper purposes are that we should serve. Once we have even a rough understanding of that, we can then look at the various business-related decisions we will have to make and see how they might, or might not, serve those purposes. Proceeding in this way can give us guidance as we think through the difficult business decisions we will inevitably face.

The Hierarchy of Moral Value

Business activity takes place within a complex set of social institutions. To understand its purpose, we must also understand its proper context. If the Aristotelian logic of a "rationally ordered moral life" holds water, then this proper context must link the daily activities of the individual businessperson all the way up to the highest-level social institutions. And if my argument so far has been sound, then this "hierarchy" must also comport with the moral values we hold dear.

Here is the structure of such a hierarchy, which I argue outlines the proper context of business and will provide its proper place in a defensible and worthy hierarchy of moral value. We start from the highest-level, or most general, ends and work our way down to the lower-level, or more specific, ends:

1. We want a *just and humane society*.
2. A just and humane society depends on a variety of *social institutions*, including political, economic, moral, cultural, and civic institutions.
3. Included in those required social institutions is a *properly functioning market economy*.
4. A properly functioning market economy requires *honorable business*.
5. Honorable business includes industries, firms, and individual businesspeople *creating value*.

Each of these steps requires elaboration and justification. Let us take them in turn.

A Just and Humane Society

Wherever we fall on the political or economic spectrums, all of us would, or perhaps should, endorse the high-level goal, and endorse it as a high-level value, to have a just and humane society. The devil, of course, is in the details: what exactly do we mean by "just and humane"? We will flesh this out more thoroughly throughout the course of this book, but let us begin by stating an important qualification. The goal of a just and humane society is offered here not as the ultimate end of any individual human being's life. According to Aristotle, that should be eudaimonia. Rather, it is offered here as the ultimate or highest *social* goal. So we are distinguishing between personal or private goals, on the one hand, and public or social goals, on the other. In a truly eudaimonic life, of course, the two will have to be linked—indeed, integrated. But for our purposes here, let us focus on the social goal. Offering a just and humane society as the highest social goal indicates that, whatever our personal or private goals, our highest public commitment is to a social order whose institutions are just and treat people humanely.

So what does it mean to treat people humanely, and what are the institutions we would regard as just? At the highest level, we want to have a society that is peaceful and prosperous, in which people are able to construct for themselves lives of meaning and purpose, and in which people are treated, both by other people and by their public institutions, with dignity and respect. We will have differing ideas about the specifics regarding all of those elements, but for the moment I propose to assume that, at least at this level of generality, substantially all of us wish to have such a society.

Social Institutions

To count as a society, as opposed to a mere collection of individuals, a community has to have public institutions; to be part of a morally praiseworthy society, these institutions must be a function of the kind of society we wish to have. The institutions set the parameters within which people in our community can live, work, associate, and prosper. But why have a society, so defined, at all—as opposed to merely living as collections of individuals? Here too we can draw on Aristotle. Aristotle argued that the first unit of society is the family, which, he says, "is the partnership constituted by nature for the needs of daily life" (2013, 36). The next unit is the village: "The first partnership arising from the union of several households and for the sake of nondaily needs is the village" (2013, 36). The next, and for Aristotle the final, unit is the state: "The partnership arising from the union of several villages that is complete is the city. It reaches a level of full self-sufficiency, so to speak; and while coming into being for the sake of living, it exists for the sake of living well" (2013, 36–37). Note that Aristotle claims that the purpose of creating the state is to enable "living well." This gives us a way to understand why we want larger systems of organization and what their purpose is.

Human beings on their own are relatively powerless. We do not have fur, claws, or wings, as other animals do, to help us get what we want. Instead we have, as Adam Smith (1723–1790) put it, "the faculties of reason and speech."[6] This means that in order to achieve our goals—from the humble, like eating today, to the lofty, like leading a good life—we need to rely on the assistance of other human beings. Humans therefore create associations of interdependent cooperation. And the more human beings with whom we can cooperate, the better. Because people are different, they have different skills and abilities; thus the more of them with whom we can cooperate, the more their differing skills and abilities can complement one another and the more of our ends we can mutually and jointly serve. A society, then, is a large-scale cooperative enterprise whose public institutions enable people to satisfy their disparate ends.[7] These institutions include political and economic institutions, private and civic institutions, as well as a shared conception of the reasonableness of the institutions themselves.[8] The last criterion is important because if people do not believe in their society's institutions, or do not believe they actually serve their intended purpose of allowing and encouraging cooperative association, their support for the institutions will wane—with the result that the institutions themselves will lose their power and hence effectiveness. The institutions, then, must reflect moral values that a broad range of citizens endorse and see as worthy of protection. To connect this reasoning to my specific argument, these institutions must be, and must be seen as, conducive to a just and humane society.

A Properly Functioning Market Economy

I suspect the previous two steps in the construction of our hierarchy of moral value are relatively uncontroversial. This third, step, however, is controversial. Before defending it, let me emphasize that a "properly functioning market

---

[6] Smith (1776) 1981, 25. Hereafter, this work is referred to as "WN."

[7] John Rawls defines society similarly: "a mutually advantageous cooperative venture" (1971, 112).

[8] See Gaus 2012.

economy" is only one member of a large set of institutions that support a just and humane society. It does not take the place of families, civic institutions, or political institutions that are also necessary. I also do not suggest that the conventions and protocols of a market economy should inform other areas of life. Things like private property rights, competition, and negotiation would not be appropriate within a family, for example. (Just imagine: "I'd like to sit on the couch. What would you take to let me do so?" That would be a disaster.) Instead, the appropriate conventions of a market economy hold principally when dealing with strangers—as people cooperating, or proposing to cooperate, in a market typically are—and when dealing with goods and services that people might buy, sell, or trade.

Given those qualifications, I offer two main reasons to support my claim that a "properly functioning market economy" is part—just one part, though an important one—of the institutions enabling a just and humane society. First, market economies are the only systems of economics we have ever discovered that enable increasing, general prosperity—what Edmund Phelps (2013) calls "mass flourishing." We will look at evidence supporting this claim, as well as the logic behind it, later, but for people who have been studying the historical creation of wealth in the world, the case now seems clear: no other system that has been tried, through many experiments over many centuries, has come close to the levels of wealth and prosperity enabled by market economies. Importantly, this wealth has accrued most substantially to the poorest segments of society. Throughout human history, pharaohs, emperors, kings, and lords have been able to arrogate to themselves wealth that their fellow community members could only dream of; by contrast, it is only with the advent of markets—beginning slowly in the sixteenth and seventeenth centuries, gaining steam in the eighteenth century, and then exploding in the nineteenth, twentieth, and twenty-first centuries—that the prosperity of the least among us has improved. And today it is at historically unprecedented levels. So the first reason I offer for why a market economy is part of the institutions that constitute a just and humane society is that it enables the poor to rise out of poverty.

The second reason is that it gives the historically disfavored groups—those at the lower ends of social classes—a dignity that is befitting a human being. In the phrase "properly functioning market economy," the word "properly" is obviously doing a lot of work. What does it mean? It has, in fact, several components, but the one relevant here is that a market economy is functioning properly if it allows everyone—including the least among us—what I call an "opt-out option." If you have something I desire, anything from your love and affection to your labor to your possessions, there are two broad ways I might get it from you. The first is to simply take it from you. I might enslave you; I might kill you or steal from you; or I might defraud you, promising to pay you but then absconding without payment. Historically, these, or some combination of them, have been the preferred ways human beings have gotten what they wanted. Think of the Egyptian pharaohs and their pyramids. How did they build those pyramids? Answer: slavery. Think of the Roman Empire and its Coliseum, its roads and aqueducts, and its vast territory. How did it get all of that? Answer: conquest, theft, and slavery. Similarly with almost all "great" civilizations in human history. Using the terminology of Acemoglu and Robinson (2012), we can call these methods "extraction." Their central defining features are (1) they involve involuntary exchange—the victims of conquest, theft, and slavery did not consent—and (2) they are "zero-sum"—they do not produce new or more wealth, they merely move wealth from one place to another. Thus they do not create genuine prosperity. If I steal your iPhone from you, certainly I benefit, but at your expense. "Plus one iPhone" for me, "minus one iPhone" for you: +1 plus –1 equals zero. Hence the term "zero-sum."

But there is another way one might get what one wants from another person: make an offer that the other may freely accept. This is what characterizes the vast majority of transactions in much of the world today. You go into Starbucks and order a double pumpkin spice mocha latte; the barista says that will be $5. You hand over the $5; the barista hands over your drink. Now, which of you benefited from that exchange? Answer: you both did! If you did not benefit—if you did not think the drink was worth the $5—you would have said, "No, thank you" and gone elsewhere. Similarly, if Starbucks did not benefit from that exchange, it would not have agreed to it either. The fact that you both voluntarily agreed means you both benefited. That means that the exchange was "positive-sum." "Plus one drink" for you, "plus $5 for Starbucks": a *positive* plus a *positive* equals a *positive*. Hence the term "positive sum." We can call such transactions "cooperation." The central defining features of cooperative exchanges are the mirror images of those characterizing extractive exchanges: (1) they are voluntary—neither of you coerced the other; and (2) they lead to mutual benefit that is positive-sum. The more such cooperative exchanges take place in a given community, the more benefit its members will enjoy—and the more prosperous the overall community will be.

Now relate this to a "properly functioning market economy" and the dignity I claimed it represents. A market economy allows and encourages cooperative exchanges, and it disallows extractive exchanges. That means that for any of its members to get something they want, they will have to make offers to other members. Moreover, each of its members will, and must, enjoy the right to say, "No, thank you" to any offer—the opt-out option I mentioned earlier. We can now make a general claim: if every member of your society has an opt-out option, and if everyone in your society must respect everyone else's decision when they say, "No, thank you," then each of us must respect the choices each other makes. But to respect others' choices, even when we disagree with their choices and even when we think they are making a mistake, just is to treat them with the dignity that being a full moral agent requires. As Milton Friedman (1970) argued, underlying markets is a moral principle of "unanimity": no transaction takes place unless all parties voluntarily agree. Thus to refrain from extractive behavior, and instead to engage only in cooperative behavior, is to show respect to all those with whom one interacts. And the moral principle that underlies this imperative to show others respect is that every human being—including the least among us—is a full and equal moral agent of dignity.

Honorable Business

What kind of business activity is allowed in a properly functioning market economy, thus defined? It is business that eschews extractive behavior and engages only in cooperative behavior, business that avoids zero-sum transactions and seeks only positive-sum transactions. That is not to say, however, that it does not seek a profit. On the contrary, it seeks *honorable profit*, which is profit gained only through positive-sum transactions that benefit all parties to the transaction.[9] I call this kind of business "honorable" because it can succeed only by benefiting others; more specifically, it can succeed only by benefiting others *as judged by those others*. In other words, honorable business does not conceive of itself as bestowing what it unilaterally considers to be benefit on others. Perhaps charity does that. In contrast, honorable business succeeds by figuring out what *you* think would benefit *you*, then figuring out a way to deliver that in such a way that you would be willing to voluntarily part with some of your limited resources in exchange for it.

Many people think that business succeeds only at the expense of others. And there are numerous examples of cases in which that is exactly what has happened. As we saw earlier, human history has demonstrated that extraction has often proved to be a preferred method that human beings have used to get what they wanted from others. It is apparently a recurring failing in the human character. Business activity conducted on the basis of extraction would be dishonorable, however, not only because it is zero-sum and thus would not lead to an increase in overall prosperity,[10] but also because it would treat other human beings as less than full moral agents. It would treat them instead as mere tools to be exploited in the service of one's own ends. It would be to show them not

---

[9] This conception of profit and honorable business is thus very different from the picture one often gets from many critics of business and business schools. For a recent example, see Martin 2018.

[10] Such activity could in fact be *negative*-sum, entailing a net decrease in resources.

respect but disrespect, to treat them not with dignity but with contempt. In a properly functioning market economy, however, getting what one wants by extraction is forestalled. Thus the only remaining option to get what one wants is through cooperation, and it must be voluntary cooperation—or else it is just another case of proscribed extraction. Business activity in such a market economy, then, can proceed only through cooperation, which means it must be based on the willing consent of all parties each of whom possesses an opt-out option. Any exchange, transaction, association, or partnership that is successfully executed under such constraints would therefore be mutually beneficial, according to the individual judgment of each party. Business operating in this way would succeed not at the expense of others, but, instead, to the benefit of others. That is what I call "honorable business."

Creating Value

The last step in our architectonic hierarchy of moral value pertains, finally, to the individual businessperson. If we want to engage in the honorable business that is required by the market economy that is part of the social institutions that enable a just and humane society, what does that mean we as individuals must do? The answer is implicit in the preceding discussions: we must seek ways to benefit ourselves only by benefiting others. That is, we must find ways to *create value*, both for ourselves and—at the same time—for others. Both parts of this equation are necessary. We must find ways to create value that others both appreciate and are willing to sacrifice their scarce resources for. At the same time, we must choose from among the many ways we might create value for others the way, or the ways, that simultaneously create value for ourselves that we think justifies the tradeoffs of the required resources.

For any voluntary exchange to take place, all parties to it must consider not only the benefit they stand to receive, but also the cost to them of what they would have to give up. Suppose you are interviewing me for a position in your company. I am considering working for you and you are considering hiring me. Each of us must make an estimation of both the potential benefit and the potential cost. I have to consider the money you would pay me, as well as the extent to which working for you would match up with and integrate into my values, purposes, and goals—in other words, into the plan I have constructed in my "rationally ordered moral life." But I also have to estimate the cost: what opportunities am I giving up to dedicate this portion of my time, talent, and treasure to work for your company? My opportunity cost is a measuring stick for determining whether what I am considering is worth doing. Ask yourself what else you would do with whatever resources you are contemplating spending in a particular way; the most highly valued alternative use, to you, of those resources is the opportunity cost. If you ask yourself this question, and it turns out that you think spending your time or other resources doing something else would be more valuable than whatever you are currently dedicating them to, you should stop and dedicate them to that other thing instead. So when deciding whether to work for you, I have to consider all the benefits, material and nonmaterial, as well as all the costs, both direct (like my time and labor) and indirect (forgone opportunities).

You have to do the same. You have to estimate how you, or your company, would benefit from having me be a part of it, and how that benefit would integrate into your larger schedule of value and purpose. But to know whether whatever benefit I could provide to you would be worth it (again, to you), you also have to estimate the cost, both direct and indirect. Direct costs include how much you would have to pay me, how much my benefits would cost, and so on; indirect costs include what you would do with those resources if you did not hire me. Might you give someone else a raise? Might you invest in research and development? Buy office equipment? And so on. Would whatever benefit you believe you or your company would receive from those alternative potential uses of your limited resources outweigh whatever benefit you judge I would provide you or your company? If the answer is yes, then you should put those resources toward those other uses; if the answer is no, you should hire me.

Successfully completing transactions like this is obviously complex. They involve many factors, on both sides, and because the values, purposes, and goals of different people are both different and changing—and because resources are limited—potential transactions often fail to come to fruition. But sometimes there is a point of intersection, some point of agreement between both, or all, sides at which all concerned believe they benefit. And when that happens, voilà! A mutually voluntary, mutually beneficial exchange takes place, and everyone involved is better off.[11] In this case value has been created, fulfilling the mandate of our individual obligations of honorable business.

Two final points about the creation of value. First, this value has a multiplier effect. When you and I successfully complete a mutually beneficial transaction, it is not only we who enjoy that benefit: others do as well. The increase in prosperity that our exchange generates is now added to the overall stock of society's prosperity, and though the increase may be only incremental from the view of all of society, nevertheless it creates new benefit that can now be used to complete

---

[11] But see J. Taylor 2017, which expresses reservations about whether mutually voluntary exchanges are necessarily also mutually beneficial. Powell and Zwolinski 2012 argue that some exchanges can be both mutually voluntary and mutually beneficial, yet still exploitive. See also Munger 2011 and Anderson 2017.

yet other mutually beneficial transactions. And as thousands, or millions, or billions of such transactions take place, each with even only a small or incremental increase in benefit in comparison to the whole, the total supply of prosperity in society also increases. The entire society thereby now enjoys the opportunity to meet more of its needs and wants, which creates yet more benefit, which can then enable opportunities to meet yet more needs and wants, and so on. The creation of value thus begets further creation of value—a virtuous cycle upward for all of society.

Second, there is another kind of benefit that the creation of value via honorable business provides for society: it can generate better relations among people. This is not a monetary value, at least not directly, but, rather, a *moral* value. When people from different backgrounds and different walks of life are able to discover mutually beneficial ways of cooperating, it tends to break down barriers that otherwise might exist to good social relations generally. There might be racial divisions in one's community, or people in one's community might be divided by religious, political, or other differences. Lamentable as they are, these kinds of divisions are often present in society, and they can lead to conflict and perhaps even violence. But division, conflict, and violence are among the greatest inhibitors to prosperity throughout human history—and they continue today to prevent many places from reaching the heights of prosperity they might otherwise generate.

One thing modern evolutionary psychology and behavioral economics seems to have discovered is that humans are a small-group species. We evolved in small, tight-knit groups that were able to survive only if everyone united behind a common purpose (usually under a common leader), and we were always on the lookout for members of competing communities who might want to enrich themselves at our expense by extraction. We today are the inheritors of the psychological instincts of tribalism and distrust of strangers that served our ancestors well but are unfortunately out of place in modern society.[12] We still readily divide the world into "us" and "them," and often it is "us" *versus* "them."[13] The mandate of creating value for ourselves only by creating value for others, however, can work against this tribalistic instinct. It can incline us to view others not as enemies but as opportunities. By restricting our available means to improving our own situation to only those that simultaneously improve the situations of others, we are incentivized to overlook racial, religious, political, and other differences, and instead seek ways of mutually beneficial cooperation. This does not mean those divisions will go away—if our apparently instinctive

[12] See Rose 2011; Frank 2012; Otteson 2012; and Gintis 2016.
[13] See Brennan 2016.

tribalism is indeed part of our genetic inheritance, they may effectively never go away[14]—but it does mean that they might be softened. What the existence of markets requiring honorable business can do, then, is give us reasons to cooperate despite our differences.

This phenomenon is not merely hypothetical. Consider what Voltaire (1694–1778) wrote in his *Philosophical Dictionary* ([1764] 1901) about what he saw while in exile in London:

> Enter into the Royal Exchange of London, a place more respectable than many courts, in which deputies from all nations assemble for the advantage of mankind. There the Jew, the Mahometan, and the Christian bargain with one another as if they were of the same religion, and bestow the name of infidel on bankrupts only. There the Presbyterian gives credit to the Anabaptist, and the votary of the establishment accepts the promise of the Quaker. On the separation of these free and pacific assemblies, some visit the synagogue, others repair to the tavern. Here one proceeds to baptize his son in a great tub, in the name of the Father, Son, and Holy Ghost; there another deprives his boy of a small portion of his foreskin, and mutters over the child some Hebrew words which he cannot understand; a third kind hasten to their chapels to wait for the inspiration of the Lord with their hats on; and all are content.[15]

The desire for mutual advantage can bring together even the strangest of bedfellows—including people who, as Voltaire goes on to say, otherwise "would seek to cut each other's throats." If we allow them to cooperate, and if we prevent them from engaging in extractive behavior, people will look for ways to overcome their other differences and benefit one another. Steven Pinker (2011) tracked the centuries-long reduction in worldwide rates of violence and discovered that it is today at all-time lows. Perhaps it is no coincidence that this has correlated remarkably with the rise and spread of markets.[16]

---

[14] See chap. 5 for further discussion of our allegedly instinctive tribalism.

[15] Voltaire (1764) 1901.

[16] This was the prediction of several early political economists, including Montesquieu (1748) 1989, Hume (1754) 1985, and Smith (1759) 1982. Hume, for example, wrote: "The more these refined arts advance, the more sociable men become [...]. Thus *industry, knowledge,* and *humanity* are linked together by an indissoluble chain" ([1754] 1985a, 271). For more recent discussions, see McDonald 2009 and Bowles and Gintis 2011.

Conclusion

As purposive creatures, human beings need to know the *why* of any activity before they come to think about the *how*. This is as true of business as it is of any other activity. As rational creatures, our purposes need to fit together in an integrated hierarchy: proximate ends should serve intermediate ends, which in turn serve long-term ends, which in turn serve ultimate ends. And as moral creatures, this hierarchy of purpose must also be a hierarchy of moral purpose. To lead a truly happy life—a eudaimonic life—we must construct for ourselves a rationally ordered moral life. In a similar way, business, which will touch all of our lives in one way or another, must also be embedded within its proper context, which means it must serve its proper role in a hierarchy of moral value.

To achieve eudaimonia requires that the ends our actions serve are themselves worthy of dedicating ourselves to. That means our actions must be virtuous, and issue from habits of behavior that are reflective of good character. To develop this character, we must develop good practical judgment that is the consequence of the freedom to make our own decisions and the responsibility of being held accountable for them. Developing this judgment enables us to integrate the various aspects of our lives into a coherent whole and to develop the overall character of virtuous people. Restricting the focus to those aspects of our lives that deal with business activity, the foregoing reasoning entails that the proper purpose of businesspeople is to create value for themselves—thereby enabling the construction of a eudaimonic life for themselves—but to do so only by creating value for others. They do this by engaging only in cooperative, never extractive, transactions, which are characterized by being mutually voluntary and mutually beneficial. When they do so, they engage in honorable business, which is part of and supported by a properly functioning market economy, which itself is part of and supported by—and in turn supports—the public and social institutions that enable a just and humane society.

Remaining Questions

Numerous questions remain to be addressed. Among them:

1. What moral and cultural institutions are required to support the hierarchy of moral value advocated in this chapter, including in particular the "properly functioning market economy"?
2. People raise many objections to market economies, as well as to the behavior of businesspeople, firms, even entire industries. What are those objections? Can the model described here plausibly address them?

3. Why should I care about a just and humane society? Or perhaps: why should I *qua businessperson* care about a just and humane society?

4. How exactly would the hierarchy of moral value described in this chapter help me to adjudicate the actual dilemmas I will face in my professional life as a business person?

5. What obstacles am I likely to face as a businessperson even if I accept this conception of honorable business?

6. What obstacles does society face in trying to construct and maintain the proper institutions?

These are the central questions that will occupy our attention for the rest of this book.

2

The Proper Context of Business

Introduction

Imagine you were transported back in time to the middle of the eighteenth century and plopped down in—to pick a place at random—Edinburgh, the capital of Scotland. Imagine you were told that the leading thinkers of the day were embroiled in heated disputes about what kinds of political and economic policies they should have. Now imagine that you are asked to write a book, the first of its kind, in which you are (1) to explain what genuine wealth really is, (2) to explain why some places are wealthier than others, and (3) to make policy recommendations about how a country could increase its overall wealth (properly defined—by you). To write your book, you have only the knowledge and resources available to you that would have been available then. Since it is the eighteenth century, you thus have no Google or Wikipedia, no internet, no computer, no telephone, and no electricity; there are no databases to consult, no work of other researchers to build upon, and probability and statistics are only early in their development. You have a good library, but most of it is made up of works of philosophy, literature, theology, and history, which are thin on empirical data. Where would you start? How would you proceed?

Focus for the moment on the question (2) above: What factors would you initially guess would play a significant role in determining why some places, even in the eighteenth century, were wealthier than others, and why some were growing in wealth more quickly than others? Some things that might occur to you: natural resources, geography, population demographics; perhaps infrastructure like roads for horses and carriages and canals for shipping (there were no airplanes or trains or cars); perhaps levels of education and technology; perhaps the forms of government; perhaps differing religious, moral, or cultural beliefs; or perhaps a factor that would have been supported by many then but that is odious for us to consider today—namely, the (alleged) natural superiority of some races and the natural inferiority of other races.

This is the world in which the Scottish moral philosopher Adam Smith found himself, and these are the questions that he set himself to answer. His conclusions, which were over a decade in the making, resulted in a book that is today widely considered the beginning of the discipline of economics: *An Inquiry into the Nature and Causes of the Wealth of Nations*, first published in London on March 9, 1776. This book, and the theories, arguments, and data contained in it, has become one of the most influential books of the last millennium, and it has garnered for Smith a place in the pantheon of humanity's greatest thinkers. To consider the proper purpose and place of business, then, perhaps it is best to start with Smith.

Adam Smith's Story of Wealth

Begin with the title of Smith's book. It is often shortened to simply *The Wealth of Nations*, but its full title indicates the broader scope of the book: he first wants to understand the "nature" of wealth, that is, wherein true or genuine wealth consists; and, second, he wants to understand what causes it. *The Wealth of Nations* (WN) is a long and wide-ranging book, discussing everything from human nature to government to where prices come from to trade policy to public debt. Smith was able to get figures for things like grain production in several countries of Europe for several centuries—no mean feat in an era without an internet, computers, or telephones. His method was relatively simple, and might even strike us today as obvious; in his day, however, it was revolutionary. He wanted to compare the production over time of various goods (like corn, for example), and then track them according to the policies the respective countries had in place over the same periods. Were there patterns that could be discovered? That is, were periods of increasing production and prosperity correlated with specific policies, and decreases likewise correlated with other specific policies? If so, then perhaps hypotheses could be formulated: "Policies like X, Y, and Z lead to increasing production and prosperity, while policies like A, B, and C lead to decreasing production and prosperity." The next step would be to gather further empirical data against which hypotheses like this could be tested; if the new data confirmed them, then a recommendation could be made: "Pursue policies like X, Y, and Z, and avoid policies like A, B, and C."

After surveying the evidence that he could gather, Smith came to the conclusion that the primary factor in explaining why some places were increasing in wealth was the division of labor. That might seem like an underwhelming conclusion. What about natural resources, infrastructure, education, or technology? Smith considered these possibilities, but he discovered that they did not account for the differentials in wealth he was observing. Take natural resources: there were some places that were rich in natural resources, like China, but that overall were not wealthy; and there were places relatively poor in natural resources, like Holland and Britain, but that were wealthy. It turned out that factors like infrastructure, education, and technology were in fact functions of wealth, not originators of it. In other words, places that were already generating wealth could afford better infrastructure, could afford more formal education, and could capitalize on technological advances; places that were not already wealthy struggled to develop or take advantage of these things. And to Smith's great credit, he also did not think that racial distinctions played any role. That was an explanation that would have been ready to hand in the eighteenth century (and in the nineteenth century as well—Darwin, for example, took "natural" distinctions among human races seriously in his *Descent of Man* [1871] 1981). But Smith believed, and premised the entire argument of WN on the claim, that all human beings were roughly equal in their motivations and abilities,[1] and thus policies that worked in one country or in one culture would, or should, work in others as well.

So what did Smith think the division of labor would accomplish? Before addressing this question directly, we need to understand what Smith meant by "wealth." Here too Smith was offering a new account. In the eighteenth century, the reigning economic theory came from a school of economic thought called mercantilism, which held that wealth consisted in gold or other pieces of metal. The more gold a country has, according to mercantilism, the wealthier it is; the less gold, the less wealthy. Given that theory, countries often implemented trade restrictions. If British citizens bought, say, wine from France, the British would get wine but the French would get gold. If wealth consists in gold, however, that would mean that Britain is getting poorer relative to France, which is getting wealthier. Thus Britain might be inclined to place restrictions on trading with other countries—which it did. Britain would want its citizens to *sell* to other countries, but not to *buy* from them. Because other countries would reason similarly, however, there would ensue a mutual race to implement as many trade restrictions as possible, with the result that overall trade would decrease.

Smith argued, by contrast, that wealth does not consist in pieces of metal: it consists rather in the relative ability to satisfy one's needs and desires. "Every man," Smith wrote, "is rich or poor according to the degree in which he can afford to enjoy the necessaries, conveniencies, and amusements of human life" (WN, 47). Because the "far greater part of them he must derive from the labour of other people," Smith continued, "he must be rich or poor according to the quantity of that labour which he can command, or which he can afford to purchase" (WN, 47). Thus Smith claims that we are rich or poor according to whether we have

---

[1] See WN, 28–30.

the means to accomplish our ends, whatever they are; true wealth, then, is the relatively higher capacity to satisfy our ends. What the mercantilist forgets is that when British citizens buy wine from France, they do give up gold, *but they get the wine*—and that is what they wanted. Thus their situations are improved, according to their own lights, and that means they are relatively wealthier on Smith's definition of wealth. Understanding wealth in this way enabled Smith to explain why people would part with pieces of metal for goods or services: if they were not thereby benefited, why would they have done so? Since each person always wishes to "better his own condition" (WN, 343), the argument of WN is that policies and public institutions should be adopted that best allow each of us to do so. In this case, it means lowering trade barriers and encouraging free and open trade, even between people of different countries.[2]

What does this have to do with the division of labor? Smith claims that dividing the labor required to complete a task enables far greater production. Consider Smith's famous example of making pins. Smith says that an individual pinmaker could, if he is a master at it, make no more than twenty pins in a day if he is responsible for the entire pin from start to finish. A shop of ten similarly tasked master pinmakers could thus make up to 200 pins per day. If, however, the various tasks involved in making pins are divided, with different people specializing on individual tasks—"One man draws out the wire, another straightens it, a third cuts it, a fourth points it, a fifth grinds it at the top for receiving the head" (WN, 15), and so on—the overall production of pins increases dramatically. Smith argues that division of labor will lead to specialization. Specialization, in turn, leads to increasing quantity of production because of three factors that Smith identifies: first, "the increase of dexterity in every particular workman"; second, "the saving of the time which is commonly lost in passing from one species of work to another"; and, third, "the invention of a great number of machines which facilitate and abridge labour, and enable one man to do the work of many" (WN, 17).

For the first factor, Smith claims that the more one does something, the better at it one gets; so focusing on a smaller range of activities, and repeating them over and over again, leads workers to get much better and faster at them. For the second factor, Smith argues that when we switch between tasks, we usually lose time. We lose our focus, and it takes some time to regain it. As Smith writes, "A man commonly saunters a little when in turning his hand from one sort of employment to another" (WN, 19). Today, when we stop one task, before

---

[2] Hume (1754) 1985b wrote that residents of other countries "consume the produce of my industry, and afford me the produce of theirs in return" (329), from which he concluded, "I shall therefore venture to acknowledge, that, not only as a man, but as a BRITISH subject, I pray for the flourishing commerce of GERMANY, SPAIN, ITALY, and even FRANCE itself" (331). Even France!

turning to another perhaps we first check Facebook, our emails, our Twitter feed, our texts, and so on—and pretty soon an hour has gone by. Doing that multiple times every day leads to a great deal of lost productivity; by contrast, remaining focused on one task, or one set of tasks, uses the otherwise lost time in productive activity. Finally, the third factor relies on human beings' natural desire to save their energy. We look for ways to get our jobs done with the least amount of time and effort possible. This naturally inclines us to seek out expedients or more efficient methods of work, and this often leads to innovations. One key aspect of this search for expedients is that they come principally from the workers themselves, not the managers or bosses. Smith thinks that innovation is primarily a bottom-up phenomenon, not a top-down one. But the managers and bosses will also search for expedients to achieve their own tasks. Thus innovations will occur throughout the entire chain of command in a firm.

These three factors, and in particular the last one—innovation—lead, Smith claims, to a "great increase of the quantity" in production. In fact, Smith claims that that same ten-person pinmaking shop could, if the labor is divided to enable specialization, make upwards of 48,000 pins per day, or the equivalent of 4,800 pins per person. That is an increase in production of 23,900 percent!

The pinmakers do not, of course, need 4,800 pins per day themselves, so what do they do with the surplus? They sell it. As the number of pins available in the market thus increases, other things being equal, the prices will decrease, which means that more and more people will be able to afford them. Now, one might be unimpressed with a greater supply of pins in the market, believing this to be is a relatively insignificant good. Smith himself calls pinmaking a "very trifling" good. But Smith argues that the same process can take place in the production of any other good: "In every other art and manufacture, the effects of the division of labour are similar to what they are in this very trifling one" (WN, 15). As the division of labor spreads to other industries, the result will therefore be the same: more and more goods available in the market, with ever-decreasing prices. This means more and more people will be able to afford more and more means to satisfy their ends, which means the overall wealth—and thus prosperity—of the society will increase. And if British pinmaking shops make more pins than British citizens need, the surplus pins can be sold to people in other countries, making the citizens of both countries better off. To summarize Smith's argument:

Step 1: Labor is divided.

Step 2: Division of labor leads to specialization, which leads to increasing production.

Step 3: Increasing production leads to decreasing prices.

Step 4: Decreasing prices lead to increasing standards of living.

That's it. That is the core of the argument Smith makes, capturing the essential elements he gleaned from his survey of centuries of human history across more than a dozen countries.

Here is Smith's own summary of his argument, which comes not ten pages into the over-one-thousand-page WN:

> It is the great multiplication of the productions of all the different arts, in consequence of the division of labour, which occasions, in a well-governed society, that universal opulence which extends itself to the lowest ranks of the people. Every workman has a great quantity of his own work to dispose of beyond what he himself has occasion for; and every other workman being exactly in the same situation, he is enabled to exchange a great quantity of his own goods for a great quantity, or, what comes to the same thing, for the price of a great quantity of theirs. He supplies them abundantly with what they have occasion for, and they accommodate him as amply with what he has occasion for, and a general plenty diffuses itself through all the different ranks of society. (WN, 22)

This passage highlights the extensive cooperation and interdependence that arises in markets: we all become dependent on one another to supply what we have "occasion for." For Smith, this is a cause of celebration. Far better to view others—including people from other countries, who speak different languages, who practice different religions, who are of different races, and so on—as opportunities rather than as enemies. Note also that Smith speaks of "universal opulence," "general plenty," and of the common "workman": all of these emphasize Smith's primary concern, namely, the least among us. His primary interest is to understand how the poor can raise their estate. Pharaohs, emperors, kings, and aristocrats have long been able to take care of themselves, and would continue to do so; Smith, instead, is worried about the everyday common man.[3]

Finally, note Smith's crucial qualifier "in a well-governed society." What constitutes a "well-governed society"? Although Smith does not specify in this passage what he means by this phrase, we can infer from what Smith has argued that a "well-governed society" is one in which the division of labor is allowed to proceed, and in which people are able to trade or sell away their surplus. What is needed for that? Here we can draw on what Smith had argued in his first book, *The Theory of Moral Sentiments* (TMS), first published in 1759. There

---

[3] Smith used only masculine pronouns throughout his writings. Because of this, and not to beg any questions, when discussing Smith's argument I follow his convention.

he distinguished between what he called "justice" and what he called "benefi-cence." Justice, Smith claimed, was a "negative" virtue, which involved primarily restraint from committing injustice (or "injury") to others—in other words, refraining from making other people worse off. Beneficence, by contrast, was a "positive" virtue, which involved taking positive action to improve the situation of others. (Note that Smith is not speaking of *benevolence*, which is the easy and costless act of merely wishing others well; he was speaking instead of *beneficence*, which is the difficult and costly expenditure of energy and resources to make others better off.) Smith's argument was that beneficence was surprisingly dif-ficult: to actually improve another's situation required extensive knowledge of the particular situation of the people involved, both that of the giver and that of the receiver. For that reason Smith thought that proper beneficence could not be directed or superintended from afar; it instead should be left to the individ-ual actors themselves who possessed the requisite local knowledge. Smith also argued that in order for beneficence to count as moral virtue, it had to be freely chosen: "Beneficence is always free, it cannot be extorted by force" (TMS, 74). If one acts beneficently only because one is forced to do so, then one receives no moral credit for it.

Justice, by contrast, was relatively easy to administer, since it was usually relatively clear when a person had been harmed or injured. Thus justice is a task that could be safely left in the hands of the state. A "well-governed society," then, was one that had public institutions that protected justice but left beneficence in the hands of private persons and local (private) groups. Smith argued that protecting justice comprised, in fact, enforcing just three rules, rules that were "precise, accurate, and indispensable" (TMS, 175): "The most sacred laws of justice, therefore, those whose violation seems to call loudest for vengeance and punishment, are [1] the laws which guard the life and person of our neighbor; [2] the next are those which guard his property and possessions; and last of all [3] come those which guard what are called his personal rights, or what is due to him from the promises of others" (TMS, 84). We can think of Smithian justice as the "three Ps": the protection of *person*, *property*, and *promise* (or contract). This constitutes a "well-governed society."[4] When everyone, even the least among us, is protected in his person, his property, and in the promises made both by him and to him, then he has the security to increase his production and the liberty to work, sell, buy, trade, negotiate, and associate as best he can in seeking to "better his condition." In that case, ventures will be launched, labor will naturally divide itself, and all the gains from the rest of Smith's story will ensue.

---

[4] See Oman 2016 for an extended discussion of the importance of the third "P," contracts.

Thus Smith's argument is that a country that wants to increase its wealth and enable its citizens to prosper must enact policies that enable the division of labor, leading to the consequences he predicted of the increase of production, the decrease of prices, and the increase in standards of living. His claim is that this process of increasing prosperity will ensue in any country, regardless of its natural resources, its geography, its antecedent levels of wealth or education or technology, or the races of its citizens. Smith's argument is therefore a universally applicable prediction: Wherever your country is today and whatever its current state, its prosperity will increase if your government protects justice but largely leaves the rest in the hands of individuals. Under such conditions, individuals will pursue activities that will benefit not only themselves but others, indeed the rest of society, as well. Crucially, Smith argues that the government should not, in fact, try to steer industries or manage markets: when they enjoy protection of their three Ps, people will figure out all on their own how to improve their conditions. Smith writes: "This division of labour, from which so many advantages are derived, is not originally the effect of any human wisdom, which foresees and intends that general opulence to which it gives occasion. It is the necessary, though very slow and gradual consequence of a certain propensity in human nature which has in view no such extensive utility; the propensity to truck, barter, and exchange one thing for another" (WN, 25).

Smith's prediction seems a rather optimistic one: the government needs only to protect "negative" justice, and does not need to take positive steps to help its citizens. But why should we think that a society characterized by Smith's extremely small (at least by today's standards) government would prosper and flourish, as he suggests? Smith substantiates his political-economic recommendations with three further, linked arguments: the *economizer argument*, the *local knowledge argument*, and the *invisible hand argument*.

I describe each of them below, but before doing so, perhaps a word a word is in order about why businesspeople should care about these arguments. Why should we care today about what Adam Smith thought over two centuries ago, and why should this discussion be part of business ethics? As the author of the *Wealth of Nations*, Adam Smith was a principal founder of the discipline we today call economics, and his arguments have had enormous influence on the subsequent development of political and economic institutions. To understand why we have what we have, then, it might be instructive to see what first launched us on this trajectory. But Smith was also a moral philosopher, and as his earlier book *The Theory of Moral Sentiments* ([1759] 1982) demonstrated, he was also deeply concerned about the nature of virtue and how to achieve it. Thus understanding how he connected economics and morality—in the united discipline he called "political economy"—is also instructive. Beyond any historical and scholarly interests, however, Smith's positions have the additional benefit of being based on arguments that are not only influential but—as I hope to show—also plausible yet today. To understand the proper context of business, then, as well as the proper conception of honorable business, examining Smith's arguments is an excellent place to start.

The Economizer Argument

Smith writes: "Every individual is continually exerting himself to find out the most advantageous employment for whatever capital he can command" (WN, 454). This is connected with Smith's discussion elsewhere (and repeatedly) of the "natural effort of every individual to better his own condition" (WN, 540), and his (again, repeated) claim that "it is the interest of every man to live as much at his ease as he can" (WN, 760). We might, somewhat less charitably, think of this as the "human laziness argument," but it is more accurately described as the claim that people naturally—that is, without being told to do so—look for more efficient means to achieve their goals, whatever they are. Do you want to learn to play the piano? To run a marathon or learn French or get a job as an attorney? Whatever your goals, the economizer argument holds that you will assess the limited resources available to you—including your time, your skills and abilities, and your money—and you will look for ways to reach your goals in the surest, fastest, most complete ways, or with the least cost to any other goals you have, given your available resources. Whatever goals you have, you look, as it were, for the best returns on your investment of resources; in other words, you *economize*.

The Local Knowledge Argument

Smith writes: "What is the species of domestick industry which his capital can employ, and of which the produce is likely to be of the greatest value, every individual, it is evident, can, in his local situation, judge much better than any statesman or lawgiver can do for him" (WN, 456). As Smith develops it, this argument proceeds as a three-step syllogism:

Premise 1: People's individual situations, along with their values, purposes, and opportunities, are known best by individuals themselves.

Premise 2: To be made wisely, decisions about allocating scarce resources must exploit knowledge of situation, value, purpose, and opportunity.

Conclusion: Therefore, the person best positioned to make such decisions about how to allocate resources wisely is . . . the individual.

Smith's claim is not that individuals are infallible or that they never make mistakes; obviously we all make mistakes, frustratingly often. And of course there might be special cases—for example, children or the infirm—where individuals are not, in fact, best positioned to make decisions in their own cases. But for the vast majority of normally functioning adults, Smith's claim is that their personal knowledge of their own situations exceeds that of others. And the further away a person is from me, the less knowledge she has about me, which means the worse is her position from which to try to make decisions for me. If making good decisions requires utilizing this detailed, particularized, and localized knowledge, then in the vast majority of cases the persons who should be making decisions is those persons themselves.

Smith goes on to claim: "The statesman, who should attempt to direct private people in what manner they ought to employ their capitals, would not only load himself with a most unnecessary attention, but assume an authority which could safely be trusted, not only to no single person but to no council or senate whatever, and which would be nowhere so dangerous as in the hands of a man who had folly and presumption enough to fancy himself fit to exercise it" (WN, 456). Smith does not mince words about the conceit of such statesmen. But look more closely at two specific claims he makes in that passage: (1) the statesman's attention is "unnecessary" and (2) would result from "folly." It is "unnecessary" because, as Smith explains in his economizer argument, people do it already: we are naturally constructed to seek out the best return we can get on our scarce resources, so the statesman does not need to attend to it. It is, moreover, "folly" because, as Smith explains in his local knowledge argument, the statesman does not possess the local knowledge of individual people's circumstances, values, goals, and resources that he would need in order to make good decisions for them. Does the statesman know whether you should work for that company, buy that car, get a hamburger or a salad for lunch—or go to law school or marry that person? No. If he presumes nonetheless that he can make good decisions for you, it is, Smith says, "folly."

The Invisible Hand Argument

Now we come to the most famous phrase in Smith's *Wealth of Nations*, indeed arguably in all of economics. Smith writes: "It is his own advantage, indeed, and not that of the society, which [each person] has in view. But the study of his own advantage naturally, or rather necessarily, leads him to prefer that employment which is most advantageous to the society" (WN, 454). Smith continues that each individual "generally, indeed, neither intends to promote the publick interest, nor knows how much he is promoting it"; "by directing that industry in such a manner as its produce may be of the greatest value, he intends only his own gain, and he is in this, as in many other cases, led by an invisible hand to promote an end which was no part of his intention" (WN, 456). What is the "end" the individual promotes that "was no part of his intention"? The "publick interest." Individuals have ends, of course, but they are personal and tend to be local. Smith's claim in this famous passage is that in seeking to accomplish their personal and local ends, individuals are led to discover ways that will serve others' ends as well—whether they care about those others or not. Thus the invisible hand argument claims to have found a way to achieve the lofty goal of helping others, indeed promoting society's general good, from the humble motivation of individual self-interest.

How is this extraordinary feat accomplished? Recall Smith's claim that the goal of increasing standards of living results from division of labor—but only within a "well-governed society." As we saw, what Smith means by a "well-governed society" is one that protects the "three Ps" of justice: person, property, and promise. In other words, it ensures that the only way I can get what I want from you is by appealing to *your* interests. If your person, property, and promise are protected, I cannot enslave you, steal from you, or defraud you. The only recourse I have, then, to get whatever goods or services you might be able to provide is by making you an offer. And since your three Ps are protected, you can, if you please, always say, "No, thank you" to any offer I might make and simply walk away. This means that if I want to exchange or cooperate with you to benefit myself, I have to ask myself: What can I offer you that *you* would think is valuable enough to cooperate with me? Given that each of us "stands at all times in need of the cooperation and assistance of great multitudes" (WN, 26), that means that each of us must, in a well-governed society, think constantly of the value we can provide to others—which we can know only if we are thinking about those others and not thinking only about ourselves. In a "well-governed society," Smith says, we therefore voluntarily become "mutually the servants of one another" (WN, 378).

To summarize: because I seek to achieve my goals in the most efficient manner possible (the economizer argument), I am incentivized to make good decisions about how to use my time, talent, and treasure to achieve my goals by cooperating with you and others (the local knowledge argument), and hence, as long as we are living in a well-governed society that debars me from acting unjustly, I will be led to discover ways to cooperate with you that will be beneficial to you as well (the invisible hand argument).

In Smith's account, neither of us can benefit at the other's expense; rather, each of us can benefit only by benefiting the other. The result of these mutually voluntary, mutually beneficial transactions is that overall wealth increases, leading to general growth in prosperity. The more people whose three Ps are protected will mean the more people all on their own entering into ever more mutually beneficial, or "positive-sum," transactions, leading to yet more wealth that can enable even more such transactions, and so on—creating a virtuous cycle of increasing prosperity for all. This is what Smith meant by the "universal opulence" and "general plenty" (WN, 22) that results in a "well-governed society."

Two final points in this discussion of Smith's story of wealth. First, consider: Who will be the chief beneficiaries of this generally increasing prosperity? On Smith's account, it will not the emperor, king, lord, or baron—they already manage to get theirs, mostly by extracting it in zero-sum transactions that benefit themselves at the expense of unwilling others. Indeed, such people might now find it more difficult to get what they want, because they will no longer be able merely to extract it from others. Instead, the primary beneficiary of this process is the everyday workman, the "common artificer or day-labourer" (WN, 22), who finds himself gradually and incrementally able to afford more and more of life's necessities and luxuries. It is his standard of living that should be our chief concern and that stands to see the greatest gains. Smith believes, indeed, that he has discovered the key to unlocking a perhaps limitless engine of prosperity. Its salutary effects on the lives of common people is the moral mandate that drove Smith's political economy. Smith's bold, even audacious, prediction in WN was that countries that adopted his recommendations would see all their citizens, including especially their poor, rise to heights of wealth and prosperity that even kings in his day could only dream of. He even went so far as to suggest, in 1776, that America, which at the time most enlightened thinkers in Europe considered a "barbaric" country, could perhaps one day surpass even the mighty British Empire in wealth (WN, 87)—a laughable claim! And yet what have the subsequent centuries demonstrated?

A second, and final, point. At the end of the very first chapter of *The Wealth of Nations*, Smith has a long paragraph discussing a "woollen coat" that "covers the day-labourer" (WN, 22). He says that this coat, "as coarse and rough as it may appear, is the produce of the joint labour of a great multitude of workmen." How many workmen? Smith's answer is worth quoting at length:

> The shepherd, the sorter of the wool, the wool-comber or carder, the dyer, the scribbler, the spinner, the weaver, the fuller, the dresser, with many others, must all join their different arts in order to complete even this homely production. How many merchants and carriers, besides, must have been employed in transporting the materials from some of those workmen to others who often live in a very distant part of the country! How much commerce and navigation in particular, how many ship-builders, sailors, sail-makers, rope-makers, must have been

employed in order to bring together the different drugs made use of by the dyer, which often come from the remotest corners of the world! What a variety of labour too is necessary in order to produce the tools of the meanest of those workmen! To say nothing of such complicated machines as the ship of the sailor, the mill of the fuller, or even the loom of the weaver, let us consider only what a variety of labour is requisite in order to form that very simple machine, the shears with which the shepherd clips the wool. The miner, the builder of the furnace for smelting the ore, the feller of the timber, the burner of the charcoal to be made use of in the smelting-house, the brick-maker, the brick-layer, the workmen who attend the furnace, the mill-wright, the forger, the smith, must all of them join their different arts in order to produce them. Were we to examine, in the same manner, all the different parts of his dress and household furniture, the coarse linen shirt which he wears next his skin, the shoes which cover his feet, the bed which he lies on, and all the different parts which compose it, the kitchen-grate at which he prepares his victuals, the coals which he makes use of for that purpose, dug from the bowels of the earth, and brought to him perhaps by a long sea and a long land carriage, all the other utensils of his kitchen, all the furniture of his table, the knives and forks, the earthen or pewter plates upon which he serves up and divides his victuals, the different hands employed in preparing his bread and his beer, the glass window which lets in the heat and the light, and keeps out the wind and the rain, with all the knowledge and art requisite for preparing that beautiful and happy invention, without which these northern parts of the world could scarce have afforded a very comfortable habitation, together with the tools of all the different workmen employed in producing those different conveniencies; if we examine, I say, all these things, and consider what a variety of labour is employed about each of them, we shall be sensible that without the assistance and co-operation of many thousands, the very meanest person in a civilized country could not be provided, even according to, what we very falsely imagine, the easy and simple manner in which he is commonly accommodated. (WN, 22–23)

This is clearly an important discussion for Smith, and it makes three principal claims. First, it is easy to underestimate the number of people who are involved in bringing to us the things we buy, use, and enjoy. Once we start tracing out all of them, it turns out, as Smith puts it, that it literally "exceeds all computation" (WN, 22). And that is just for a humble wool coat—imagine what the list would look like if tried to trace out all the people who had a hand in creating, say, an iPhone. Second, the astonishing number of people Smith enumerates—people of different trades and crafts, from different localities and even nations, who speak different languages, worship different gods, are of different races, and so on—cooperate with one another without any overall manager or boss directing them all. No one of them knows all the others, no one of them knows all the parts in these long chains of production, and no one of them is directing it all. It happens spontaneously, as people exploit their own local knowledge to serve their own ends, but only by at the same time serving the ends of others.

And third, in this passage Smith is highlighting the extent to which in a market economy all of us are interdependent on one another. Some thinkers in Smith's day, for example Jean-Jacques Rousseau (1712–1778), had argued that the goal for human beings should be an individual freedom characterized as complete self-sufficiency. In his *Discourse on the Origin of Inequality* ([1755] 1992), Rousseau idealized the man who could supply for himself everything he needed, and who needed only what he himself could supply. In Rousseau's romanticized telling, "savage" man fulfilled this ideal: he had few needs and was able to supply all of them himself; he needed no one else and was dependent on no one else; and hence he was, at least in Rousseau's vision, truly free. For Rousseau, dependence on others, even interdependence as Adam Smith describes it, was tantamount to slavery. Smith champions a different story. For Smith, the completely self-sufficient man is one who is poor and leads a miserable and short existence. He may not be dependent on others, but what he gets for it is poverty and misery. As Smith's "woollen coat" passage demonstrates, Smith believes that that tradeoff is not worth it. The increasing interdependence of people who exchange in markets is, for Smith, not a cause for lamentation but rather a cause for celebration. It means we can all benefit from the "dissimilar geniuses"—meaning the different skills and talents—human beings have (WN, 30), making all of our lives better off. In addition, Smith thinks that the extensive cooperation that markets enable among peoples from around the country, even around the world, is a great good for humanity: it expands our horizons, it softens our prejudices, and it reduces animosities and even violence. We come to see one another not as enemies but as opportunities, leading to both material and moral progress.

The Results of Smithian Institutions

Was Smith right? Were his predictions correct about the increases in prosperity to which the division of labor in a well-governed society would lead? We now have over two centuries of experience by which to judge, and in the last forty years or so economic historians have been able to gather and assess data from countries around the world going back not just to Smith's time in the eighteenth century, but over the last several millennia. Indeed, some economic historians believe we can make educated guesses about levels of wealth and production in the world going back as far as one million years ago, to early hominins on the planet.[5] We now have data that Smith could never have imagined, and we have developed sophisticated tools for assessing and analyzing that data that Smith could only have dreamed of. So what have we found?

The first thing to note is the spectacular, and historically unprecedented, increase in wealth and prosperity the world has seen since the eighteenth century. Before that time, the average levels of wealth, going all the way back to year 1, and further to 10,000 BC, was, in contemporary dollars, between $1 and $3 per day per person. Historically and worldwide, the average was both remarkably low and remarkably consistent. That level of wealth is barely subsistence. The United Nations calls that level of wealth "absolute poverty," which it defines as "a condition characterised by severe deprivation of basic human needs, including food, safe drinking water, sanitation facilities, health, shelter, education and information."[6] As Gregory Clark (2007) shows, the average person in AD 1800 was no better off than the average person in 100,000 BC. And as Robert Fogel (2004) demonstrates, most people prior to 1800 had so few resources that they were not able to ingest enough calories to engage in much work. So even if they had ideas for inventions, technology, or new developments, they were often too sick, injured, or undernourished to pursue or develop them to any great length. And there was little capital available for investment, research, or development. On top of that, there was the ever-present fear of predation from others. Because people were often so insecure in their persons and possessions, they faced a substantial disincentive to accumulate anything that others might value. If you had anything beyond what others had, they would as often as not simply take it from you, perhaps enslaving or killing you in the process. The rates of death from violence were significantly higher—indeed, as Pinker (2011) has demonstrated, often orders of magnitude higher—than they are today. And do not forget that there were also no antibiotics, let alone cancer treatments or inoculations. So if you got sick or injured, you probably just died.

And what has happened in the world since 1800? Not just technology and innovation, not just medicine and cars and planes and air conditioning and space exploration and the internet and smartphones, but a spectacular explosion of both prosperity and population. We are now live richer, longer, and healthier than any humans have ever lived.[7] Or, consider just the United States, which in

---

[5] See DeLong 1998; Landes 1999; Clark 2007; and Maddison 2007.

[6] See Mack 2016.

[7] See McCloskey 2006, "Apology," for a discussion of how much better people today fare in comparison to previous generations. For an updated and expanded discussion, see McCloskey 2016a, chaps. 1–6. See also Pinker 2018 and Rosling, Rosling, and Rönnlund 2018.

the period since Smith published his *Wealth of Nations* in 1776 has perhaps more closely approximated his recommendations than any other country. In 1800, the total population of what is now the continental United States was 5.8 million.[8] The average life expectancy at birth was a shocking thirty-nine years, and the annual gross domestic product per capita stood at $1,343 (in 2010$), or $3.68 per person per day. And today? As of 2017, the population of the United States was 327 million, the life expectancy at birth was eighty, and the annual gross domestic product per capita was $59,500 (in constant dollars), or $163.01 per person per day.[9] That means that over the last 217 years, as population increased nearly fifty-six-fold, life expectancy at birth doubled and real GDP per capita increased an astonishing forty-four-fold. As McCloskey notes, "By 2011 the average resident of the United States consumed, correcting for inflation, $132 a day, sixty-six times more housing, food, education, furniture than in 1620—a betterment of 6,500%" (2016a, 34). She continues: "Such a figure [i.e., 6,500%] is conservatively measured, not allowing for the better quality of today's goods and services"; she suggests that taking improvements in quality and infrastructure into account would indicate that today's average American's real betterment since 1800 is on the order of an astonishing one hundred times.[10]

And yet even this does not tell the full story, because many goods and services we enjoy today were simply unavailable in the relatively recent past—at any price. The industrialist Andrew Carnegie, for example, was one of the world's richest men at the end of the nineteenth century. He sold his empire to J. P. Morgan in 1901 for $480 million—approximately equivalent to $14 billion today. Yet for all his wealth, he still could not save his beloved mother from dying of pneumonia, because the necessary antibiotics simply did not exist.[11] Yet the treatments for pneumonia not only exist today but have become so inexpensive that they can be obtained easily, and if necessary free of charge, in virtually any hospital in America. In 1924, former American president Calvin Coolidge's son, Calvin Coolidge Jr., was playing tennis with his brother on the White House lawn. The sixteen-year-old Calvin developed a blister on the third toe of his right foot. He soon began to feel ill and ran a fever. He had incurred a staph infection, and he was dead within a week.[12] Even the president of the United States could not save his son from an infection that could have been easily treated today—again because those treatments were not available in 1924 at any price.

---

[8] This figure includes an estimate of 450,000 Native Americans.

[9] See Central Intelligence Agency, n.d.

[10] McCloskey 2016a, 34. Nordhaus 1996 gives a similar estimate. See also Rosling, Rosling, and Rönnlund 2018 for a description of the current state of the world in comparison to previous eras.

[11] See Bostaph 2017 and Krass 2002.

[12] See Shlaes 2014.

Or consider the internet. A few years ago, Michael Cox, an economist at Southern Methodist University, decided to ask his students how much money they would want in exchange for never going on the internet again for the rest of their lives.[13] Their answers were huge: $10 million, $100 million, even $1 billion. Yet, as Cox pointed out, what do those same students actually pay to get access to the internet? It costs only a few cents per day (and prices continue to decline), and many of them pay nothing at all—the service is provided for them by their parents, by their schools, by coffee shops, and so on. So something that they value in the millions, even billions of dollars, costs them virtually nothing. This gives an indication of the productive powers of markets to create value, but it also, and more to the point here, is an indication of the "hidden wealth" we possess. How can we measure the increase in productivity that the internet has provided to humanity? Or cell phones: the first commercial cell phone was the Motorola DynaTAC, which was introduced in 1983 with a price tag of $4,000 (equivalent to approximately $10,000 today). Only the superrich could afford them. Today, nearly everyone has one (in 2011, there were more cell phones owned in America than there were citizens), and today's cell phones can do a lot more than that original DynaTAC, which could only place calls. Today's cell phones send texts, take pictures and videos—and access the internet. Virtually the entirety of human learning is available to us in seconds for pennies per day— in our pockets. We thus today have access to wealth and resources far beyond what people even only a generation or two ago could only have imagined.[14]

These are anecdotes, which by themselves do not vindicate Smith. But there is more systematic evidence. International teams of economists have for the last forty years been ranking countries according to how closely their institutions approximate Smith's recommendations. One such ranking, the Economic Freedom of the World Index (EFWI), which is published by the Fraser Institute in Canada, has been ranking countries since 1975 on the degree to which their citizens enjoy "economic freedom," which they define in the following way: "Individuals have economic freedom when property they acquire without the use of force, fraud, or theft is protected from physical invasions by others and they are free to use, exchange, or give their property as long as their actions do not violate the identical rights of others" (Gwartney, Lawson, and Hall 2017). This definition of "economic freedom" is quite close to Smith's definition of "justice" and his recommended duties of government; thus their results are a fair ranking not just of "economic freedom" but of "Smithian institutions." In their most recent report (2017), which ranks 159 countries, the top ten countries

---

[13] See Fund for American Studies, n.d.
[14] See Cox and Alm 1999.

in "economic freedom" / "Smithian institutions" are, in order: Hong Kong, Singapore, New Zealand, Switzerland, Ireland, the United Kingdom, Mauritius, Georgia, Australia, and Estonia (the United States, which was as high as number 2 in 1980, and was number 2 again in 2000, slid out of the top ten in 2010 and now stands tied with Canada at number 11). The bottom ten countries, in order, are Iran, Chad, Myanmar, Syria, Libya, Argentina, Algeria, Republic of Congo, Central African Republic, and, coming in dead last, Venezuela.[15]

The EFWI shows a relatively smoothly sliding scale from most "economically free" to least, indicating, as we would expect, not a simple presence or absence of Smithian institutions, but, rather, a continuum from one end of the spectrum to the other. But that is only half the story. The other, and perhaps much more significant, aspect is that we can compare this ranking to various indices measuring human welfare. It turns out that on almost all the ways we have been able to come up with to measure human well-being, they track the economic freedom ranking. That is, the higher up a country is on the ranking, the better off its citizens are; the lower a country is on the ranking, the worse off its citizens are. And this tracks consistently all the way up and down the ranking. This holds for real GDP per capita, real income for the poor, the United Nations Development Index, environmental sustainable-use practices, life expectancy, infant survival, child nutrition, literacy rates, food production, access to safe water, access to healthcare, political stability, peace, self-reported life satisfaction, civil rights protections, resources dedicated to research and development, even numbers of toothbrushes per household.[16] On all these criteria, the more economically free a country is, the better it scores—and the less economically free a country is, the worse it scores. Now, correlation is not causation, and these are all correlations. But when this many correlations all point in similar directions, it begins to look like we might be on to something.

Did the Government Do It?

Over the past ninety years or so, at least since the outset of President Roosevelt's New Deal, the United States federal government has taken an increasingly large role in the American economy, taxing and redistributing wealth in an effort to provide charity and subsidy for an increasing number and proportion of Americans. President Johnson's War on Poverty accelerated this. Over that same

---

[15] The EFWI does not rank Cuba or North Korea, because they are unable to get independently verifiable data about those countries.

[16] See Hall and Lawson 2014.

period, however, the American economy grew substantially. With the exception of the Great Depression years and the Great Recession of 2008, America's GDP has been positive every single year. This might raise the question of whether America's economic growth might actually be *because of* this (increasing) government intervention.

More systematic and fine-grained empirical analysis suggests, however, that America's growth was not in fact because of this government intervention but despite it.[17] The causal factors are complex, of course, and involve cultural and historical factors that are hard to quantify, hard to specify, and thus hard to account for. But cross-country comparisons provide strong evidence that, in general, economic performance is inversely correlated with government intervention in the market. People do much better, and a country's poorest especially fare better, when the government concentrates on protecting the institutions of Smithian justice than when the government engages in wealth redistribution. Redistributive programs lead to localized and short-term benefit but tend to do so at the expense of general and long-term benefit. This is the lesson to draw from the Economic Freedom of the World Index and its analyses, as well as other similar analyses.[18] The conclusion is that, however much prosperity a country generates with government redistribution of wealth, it is less than the country otherwise would have generated. We perhaps cannot know exactly how much less,[19] but we can be sure it would otherwise have been higher.

And this is suggested not only by the empirical correlations, but also by the logic of redistribution. Every mandated redistribution involves opportunity cost, that is, the loss of whatever benefit the redistributed resources would have provided had they not been redistributed. If instead of taxing that wealth away from citizens the government had left it in the hands of taxpayers, taxpayers would have done something with it. They would not have buried it in the backyard or stuffed it into their mattresses: it would have been spent on other

---

[17] For a discussion of the interventions and their effects under Roosevelt, see Shlaes 2008. For an examination of America's economic performance and the effects of its federal government's interventions over the twentieth century, see Higgs 2013. See also Friedman and Schwartz 1969; Cameron and Neal 2003; and Gordon 2016.

[18] See the Economic Freedom Index published annually by the Heritage Foundation: http://www.heritage.org/index/. See also the wealth of data and analysis provided by HumanProgress: http://humanprogress.org/.

[19] But see Dawson and Seater 2013, which hazards some educated guesses. They estimate that federal regulations in the United States have prevented its gross domestic product, which is currently just under $20 trillion, from being approximately $54 trillion (in constant dollars). That means the median household income in the United States could have been, instead of its current actual $59,500, an incredible $330,000 (again, in constant dollars).

goods or services, saved, or invested.[20] It is moreover likely that the wealth put to any of these uses would have led to yet greater overall benefit than that to which the government would have put it—otherwise, the individual citizens would have already put those resources to the ends to which the government programs puts them. We cannot know that for sure, because it might be that individual citizens are not aware of some of the facts that government experts know about problems or possibilities elsewhere in their country. By the same token, however, government experts are not in possession of facts about problems or possibilities that individual citizens are. The suggestion from the local knowledge argument is that individual citizens are in fact better judges of how best to deploy their limited resources, because of their knowledge of their own situations and of others' local situations, and that thus they might be better positioned and equipped to make good use of those resources. They also face incentives that are better aligned to give them appropriate feedback for their decisions. A person spending her own money on things she believes are worthwhile is incentivized to get it right—on pain of wasting her own resources, a cost she would herself bear—whereas legislators, who are directing others on how to spend their (the others') money, do not themselves bear the cost of having spent unwisely and thus do not face the same natural discipline to put in the hard work of figuring out how best to use limited resources.

The logic of opportunity cost and the incentives involved with individual decision-making about one's own resources predicts that the more that a country's economy proceeds on the basis of decentralized, individual decision-making, the more prosperous it will be; by contrast, the more that a country's economy proceeds on the basis of centralized decision-making, the less prosperous it will be. And that is exactly what empirical investigation has found.[21] On the basis of this argument and evidence, I conclude that adoption of Smithian institutions has led to increases in human welfare that are historically unprecedented. Still, perhaps this evidence has not yet definitively proved the case. Given that we cannot have controlled experiments with human beings and human societies, it would be extremely difficult to develop a definitive case. Nevertheless, this evidence cannot be ignored. If it does not end the argument, I would argue that it must be at least the starting point of any discussion about comparative political economy. Given the large and increasing body of evidence, the burden of proof has shifted to the critic of Smithian institutions to explain why this evidence is not dispositive.

[20] See Balkin 2015.
[21] See Otteson 2014.

Business in Context

In chapter 1, I argued that the proper purpose of business is to create value. I argued that it could serve this purpose only if it is embedded in a hierarchy of moral value that begins with the highest and most general social goals we should have—namely, a just and humane society—that informs the institutions, including economic institutions, we should have, and that offers guidance even to the individual businessperson. With the discussion in this chapter of Adam Smith's conception of the proper political-economic institutions, and of the empirical evidence supporting the predictions Smith made on behalf of his recommended institutions, we are now in a position to close the loop of the argument.

The Duties of Government

Let us begin by specifying more concretely what the required institutions are that can enable honorable business. Begin with the governmental institutions. As we saw, Adam Smith argued that the proper conception of "justice" comprises protection of principally three things—the "three Ps"—namely, person, property, and promise. Because Smith argues that these protections should rightly be accorded to all citizens, not merely to the rich or powerful, this constitutes an argument in favor of extensive private property rights that all citizens would enjoy. Moreover, because Smith argued that the duties of "beneficence" cannot be effectively managed by distant third parties like legislators and should instead be left to the care and consideration of those who are equipped to do so—namely, private individuals themselves and the voluntary private groups they form—the government is discharged from directing people in beneficence. To do otherwise would be, in Smith's words, to "assume an authority which could safely be trusted, not only to no single person, but to no council or senate whatever, and which would nowhere be so dangerous as in the hands of a man who had folly and presumption enough to fancy himself fit to exercise it" (WN, 456). Hence, on Smith's account, the government's principal duty is to protect justice, and it should allow people to work, exchange, partner, trade, cooperate, innovate, buy, sell, barter, or give, freely and without interference from the government or other uninvolved third parties. That, he believes, is the path to prosperity, and limiting the government to protecting justice is both necessary and sufficient to enable any people or country to increase its prosperity.

When Smith comes to describe what he believes is the proper role of government, here is how he begins: "All systems of either preference or restraint, therefore, being thus completely taken away, the obvious and simple system of natural liberty establishes itself of its own accord" (WN, 687). Smith continues:

Every man, as long he does not violate the laws of justice, is left perfectly
free to pursue his own interest his own way, and to bring both his industry and his capital into competition with those of every other man, or
order of men. The sovereign is completely discharged from a duty, in
the attempting to perform which he must always be exposed to innumerable delusions, and for the proper performance of which no human
wisdom or knowledge could ever be sufficient; the duty of superintending the industry of private people, and of directing it towards the
employments most suitable to the interest of society. (WN, 687)

What, specifically, are the governmental institutions required by Smith's "obvious and simple system of natural liberty"? Smith identifies three. The first two
are (1) "the duty of protecting the society from the violence and invasion of
other independent societies"; and (2) "the duty of protecting, as far as possible,
every member of the society from the injustice or oppression of every other
member of it" (WN, 687). Each of these straightforwardly follows from Smith's
conception of "justice," and in fact they are best understood as charging the government with protecting us from violations of our persons, property, and promises, whether by foreign or domestic malefactors. Smith suggests that the first
duty requires a military, while the second requires a court system and police.
And Smith argues that general taxation of the populace is justified to support
these functions of government, since all of us, no matter what our goals in life
are, will not succeed unless we enjoy the security and protection of our persons,
property, and promises.

Smith's third and final duty of government, however, is different. He describes
it as "the duty of erecting and maintaining certain publick works and certain publick institutions, which it can never be for the interest of any individual, or small
number of individuals, to erect and maintain; because the profit could never
repay the expense to any individual or small number of individuals, though it
may frequently do much more than repay it to a great society" (WN, 687–88).
This duty of government, unlike the first two, seems to go beyond the duties
of merely protecting "negative" justice, and to take it into the realm of positive
intervention in the market; further, it would seem to warrant taxation beyond
that required to maintain a military, police, and courts. It also seems to open a
door that Smith elsewhere seemed to want to keep closed: if the government
may provide public works and public institutions, are there any realms of goods
or services that it may not—on principle, as it were—enter? Might this not also
empower the government to enter into the realm of beneficence, which Smith
had argued should be left to private individuals and groups?

Perhaps having the government intervene in markets, either to steer it in
certain preferred directions or to take some of its produce and redistribute it

to needy citizens, is a good idea—or at least might be a good idea, depending on how well its intervention is managed and how good or important the ends are to which it is put. Let us postpone addressing this general question for the moment and first clarify Smith's position. As an empirical political economist, Smith's goal is prosperity, however it turns out that that can be achieved. Smith is no ideologue. Therefore he quite appropriately wishes to remain open to whatever the evidence shows, including the possibility that the government might do more than protect his negative conception of justice. But note that he imposes strict qualifications on when such government intervention might be allowed: only when "it can never be for the interest of any individual, or small number of individuals to erect and maintain; because the profit could never repay the expence to any individual or small number of individuals, though it may frequently do much more than repay it to a great society." Thus Smith argues that to justify such intervention, the advocate of government action must meet the burden of making *both* of two claims: (1) the proposed public work or public institution would have to be unable to be provided by private enterprise; *and* (2) it would have to benefit substantially the whole of the "great society," not merely one group at the expense of another.

While Smith has not ruled out such intervention, then, the threshold is high: if you believe the government should take positive action to provide a public work or institution, you would have to demonstrate both that private enterprise could not supply it (note: not simply that it *currently does not*, but that it *could not*) and that substantially everyone would benefit. What government programs would meet those two criteria? Upon reflection, it would appear the answer is not many. Smith himself goes on to entertain some possibilities. He considers, for example, infrastructure such as roads, canals, and bridges, though he notes that the roads, canals, and bridges provided by private enterprise—and there were such in his day, as in ours—are typically of better quality and more efficiently maintained than publicly provided infrastructure.[22]

Smith also considers education. Smith worried that if people received no education and instead spent their lives working in one narrow operation created by extensive division of labor—perhaps they spent their entire professional adult lives doing nothing but putting heads on the top of pins—they could become, in Smith's vivid and almost apocalyptic language, "as stupid and ignorant as it is possible for a human creature to become" (WN, 782). But what does Smith propose as a remedy for such a potential malady? Not publicly funding college education, not even publicly funding high school education: instead, only *partially* subsidized *primary* schooling (WN, 785). He even supported school vouchers

---

[22] WN, 724–31.

and competition (WN, 763). Smith considers that the only aspects of education that everyone would need, regardless of the occupation or field or industry into which one goes, are reading, writing, and what he calls "accounting," or
arithmetic (WN, 785). The necessity of anything beyond that would depend
on one's particular needs given the field in which one works—and would thus
be different for different people. Thus Smith suggested that public funding for
the "three Rs" might be a justifiable government intervention. Even here, however, he thought the public subsidy should be less than half the total cost—the
rest being borne by the students themselves (or their families or sponsors)—to
make sure that incentives are aligned properly. Teachers, Smith thought, would,
like anyone else, naturally pay more attention to whoever is paying the majority
of their fees. If that is the government, they will pay more attention to, and be
more solicitous of, the government than they would be of students. If, on the
other hand, students (or their families or sponsors) pay the majority of their
fees, teachers will naturally pay more attention to the students (families, sponsors)—which they should.

So although Smith is open to considering positive government intervention
in the economy and taxation for things other than to protect justice, many things
that governments routinely provide in the world today would be disqualified
by Smith's account. Retirement funding (Social Security, for example), welfare
benefits, job training, disability, public libraries or universities, national parks,
healthcare, and many other government programs, including trade tariffs or quotas, subsidies, and protections from competition, would likely be disallowed—
all because they could be provided privately, would benefit one group at the
expense of another, or both. To demand that they be provided by the government, rather than through private and voluntary initiative, would also be to
violate justice toward those required to pay but who did not want to because it
would violate their property and possessions.

The conclusions of WN are therefore largely in favor of limiting political
interference in markets.[23] Each individual knows his own situation—including
his goals and desires, as well as the opportunities available to him—better
than anyone else does, and certainly better than any distant legislator. Hence
Smith argues that individuals themselves should be allowed to decide how best
to apply and sell their labor or goods, with whom to trade and on what terms,
and so on. Smith is withering in his condemnation of meddling legislators who
overestimate their ability to direct the lives of others, who legislatively substitute
their own distant judgment for that of the individuals with actual local knowledge

---

[23] For a contrasting view of Smith, see Fleischacker 2016.

over whom they rule, and who then use the predictable failures of their decisions as reasons for yet more potentially imprudent intervention.

Yet Smith is equally condemnatory of grasping merchants and businesspeople who seek legal protections of their industries or prices. "People of the same trade seldom meet together," Smith writes, "even for merriment and diversion, but the conversation ends in a conspiracy against the publick, or in some contrivance to raise prices" (WN, 145). Such merchants proclaim that trade barriers, tariffs, and other legal protections are for the good of the country, but Smith exposes these claims as special pleading, since they work in practice to increase those particular merchants' profits at the expense not only of their competitors but also of consumers. Keeping prices up and limiting competition will certainly benefit the favored businesses, but such policies impose artificial costs on everyone else. Smith argues that the way to deal with such attempts at legally guaranteed extractive benefit—what we might today call "cronyism"—is typically not to regulate them, however, but rather to disallow legally enforced privileges in the first place. Markets and open competition are, Smith thinks, typically better providers of social benefit than regulation by politically motivated legislators—who are, after all, often remunerated handsomely by the very merchants and businesses from whom they profess to protect the public.

The Duties of Society

Governmental institutions are not the only institutions in society, and they do not enforce themselves. For them to work as they are intended to, they must be supported by a wide consensus among citizens that the institutions are the proper ones and are worth supporting. Among the chief obstacles that societies have faced in creating and maintaining the institutions that enable growing prosperity is what we might call *opportunism*.[24] Opportunism comes in different varieties. One kind of opportunism is simply reneging on an agreement, contract, or promise. You and I agreed that you would provide me a good and I would pay you. You trusted me and provided the good; I take receipt of the good, but then I do not pay. A case like this is usually easy to detect, however, and, as a straightforward violation of Smithian justice, it would fall under the government's duty to protect against and punish when it happens. A subtler case of opportunism is when you and I make an agreement, but while you fulfill your end of it, I find a loophole and fulfill the letter of the agreement but not its spirit. Such cases are more difficult to detect and prove, and remedying them may require costly assistance from lawyers and courts—reducing the overall benefit we stood to gain.

---

[24] I draw here on Rose 2011.

A final, still subtler case of opportunism: you and I make an agreement, and both of us fulfill both the letter and spirit of it. As I do my work, however, I figure out a way I could have done even more for you, but I decide not to do so because I do not want to put in the effort. Suppose you hire me to work for you and you put me in charge of handling some aspect of your firm's operations. Once I get into the job, I discover a way of doing things that would provide even more returns to you and to the firm, beyond what you anticipated or expected. I decide not to pursue that new, more productive, process, however, because it would require me to work harder than I want to; instead, I give you only what you expected. You are happy, because you do not know about what I discovered. But you are not as happy as you could have been, and the firm is not as productive as it might have been.

Only the first of these kinds of opportunism is a clear violation of Smithian justice; the second might be, but it is a harder case. It is not clear that the third is a violation at all. Yet in all three, prosperity is left on the table: there were gains that could have been realized but, alas, were not. Hence all three opportunisms are obstacles to the prosperity that Smithian political economy proposes.

Another obstacle arises from free riding. Suppose we all agree that we would all benefit if everyone follows Smith's rules of justice. But suppose I discover that I can violate one or more of the rules in such a way that I know I will not be discovered. Perhaps I want to take some reams of paper home from the office for my personal use, and I discover that there are times I could do so when I know I would not be caught. Perhaps it is the case that not only would I not be caught, but no one would even notice the difference. Cases like these, which are far more common than one might initially suspect, are what Robert Frank (1988) calls "golden opportunities." I have a golden opportunity when I could benefit myself by breaking a rule I expect everyone else to follow, but (*a*) I would not get caught and (*b*) no one else would notice or detect.

Consider a case drawn from my own life. In 2014, I was rear-ended while stopped at a red traffic light. Thankfully, no one was hurt. The accident was clearly the other driver's fault, so her insurance had to pay for the damage. When I took my car to the authorized body shop for repair, the repairman told me it would cost $1,500 to repair the damage. "But," he said, "I noticed that you have a ding on your driver's side door." Indeed I did. He continued, "I could fix that for you too, add $500 to the bill, and claim it as part of the accident repair." Now consider: the person who hit me was insured by Allstate, which has a market capitalization of over $33 billion. The extra $500 on this particular bill is so small in relation to the company's overall activities that Allstate would probably be literally unable to detect it. And whatever increase in insurance premiums this accident would cause for the driver who hit me would probably be unaffected by whether the claim was $1,500 or $2,000. So there would be clear beneficiaries to my repairman's proposal: he and his shop would benefit from the extra work and money, and I would benefit from having the ding on my door also repaired. And he could easily ensure that neither of us would be caught. Moreover, who would be harmed by it? Not the person who hit me—the extra $500 would make no additional difference to her premiums. And not even Allstate—the difference is too small for such a large company to even be able to detect it. Thus I faced a golden opportunity. I did not take it. But should I have? If not, why not, exactly? And what reason would I, or anyone else similarly situated, have for not taking it?

This presents us with a new kind of difficulty. Exploiting such golden opportunities would clearly violate Smithian justice, and if everyone exploited such opportunities, overall prosperity would be forsaken. We would all be worse off for it. But I might reason that if only one person did so—namely, me—that would hardly make any negative difference in the world. Like micturating in the ocean, no one would know or be able to detect the difference. So why should I not do it? Note, however, that every other single person could reason similarly, in which case there could ensue a rapidly descending spiral of lost prosperity. What would, or could, prevent such a thing from happening?

Empirical investigation has shown that one of the most important factors for explaining which societies are prospering and which are not is trust.[25] Getting the right institutions is necessary, but not sufficient, because the officially authorized people enforcing the institutions—police, for example—are not always present. Thus if we engage in mutually beneficial exchange only when police or other authorities are monitoring us, much potential exchange will be forgone, meaning lost prosperity. What is required, then, is for people to trust one another to do the right thing even when no one is looking and no one would notice a breach. In other words, people need to trust that their fellow citizens will not exploit the myriad golden opportunities that arise. Suppose you make me an offer and I am considering accepting it, but I am not sure whether you are an opportunist or not. That is, I am not sure whether you would engage in opportunism or exploit a golden opportunity if given the chance. If I do not trust you, I will be far less inclined to make any kind of agreement with you. Even if we both would have benefited from the agreement, I may well not agree if I do not trust you—and we will both be worse off than we otherwise would have been. If many people in our society do not trust their compatriots, this acts as a significant disincentive to cooperate, trade, and exchange, all the things necessary for growing prosperity. Thus lack of trust is a substantial obstacle to prosperity.

And this is what we find empirically. If we rank countries according to how much their citizens trust one another, from the most trusting (like Norway) to

[25] See Zak 2017.

the least trusting (like Brazil),[26] we find that it correlates with their respective levels of prosperity. The fit is not perfect, but it seems to be the case that background levels of trust account for some substantial part of a country's overall prosperity.[27] By far the best way to generate this necessary background default of trust, however, is for the people in one's society to be actually trustworthy. People become trustworthy by acting in trustworthy manners, and we come to trust others when they do the right thing not only when it is in their interest to do so but because it is the right thing to do—even when they would benefit from not doing so. How do we get people to do that? The short answer is culture.[28] And here is a primary obligation of society that goes beyond the society's formal or public (that is, governmental) institutions: to foster and maintain a culture that inculcates in people the idea that they are morally required to do the right thing—period, as a matter of principle, and not as a result of a utilitarian calculation or on-the-spot cost-benefit analysis. And this is a key part of what will become part of the code of business ethics I will argue in chapter 3 that all businesspeople should accept. If I think you are the sort of person who, once you make an agreement, will then run a utilitarian calculation or cost-benefit analysis to decide whether you will keep your word or instead engage in opportunism or exploit a golden opportunity, I may not be able to predict what you will do in *this* case. Such uncertainty creates a disincentive to working with you. And if you thought the same about me, you would have a similar disincentive to working with me. The more such people we have in our society, the more potentially mutually beneficial transactions are not undertaken and the more prosperity is forgone.

The way to combat this destructive obstacle to prosperity, then, is by having more and more people in our community—society, country, world—who will not engage in opportunism or exploit golden opportunities as a matter of principle. In other words, they refuse to do so not because it is inconvenient or someone might notice or someone might get harmed, but, instead, because they have internalized a commitment to following such rules, and they now would refuse to do so—would not even consider doing so—through the force of their own character.

How do we create a society like this? How do we create a society in which people are trustworthy and thus engender trust in their fellow citizens? If we wish to have a society that realizes the potential gains of prosperity from mutually voluntary and mutually beneficial cooperation, it is our social duty to foster people of such character, even beyond what our formal institutions do. We need

[26] See Ortiz-Ospina and Roser 2016.
[27] See Rose 2011, chap. 9.
[28] See Rose 2019.

not only the formal institutions that Smith described—namely, institutions that protect justice, that is, the person, property, and promises of each citizen—but we must also have a society whose culture extols a moral character that is both honest and trustworthy.[29] The main culture organs of our society must encourage everyone to adopt an internalized code of behavior that respects others' persons, property and possessions, and promises and contracts, and that refuses to engage in behavior that benefits one person or party at the expense of others, instead looking for and pursuing behavior that creates value for all concerned. How do we do that? This question brings us to the duties of the individual.

The Duties of the Individual

The final piece of the argument concerns the behavior of the individual person—of you and of me. A society will have the informal cultural and moral character that its individual members have. Getting the formal institutions right is the necessary first step but by itself is not sufficient. People must trust one another, which means that people must behave in ways that engender trust. How do we get all the members of our society to behave in such ways? The perhaps disappointing answer is that we do not know. Individually, we have little control over the character of our culture, because we have little control over what others will do. We may have some influence over our own children,[30] and we may have some limited influence over our family and friends. But we do have a great deal of influence over one unit of society: ourselves. We may not be able to control what others do, but we can control what we ourselves do. And if we come to an understanding of the kinds of behavior that we can engage in that will increase the chances of mutually beneficial cooperation, then we can present society with at least one improved unit: ourselves.

The first duty of the individual, then—that is, your duty and my duty—is to make a commitment to ourselves that we will never engage in injustice; neither will we engage in opportunism or exploit golden opportunities. If we have understood the logical chain running from a just and humane society, through the institutions required to sustain such a society, to the nature of honorable business, and to business's purpose of creating value, then we understand that all the actions we engage in must be such that they are part of this hierarchy of moral value. That means it is now incumbent on each of us, as individuals, to exercise what Adam Smith called "self-command" to ensure that all of our actions are

---

[29] See Miller 2014 and 2017 on the nature and proper development of such character.

[30] But see Caplan 2012 for surprising, and perhaps depressing, evidence for how little effect parents actually have on the ultimate personalities even of their own children.

consistent with this moral vision. Smith wrote: "Self-command is not only itself a great virtue, but from it all the other virtues seem to derive their principal lustre" (TMS, 241). Now we can see why both of those claims are true. Possession of self-command is what enables us to guide our own behavior in the right directions, and what, when systematically deployed and developed, gives rise to habits of behavior that eventually form our characters. Moreover, we can achieve the other virtues—Smith singles out prudence, justice, and beneficence[31]—only if we act not by accident or even by natural inclination but instead by principled adherence to the internal dictates of our well-formed character. This means we will have had to develop our character through decisions and actions we freely chose but that we were held responsible for, and, on the basis of the feedback we received, developed judgment sufficient to guide our future actions. And we will have had to develop a deliberate control of our behavior to ensure that it comports with the dictates of our conscience. This "deliberate control of our behavior" just is what Smith means by "self-command," and its role as a necessary prerequisite to achieve all the other virtues is why Smith says it gives the other virtues "their principal lustre."

But a substantial worry arises here. Suppose that we are convinced by this argument, and we have decided to constrain our actions and decisions so that we will on principle never behave unjustly, never engage in opportunism, and never exploit golden opportunities. But suppose that the society in which we live is not similarly constituted. Suppose our society contains people who are not similarly principled, and who will, when given the chance, behave opportunistically. In such a case, would we merely be setting ourselves up for being exploited? Would those unscrupulous others, once they realize what kind of person we are, decide to lie to us in order to take advantage of us? A conman survives and flourishes in a community of people who are not conmen—in a society, that is, in which people keep their word and trust others to do the same. A lie works only if it is told in an environment in which everyone else tells the truth and expects that others will do the same. If you expect that I will lie or will not keep my word, then you will not trust me regardless of what I say. So I cannot get whatever I wanted to get by lying if you expect and are prepared for me to lie. By contrast, if you assume that I am trustworthy and expect that I will keep my word, then that is the perfect situation for me to lie and defraud you, if I am of a mind to do so. So if I follow the argument of this chapter and accept the duties it argues I should, am I just setting myself up to be taken advantage of?

There are two devices that mitigate this worry. The first arises from what is perhaps the foundational claim Adam Smith made in his first book, *The Theory*

---

[31] See also McCloskey 2006.

of Moral Sentiments, namely, that each of us desires what Smith called "mutual sympathy of sentiments." The first sentence of TMS is, "How selfish soever man may be supposed, there are evidently some principles in his nature that interest him in the fortune of others, and render their happiness necessary to him, though he derives nothing from it except the pleasure of seeing it" (TMS, 9). Smith argues that it is an empirical fact of human nature that we are interested in others. More than that, Smith argues that our psychology is so constructed that we feel pleasure when we know that our sentiments are echoed in or harmonize with those of others. By "sympathy" Smith does not mean pity; following the word's etymological roots, he means "feeling with" or perhaps "empathizing." We naturally seek others' approval—about everything from how we dress to what we read to how we behave. What Smith means by a "sympathy of sentiments" is that our own thoughts, preferences, and tastes are shared by others we care about. When we discover that others do not share our sentiments, it creates a jarring and unpleasant feeling in us. This unpleasantness is valuable feedback. It tells us that others do not approve of what we did, and it gives us reason to alter our behavior in the future.

One of Smith's favorite examples to illustrate this phenomenon is joke-telling and laughing at jokes (see, e.g., TMS, 14, 16, 17, and 112). He writes: "A man is mortified when, after having endeavoured to divert the company, he looks round and sees that nobody laughs at his jests but himself. On the contrary, the mirth of the company is highly agreeable to him, and he regards this correspondence of their sentiments with his own as the greatest applause" (TMS, 14). If you went out with your friends one evening and told the group a joke, and you laughed after telling your joke, but then you noticed that no one else was laughing, how would you feel? That awkward unpleasantness would tell you: *Don't do that again.* Consider the example from another angle: are there jokes you could think of that would be inappropriate to tell in a professional business setting? Of course there are. Are there jokes you could think of that would be appropriate to tell in such a setting? Again, of course there are. How do you know the difference? How did we all learn this? There is no manual we can consult, and the rules are not written down anywhere. Similarly, is there such a thing as laughing *too long* at a joke someone else tells? Or realizing that one ought not to laugh at a joke someone just told? In both cases, the answer, again, is yes. Again, how do we know this? How did we come to understand these rules—rules that we probably could not write down or even articulate, rules that indeed change over time? Smith's answer is that we develop judgment about joke-telling and laughing based on the numberless experiences we have had with people (including ourselves) telling jokes and observing how others (and we ourselves) react. Our sense of what is appropriate or inappropriate in such cases is the result of trial-and-error experiment in which people make attempts, get feedback, and hone their judgment accordingly. Smith's claim is that this example illustrates a more general phenomenon, namely, the process by which we come to have a sense— Smith calls it our "moral sentiments"—of what is proper or improper behavior in the whole range of activities in which we engage, from the smaller matters of etiquette to the most important moral duties.

What is particularly relevant for our purposes here is that this process of developing and training our moral sentiments by interactions with others proceeds only on the basis of our "desire for mutual sympathy of sentiments." If we did not receive pleasure from a "mutual sympathy of sentiments," we would not care what others thought of our conduct—and in that case we would not develop moral judgment. But we do care about what others think of our conduct because we do receive pleasure from mutual sympathy of sentiments, just as we feel displeasure when we become aware of an "antipathy" of moral sentiments between ourselves and others. It turns out that contemporary empirical study has confirmed Smith's analysis: we do, in fact, seek sympathy of mutual sentiments with others, and we do, in fact, receive pleasure when we realize a sympathy.[32] Though there is some very small proportion of people who seem not to be moved by others' approval or disapproval,[33] the fact that Smith's analysis applies to the overwhelming majority of human beings helps address the concern that gave rise to this discussion.

Thus the first factor that mitigates the worry about being systematically exploited if one commits to engaging only in honorable business is that the vast majority of people will feel the sting of negative judgment if they take advantage of us. Even if they are not caught, their awareness that they would be negatively judged if they were caught often generates guilt and remorse in them.[34] This creates a powerful incentive for them—and for us—not to exploit others. It is not a perfect mechanism, of course, and there are people who will try to get away with opportunism nonetheless. But if we are wronged, we should express our negative judgment. If we see others being wronged, we should express our negative judgment. And if we see someone contemplating wronging another, we should again express our negative judgment—and, as the case may be, refuse to take part.

The second defense against being exploited follows from the first. If I betray you, or if I manage to otherwise exploit you because of your willingness to trust

[32] See, for example, Zak 2012. Zak claims the pleasure we feel on realizing a mutual sympathy of sentiments is connected with the release of oxytocin. See also Pinker 2002; Ramachandran 2003; de Waal 2006; Harris 2006; Joyce 2006; and Tomasello 2016.

[33] Contemporary psychologists estimate such people to be approximately 1 percent of the population. See *Psychology Today*, n.d.

[34] See Bowles and Gintis 2006 and 2011.

others and your principled unwillingness to behave dishonorably, you should, as we just said, express your negative judgment of my behavior. But you should not only express it to me: you should express it to others as well, including in particular other people I might potentially try to work with in the future. In this way I will develop a reputation, and this too is a very powerful social force. Another aspect of human psychology is apparently that we are very keen to learn about others' failings.[35] This has a dark side, as it inclines us to gossip about others, sometimes in destructive ways. But it has a beneficial side as well: if I defraud others, betray their trust, or renege on my promises, I will quickly develop a reputation for being such a person. And that word will spread like wildfire. A negative reputation is extremely costly because it is extremely difficult to overcome. People will forget about the hundred times I kept my word, but they will remember the one time I did not.[36] They may or may not bother to tell others about when I behaved honorably, but they will almost certainly tell others when I behave dishonorably.

This second line of defense—reputation—is increasingly important today, when communication of information about past behavior is so easy and so permanent. The internet and social media have made it essentially costless to convey this information, and even a few bad tweets, let alone a video about a bad encounter, can be enough to bring down a CEO or even an entire company. Think of how concerned sellers are of their ratings on eBay, or of how concerned proprietors are of their ratings on TripAdvisor or Yelp. Now, it is certainly true that not all the information on those sites is reliable. That is true for gossip generally. One part of developing judgment is learning to be appropriately skeptical about what one hears or reads so that one can separate the signal from the noise. But our keen interest in the information (good or bad, reliable or unreliable) contained in such venues indicates how powerful a mechanism the desire for a good reputation can be. And because there are so many people contributing to the conversation now—not only the handful of people personally known to those involved, but the thousands and millions who might hear or see what is posted on the internet—it is increasingly difficult for anyone to get away with systematic opportunism for any length of time. Someone will discover what you are doing, and word will get out.

So is it possible that we might be taken advantage of if we maintain our principled adherence to honorable business? Yes. But the social incentives are such that more and more pressures will be brought to bear against people trying to take advantage of us, and the judgment we develop from past experience will

---

[35] See Dunbar 1998 and 2010.
[36] See Hanson 2013.

help us sort the wheat from the chaff in the future. Moreover, on the positive side, the benefits not only to us but to those with whom we cooperate—and, indeed, to the rest of society—by having someone like you engage in honorable business are substantial. You are better for it—not only materially, because you will get people lining up to associate with you to engage in mutually beneficial cooperation, but also psychologically, because you will not have the guilt or remorse from knowing that you behaved dishonorably. And the rest of us will be better as well, for all the same reasons.

Conclusion

Adam Smith's *Wealth of Nations* gives one of the first systematic accounts of the nature of true wealth and of the reasons why some places are wealthier than others. Not only was his account extremely influential, but, despite its age, its main elements and its central predictions have enjoyed considerable historical and empirical confirmation. Smith locates the main cause of increasing prosperity as division of labor, which leads to increasing production, decreasing prices, and hence rising standards of living. But this can happen, Smith argues, only in a "well-governed society," by which he means a society that protects "justice," or the persons, property, and promises of all of its citizens. Smith's negative conception of justice is, he argues, both necessary and sufficient for society survive. By contrast, the positive duties of beneficence are neither necessary nor sufficient and are best left to individuals.

Smith's political economy proceeds on the basis of three central arguments: the economizer argument, the local knowledge argument, and the invisible hand argument. Together, these arguments make a strong case for limiting government and other third-party interference in the economic decision-making of individuals. It is an argument against centralization and in favor of decentralization. Smith's claim is that this system of political economy will lead to "universal opulence," including especially for the poor—Smith's main concern.[37] It also, he argues, extends the frontiers of human cooperation, resulting in a wide-ranging interdependence that capitalizes on different individuals' "dissimilar geniuses."

There is substantial empirical evidence today that Smithian political economy has indeed led to the spectacular increases in prosperity that the world has seen since Smith's time. This evidence further suggests that the growth in prosperity has been despite, not because of, government intervention in economic

---

[37] See Hanley 2016.

decision-making. On the basis of Smith's argument and the now large body of empirical research, I argued that the principal duty of government should be to protect Smithian negative justice. Anything beyond that must be specially defended, taking all tradeoffs and costs—including opportunity costs—into account.

But we do have obligations beyond merely respecting justice. This includes manifesting in ourselves and inculcating in others a principled refusal to engage in opportunism or to exploit golden opportunities. In this way we can foster trust, which is a crucial ingredient in a culture that enables prosperity. I argued that even if one's larger culture does not promote the proper moral principles, one should follow these principles oneself nonetheless. There are reasons to believe that doing so could benefit not only us but also others, reasons arising from Smith's claim that human beings have a strong desire for "mutual sympathy of sentiments" and concerns about reputation. These also give us reason to believe that under a "well-governed society," both individuals and firms will be incentivized to behave honorably, which includes charitably.

Can we, then, develop a code of behavior from these considerations? Might we be able to develop even a code of business ethics? The answer is yes. We turn to that in the next chapter.

3

A Code of Business Ethics

Introduction

It might surprise you to discover—or, then again, perhaps it would not surprise you—that there is no generally accepted code of ethics for business.[1] Many other fields have such codes. Medicine, for example, has its Hippocratic Oath, and law has a code of professional ethics as well. Some specific areas of business, like accounting, have codes. But not business in general or overall. Why not? The easy answer is that businesspeople are not ethical. However easy that answer might be, it is false—demonstrably so. Although there are bad actors in business, the vast majority of businesspeople behave honorably. And of course there are bad actors in all walks of life, in everything from medicine and law to government to education to charities to car repair. Indeed, it would seem to be an enduring feature of human action: wherever there are humans, there will be at least some bad action. Perhaps the bigger surprise, given this reality, is that so many people manage to behave honorably nonetheless.

I submit instead that one main reason why there is no overall code of ethics for business is that there is little consensus regarding the overall *purpose* of business. Why do firms exist? Why do industries exist? Why do we engage in production, exchange, trade, partnership, and so on? I have tried to address some of these questions in the previous two chapters, but the larger point here is that one cannot know how one should behave within an organization, or hence what constitutes acceptable or unacceptable behavior for or within the organization itself, without first knowing what the overall purpose of the organization is. If we say that we engage in production, exchange, and so on because we want to improve our lives by getting more of the things we want, that might be true, but it does not get us very far. Because the things that each of us want vary, because our ends and values vary, and because our preferences and experiences

---

[1] Though see DeMartino and McCloskey 2016, esp. chap. 37. See also Davis and Stark 2001.

vary, referring to "what we want" is far too large a category to give any concrete guidance—and by itself it would allow far too great a range of potential
behavior. After all, extraction—taking from others without their consent—can
enable us to "get what we want" too. This wide range of differing and sometimes
conflicting goals, and perhaps also the common view that business is morally
suspect, combine to stymie efforts to develop a general code of business ethics.

So let us draw on the argument of the previous two chapters to narrow the
discussion. By isolating and identifying the connection between the kind of
society we would like to have—a just and humane society—and the kind of
business behavior this entails—honorable business—we can begin to construct
a code of business ethics. There are three parts of such a code: (1) the role it
plays, or should play, in the mission statement of a firm; (2) the role it plays, or
should play, in guiding the actions of the individual businessperson; and (3) the
role it plays, or should play, in informing the formal public institutions of the
society in which it operates. In this chapter, we will take up the first two. In later
chapters, we will have an opportunity to address the third and draw out some
of the political-economic implications this conception of business ethics has,
as well as entertain and address some objections some have raised to business.

Your Firm's Mission Statement

Over the last century or so,[2] there has been a lot of discussion, both historical
and theoretical, about the origins and nature of firms. There have not always
been firms, after all. There has probably always been bartering and trading, at
least as long as there have been humans;[3] and for millennia there have been people who partnered with or employed others to help them conduct their business.
But the firm as a separate legal entity, almost a legal person, has existed for only
the past couple centuries. Why did it come into existence? And why did it do so
only relatively recently?

If your first thought is that legal institutions were changed to allow firms to
emerge, you probably got the cart before the horse. In this case, as in many others, human experiences, preferences, and behaviors changed, and institutions
then changed in response. We frequently get the order of causation backward
when trying to account for large-scale social institutions or changes. Think,
for example, of the fabled accounts of quasi-divine lawmakers like Solon of
Athens or Lycurgus of Sparta, who are portrayed as if they, in all their wisdom,

---

[2] At least since Coase's canonical 1937 article.
[3] See Greif 2006 and Ridley 2011.

excogitated nearly perfect systems of law that they then vouchsafed to their commonwealths, creating their respective subsequent success. Or take a much more recent example: America's civil rights legislation. The 1964 Civil Rights Act is often spoken about as if it fundamentally changed American culture, as if the legislators were wise far beyond the rest of us and brought us to share in their enlightenment. In fact, almost the reverse is true: the 1964 act was demanded by American culture, and the legislators bowed to, rather than creating, that change in sentiment.[4] The Supreme Court decision legalizing same-sex marriage is another example of government acceding to a cultural change that had already taken place.[5] One ingenious aspect of Adam Smith's investigation into human social institutions was his suggestion that they were "spontaneous orders": language, law, and economies largely emerge by the independent and decentralized actions and decisions of individual people, not by the edicts of any privileged person or persons.

So we should expect that firms emerged because they served some new need or demand that people had. What would that be? Recall that human beings are relatively weak in comparison to other animals. We do not have fur, claws, wings, and so on to aid us in supplying our needs and wants. Instead, what we have is, as Smith put it, "faculties of reason and speech" (WN, 25). To procure what we need, we have to use reason and speech, which means that our comparative advantage is to cooperate with one another. Whatever you want, you are much more likely to get it by working in cooperation with others and using your faculties of reason and speech to articulate your goals and work out cooperative arrangements to achieve them—along with others who similarly use their own reason and speech. The extent to which we have been able to flourish, and to create large-scale social institutions enabling prosperity, is testament to the power of our reason and speech.

What, then, is the purpose of a firm? Fundamentally, it is to enable more cooperation. The more people who can cooperate with one another, the more prosperity we can generate. This is reflected in Smith's claim that the division of labor is limited by the extent of the market (WN, book 1, chap. 3): the larger the market, the more division of labor that is enabled; the more division of labor, the more prosperity. Similarly, the more people who can cooperate, the more prosperity. One of the barriers to cooperation is what economists call transaction costs.[6] If you and I are far away from one another, or cannot communicate easily, it is difficult for us to cooperate. If, on the other hand, we are close to one

[4] See Epstein 1992 and Bernstein and Somin 2004.

[5] *Obergefell v. Hodges* 2015. I note that I argued for legalization of same-sex marriage over a decade ago; see Otteson 2006, chap. 8.

[6] See Coase 1937.

another and can communicate easily, the costs of carrying out a transaction—
that is, the costs of cooperating—are reduced, which means the gains from
cooperating can be larger. That is what a firm does. It brings people into close
proximity with one another so that they can cooperate much more effectively.
It also enables people to develop and capitalize on new ideas: we discover new
ways of doing things, and even new things to do, and because we are working
together, we both—we all—benefit. So the firm acts as a node of cooperation,
enabling it and amplifying it.

In this, firms are like hospitals. Why would many doctors, nurses, and technicians, as well as pharmacies and physical therapists, want to be in one place? Or
like malls: why would many stores, even stores that compete with one another,
want to be in one place? Or universities: why do so many scholars of different
fields like to be in one place? Or cities: why do so many people pursuing disparate life projects want to live in cities? In all these cases, and many more besides,
having many people in close proximity enables many more opportunities for
exchange and interaction, and the wholes are much greater than the sum of the
parts. Think again of Smith's discussion of the division of labor. Suppose you and
I are bakers. Alone you make ten loaves of bread, and alone I make ten loaves;
together, if we divide the labor, we make not twenty but twenty-seven loaves.
Adding even more people makes the gains from cooperation even greater.[7] The
more of this there is, the more gains to everyone concerned.

Thus firms—like hospitals, malls, and cities—play a crucial role in generating
prosperity. This gives us a first start in understanding the purpose of a firm: to
reduce transaction costs and thereby enable and encourage larger-scale cooperation. But there must be more to the story. One can imagine a firm dedicated
not to cooperation but to extraction. Think of a criminal enterprise—a mafia or
crime syndicate. There you have cooperation among the members of the syndicate, but its larger purpose is to engage in extraction from others. Its goal is to
prosper not by *benefiting* others but *at the expense of* others. But this kind of activity is zero-sum and thus does not lead to prosperity. It can certainly enrich the
members of the syndicate, but that is not the mass flourishing with which we are
concerned: it is wealth redistribution, not wealth generation. In the hierarchy
of moral value we developed in chapter 1, such activity would short-circuit the
creation of value for others, which means it would ultimately not conduce to a
just and humane society but would instead undercut it.

Crime/extraction

---

[7] On Adam Smith's reasoning in his pin-factory example, we could, by dividing labor, make orders
of magnitude more loaves.

So the kind of cooperation that should be the aim of a firm is not merely cooperation among its employees but cooperation with its customers and clients. It would have to aim at creating value not only for itself but for others as well. How would we know if a firm is doing that? One way to tell is if people voluntarily wish to associate with it. If people retain their (opt-out option) and yet voluntarily decide to part with some of their limited resources to buy what the firm is selling, to work for the firm, to employ the firm's services, and so on, that is a strong signal that a firm is indeed creating value for others. A firm might claim that it is providing value, or third parties might claim that they are providing value, but if people do not want their goods or services, or not at the price or under the conditions that the firm is offering them, that tells us that the firm is either not creating value or is not creating it in such a way that others believe they benefit sufficiently from it.

Every firm's mission statement, therefore, regardless of the particular goods or services it aims to provide, should include the mandate to *create value for others that others themselves find worthwhile.* This not only shows respect to others as persons of dignity who have the right to order their lives and expend their limited resources as they see fit, but also disciplines the firms and their members to pay constant attention to those they presume to benefit. This places an extraordinarily difficult burden on firms, but it should. There are only limited resources in the world; that means we cannot, alas, have everything we want at the same time—when resources are put in one place, it means those same resources cannot be put somewhere else. If we wish to use our resources as wisely as possible, we must constantly search for new and better ways to use what resources we have, and we should be vigilant against wasteful or inefficient use of resources. One way to encourage that is to require that firms demonstrate to the rest of us the value they can contribute with their efforts, with the implication that if they get things right, they succeed—and if they get things wrong, they fail. And the best way to do that is by making sure that everyone has the right to say "No, thank you" and go elsewhere.

This mission of business—to create value for others that those others find worthwhile—follows from our hierarchy of moral value that connects the just and humane society to the duties of the individual businessperson. But it also has implications for government and the role it should play in the politics and economics of society. In particular, it has implications about profit, about the role of prices, and about protection of business interests. We will address those in a moment. Next, however, let us look at the implications that the proper mission of business has for the individual businessperson.

Your Code of Ethics

Your business's highest purpose should be to create value for everyone involved—owners, investors, employees, customers, clients, partners, associates. If you work for a company, however, what should your own code of ethics be? Based on the argument so far, I suggest that there are five core foundational principles that your own professional behavior as a businessperson should follow. There will be other things you will have to do as well, but none of them matter unless and until you follow these five. Here they are:[8]

1. You are always morally responsible for your actions.
2. You should refrain from using coercion and the threat of injury.
3. You should refrain from fraud, deception, and unjust exploitation.
4. You should treat all parties with equal respect for their autonomy and dignity.
5. You should honor all terms of your promises and contracts, including your fiduciary responsibilities.

Let us explain and justify each.

Principle 1: Individual Moral Responsibility

As a moral agent, you enjoy the liberty of deciding what actions to take, but you are also properly held responsible for those decisions. This conception of moral agency is contained already in the very idea of moral evaluation. If you could not choose otherwise, you could not be held responsible for your choice. This is why we do not morally condemn the dog that bites a child: we might regret what happened, and we might seek to correct the dog's behavior (or even put the dog down); but we do not morally condemn the dog because the dog is not a moral agent. You, by contrast, are a moral agent. Unless you are coerced by another person, you can choose to do otherwise. This is why you deserve moral credit when you choose well, and you deserve moral blame when you choose poorly.

Now there are difficult cases when it is not clear that a person actually had a choice. We are not here considering cases in which the circumstances of the world placed constraints on you that were no one's conscious or intentional doing.[9] I may not have the natural abilities to play in the NBA, but that does not mean I am not free to try. You may not be able to bench press 500 pounds, but

---

[8] Hasnas 2013 offers a list similar to this, though not exactly the same. I draw partly on his argument in what follows.

[9] See Hayek (1960) 2011.

that does not mean you are not free to do so—or at least try. Most people (myself included) do not have the ability to be theoretical physicists, but that does not mean that anyone is preventing them. The aspect of free choice relevant here, rather, is the ability to say, "No, thank you" to an offer someone makes. Except in extraordinary cases like threats or force, we have this ability. Even here, however, there are difficult cases: sometimes people can be pushy or insistent, and we can feel as though we were "talked into" or even "shamed into" something that we did not want to do. We have probably all had unpleasant interactions with particularly unrelenting salespeople, for example. Consider this spectrum of influence from others: disinterested provision of information, persuasion, intimidating, bullying, threatening, coercing. The first two are perfectly acceptable; the latter two are not. Yet the point at which attempting to persuade someone turns into intimidating or bullying them can sometimes be hard to distinguish. And people might have good-faith disagreements about whether a particular case falls on one side of that divide or the other.

Luckily, however, we do not have to settle those hard cases to make our point here. We can instead advert to a general principle of asking whose will is the one that effectuated the decision or action: was it your will or another's? If you were threatened or coerced, it was another's will; otherwise, it was your will. Unless you were actually threatened or coerced, you could say no. That means you are responsible for what you do, even if someone else told you to do it, even if—within reasonable limits—you were pressured. Did your boss tell you, or even order you, to do that? Fair enough, but if you did it, you are responsible for what you did. You are a moral agent, and so, in the absence of actual coercion or threat, you must own your decisions and actions. Holding you accountable for them is not punishing you but, on the contrary, is the way the rest of us respect you as a moral agent with dignity. Indeed, *not* holding you responsible is precisely to treat you as something other than you are, namely, a full and free moral agent.

Principle 2: Refraining from Coercion and Threats

This principle follows directly from, and is an extension of, principle 1. We do not want people to coerce or threaten us, because in doing so they disrespect us as moral agents. By demanding the liberty to make decisions for ourselves, we declare and represent ourselves as full and free moral agents, equal to anyone else in this regard. Principle 2 requires us merely to extend the same respect to everyone else that we demand for ourselves. We are welcome to explain our positions or preferences, and we are welcome to try to convince others we are right. We are even welcome to try to talk another person into exchanging or partnering with us. But this is subject to two important qualifications. First, we may not badger, harangue, bully, or intimidate another, and we may certainly not threaten or coerce another. Doing so would not only compromise the person's moral agency, but it would be tantamount to, or actually constitute, a zero-sum rather than a positive-sum exchange. Second, if we are trying to convince another to exchange or partner with us, it must be for something we actually believe will be mutually beneficial—something we believe will truly create value not only for us but for others as well.

Principle 3: Fraud, Deception, and Unjust Exploitation

Sometimes we might be able to get others to do what we want by defrauding or deceiving them. Doing so would, like threatening or coercing, be to disrespect them as moral agents—and hence is disallowed. Fraud and deception both involve lying, which achieves its end by falsely representing ourselves to others. If, in response to our deceptive representations, others make decisions that they would not otherwise have made, this amounts to an extraction—an exchange, partnership, or transaction without their fully willing consent. An exchange or transfer effectuated through fraud or deception would thus benefit one party at the expense of the other—and hence, again, is disallowed. We must represent ourselves to others honestly and keep whatever promises or commitments we make.

Principle 3 also addresses some aspects of the opportunism discussed in chapter 2. Reneging on promises, agreements, commitments, or contracts is an obvious violation of this principle, but so is looking for ways to keep to the letter of an agreement while violating its spirit. Principle 3 calls on us to enter into agreements only in good faith, and to interpret the elements of the agreement in light of what the other parties to it are likely to have expected or understood it to hold. Trying to "game" an agreement or look for loopholes that enable us to benefit ourselves at the other parties' expense may not be forbidden by the letter of an insufficiently exhaustive agreement. But no agreement can be completely exhaustive, covering all possible contingencies. And of course we cannot take full responsibility for other parties' interests—they must take responsibility for their own. The principle of caveat emptor—"Let the buyer beware"—is legitimate within reason. The problem arises when we pass from "It is your responsibility to know what your interests are and how to protect and serve them" to "You cannot reasonably be assumed to have thought of or known this." Such cases are sometimes very hard to adjudicate, even in good faith. But a heuristic for determining when this important line has been crossed is to ask oneself this: *Knowing what I know, would I still be willing to engage in this exchange (partnership, etc.) if I were on the other side of the exchange?* If the answer is yes, then what you are proposing is likely mutually beneficial; if the answer is no, then what you are proposing is likely beneficial only to you, and quite possibly at the other's expense. The third level of opportunism we discussed in chapter 2, when you meet both the letter and the spirit of the agreement but nevertheless do not benefit the other party as much as you discover you might be able to, falls under this principle as well. If the other party expects you to do your best, then you should do your best. But that expectation too must be subject to reasonable limits. A heuristic similar to that above would also help adjudicate cases like these. Ask yourself: *Knowing what I know, if I were in the other party's shoes, would I be happy with my efforts?* If the answer is yes, then you are likely doing everything one could reasonably expect of you; if the answer is no, then perhaps you should reconsider.

The last part of principle 3 is to refrain from "unjust exploitation." The quali-fier "unjust" is required because "exploitation" can sometimes be neutral or even benign.[10] If I take an Uber to the airport, I am "exploiting" the Uber driver's time and car. But this "exploitation" is allowed because the driver—presumably—has the ability to say "No, thank you" if she wishes. This is a benign sense of "exploi-tation," because no one was defrauded or deceived, and both parties benefited. Similarly, we speak of "exploiting" opportunities—say, when we realize there is an unmet demand in the market and we start a business or venture to address it. This too is a benign, or at least neutral, sense of "exploitation." The morally unacceptable sense of exploitation, however, is when one party knows material factors that the other party does not, and the former uses this asymmetry of knowledge to its own advantage.[11] I may have technical or proprietary or other knowledge about what we are contemplating that you do not possess. In such cases, it might be easy for me to convince you of something that you would not agree to if you knew what I know.

Mere *differences* in knowledge, however—like differences in skills or abilities—are not problematic. Indeed, it is precisely because we all have uniquely different knowledge, skills, and abilities that we can gain from cooper-ating with one another. In such cases, the differences complement one another and lead to overall increases in benefit. But there are other cases in which I know that if you knew what I know, you would not agree. If I move forward under such circumstances, I am unjustly exploiting you. A heuristic can help here as well. Ask yourself: *Knowing what I know, would I move forward with the agreement if I were in the other person's shoes?* There are, of course, limits to this: as the local knowledge argument shows, the other person has personal, localized knowledge about his own situation that I do not have, and the other person might also have

---

[10] See Powell and Zwolinski 2012.

[11] I discuss problems associated with asymmetrical knowledge in more detail in chapter 5.

interests, preferences, and values that are different from mine. So the other person might be willing to do things or accept agreements that I would not—and that is perfectly acceptable. Again, that is how we can be of benefit to each other through complementary cooperation. People are different, and they are entitled to make decisions in their own lives even when we disagree and even when we would not. Still, if I think there is a good chance the person would not agree with what I am proposing if that person knew what I know, then that is a red flag that should cause me to reconsider. Of course, one effective way to know for sure is simply to inform the other prospective party of what one knows.

Principle 4: Autonomy and Dignity

We should treat others as we wish to be treated. That does not mean that we should expect everyone to be just like us. It means, instead, that just as we wish to be the captains of our own lives, and to have the freedom and responsibility to construct for ourselves lives of meaning and purpose that are unique and appropriate to us, we should respect others' wishes for the same. This has two immediate implications. First, we should demand that others respect our opt-out option. We have the right to say, "No, thank you" to any offer made to us, full stop. Second, we must respect others' opt-out option as well. If they say "No, thank you" to us, we must respect their decision, and trust that, as full moral agents, they have reasons for their decision—even if we do not know or understand those reasons, and even if we do know and understand the reasons but disagree with them. If we are fully convinced that the other person is making a mistake, even if we are *right* that the other person is making a mistake, as a full moral agent that other person still has the right to make her own decisions. Principle 4 holds that we must respect them.

A note of caution here. Others have the right to demand that we respect their decisions, whether we agree with them or not. They do not have the right, however, to demand that we support those decisions. If another person makes decisions we think are wrong, we are free to express our dissenting view, which includes the freedom to decline to support or approve the other's decision. Respecting autonomy is a two-way street. Just as I may not threaten, coerce, or deceive you, you may not do so to me; and just as I must respect your decisions, so too you must respect mine. Now, this issue has several complicating factors. One is the law. Perhaps the law forbids me from refusing service on the basis of certain categories—race, sex, and so on. The argument here addresses not legal obligations but moral obligations, and these are often not the same. But even the moral obligations might change over time. In today's economy, as opposed to the relatively recent past, for almost all goods and services there are numerous, even thousands, of potential buyers and sellers. So if one declines to provide its service to me, in most cases I have many other options. And here we see one of the great, if unexpected, benefits of a market economy. If you decline service to me, that means I will go elsewhere and someone else will get my business. And the more people to whom you decline service, the more business will go to others—your competitors. In other words, in markets, where people have options and where there are no legal requirements that we deal only with one firm or where there are no barriers to others to supply goods and services, your prejudices will cost you money. If you wish simply to bear those costs because it is worth it to you, you may be within your rights; but the financial incentives will be such that there will likely be others who will be only too happy to have my business. You end up having to pay for your prejudices, while others, who are not willing to pay for such prejudices, benefit. In such a case, everyone's moral agency is protected and respected, and resources flow in directions reflecting everyone's preferences and decisions.[12]

A recent example that illustrates this phenomenon is the new, planned Palestinian city of Rawabi. Bashar Masri, a Palestinian businessman, decided he wanted to help Palestinians develop an identity that was independent of opposition to Israel, an identity that would be more hopeful and positive about their future. So Masri, along with several partners, bought some land in Palestine and began in 2012 building a city called Rawabi that would be, as he puts it, a liberal, secular, cosmopolitan Silicon Valley of Palestine. Masri's hope is to eventually have some forty thousand people living in Rawabi; it currently has approximately three thousand. But they are building condominiums and apartments, shopping malls, schools, mosques and synagogues and churches, and recreation areas complete with zip lines and amphitheaters. Masri's project is controversial and faces considerable challenges, especially in that fraught area of the world; time will tell whether this experiment will be successful.[13] But one interesting aspect of the experiment bears on our conversation here. Reflecting his liberal and secular aims, Masri wanted to hire not only male construction workers and engineers, but females also—a rare practice there. When he did so, some male workers and engineers quit in protest; but those who stayed have worked with the females, and they have made tremendous progress in building out the structures that are becoming a complete city. Masri discovered not only that he would receive numerous applications from female engineers, but that the success he has had working with them is now beginning to put pressure on

Female workers in Palestine

---

[12] For an illustration of how this reasoning played out in the economics of segregation in the Jim Crow era, see Higgs 1980 and Morse 1984 and 1986.

[13] See Schwartz 2016 for an overview. See also Rawabi's website: http://www.rawabi.ps/about.php.

other areas of Palestine: female engineers in other cities have begun asking aloud why, if Rawabi would hire them, developers in their own cities would not. And now other developers are beginning to overcome their own prejudices and hire women as well.[14]

It is important to note that decisions about from whom to buy, to whom to sell, with whom to partner or exchange, and so on frequently reflect not just the economic but the moral values of respective parties. Perhaps you are willing to pay a bit more to get recycled goods, because recycling is an important moral value to you. Perhaps you are willing to pay a bit more for coffee or clothing because you wish to buy from firms that pay their workers or suppliers more. Perhaps you are willing to pay a bit more for your food because you want organic food. In these and many other cases, you are making decisions that reflect your schedule of value, and you are entirely within your rights to do so. Others may make different decisions, however, owing to their differing schedules of value— and they are within their rights to do so as well.

One final note on principle 4. Respecting others' autonomy and dignity means, as I have argued, respecting the choices they make. That includes choices about with whom to partner or exchange, which includes decisions about whom to hire. Suppose I want to work for your company, but you for whatever reason do not want to hire me. You have a right to say, "No, thank you," just as I have a right to say, "No, thank you" to any offer you might make. So I have no right to a job at your company, and I have no right to any particular package of salary and benefits. To demand that you hire me, or that you pay me a certain amount or give me certain benefits, is to disrespect you as a moral agent because it removes your opt-out option. We can of course negotiate, and both of us can make offers to the other; but if either of us decides to decline, the other must respect this decision. And third parties who are not directly involved in the negotiation between you and me should also respect our decisions. If you and I come to a voluntary agreement, which we presume is mutually beneficial to both you and me, but a third party does not like the agreement, that third party is free to voice disapproval but must not threaten or coercively prevent us from executing our agreement. As long as I am not forced to participate, your values and your decisions are none of my business. Precisely the same reasoning holds in the case of hiring, associating, partnering, and so on. If you think I should not accept that job, or should not accept it on those terms, you are entitled to your opinion and may voice it if you so choose; but if another person and I voluntarily agree to terms, and you are not forced to participate, then our

---

[14] This information is based on a personal interview conducted with Masri and others involved with the Rawabi project during an on-site observation I made in March 2018.

decision is none of your business. This holds for the vast majority of exchanges, associations, and partnerships in which people decide to partake. They are their own and not others' business. To respect their autonomy and dignity, we must respect their decisions, and we should assume that they have their reasons for what they do, even if we disagree.

Principle 5: Promises and Responsibilities

When you make a commitment to another person, that other person then makes other decisions about her life based on your commitment. Specifically, that other person will begin to reallocate her resources—including her time, talent, and treasure—based on the commitment you made. If you then renege on your commitment, you will have imposed a cost on her, a cost for which you are now responsible. Even if you compensate her for that cost, this will typically have resulted in a net loss of resources: you are moving resources around to bring a person back to where she was before, not to improve her (or your) situation. If you make a habit of breaking commitments, the losses compound.

That is, as we might say, an economic argument: breaking promises and failing to fulfill commitments and contracts are costly. In the best case, they constitute forgone prosperity; in the worst case, they lead to actual loss. But breaking one's commitment is also a violation of a moral mandate to treat others with respect. They trusted you and agreed to a commitment based on their trust that you would fulfill your obligation. By failing to do so, you violated their trust and in effect defrauded them. You made a representation to them about your ability and willingness to cooperate, but your representation turned out to be false. Sometimes we cannot help breaking a commitment. Sometimes unexpected or unpredictable exigencies arise that require us to break a commitment. In such cases, we must do our best to make the other person whole and to learn from the experience to minimize the chances that it could happen again in the future. But the loss is still costly and thus regrettable. By contrast, sometimes we just get another offer, or another opportunity arises, and we decide we would benefit more from reneging. That is what is not allowed. Even if we would benefit from reneging, we would be imposing unwilling and unwelcome costs on the party with whom we had entered into an agreement; that means we would be benefiting at that party's expense. We should employ our judgment carefully, giving due and proper forethought, before entering into agreements with others. We should review and consider the likely consequences, and deliberate on them duly before agreeing. But once we agree, we have made a promise, and we should fulfill it. This is necessary both to respect the other party's autonomy and dignity as a full moral agent, and to preserve and maintain the culture of promise-keeping and trustworthiness that underpins the just and humane society that we ourselves not only want but from which we also benefit.

This principle also calls on us to fulfill our fiduciary responsibilities. A fiduciary responsibility is a "good faith" responsibility to fulfill the spirit of whatever agreement we made. Often agreements and contracts leave a wide scope of discretion. My contract with Wake Forest University, for example, does not stipulate what I am to do every minute of every day; instead, it outlines broad goals and tasks—like conducting research, teaching, and administrative service to the university—that I agree to use my discretion to fulfill. When I signed it, both Wake Forest and I understood that I would use my judgment, my skills, my abilities, my expertise, and so on to contribute to the best of my ability to Wake Forest's overall educational mission. But that still leaves a lot unspecified. Consider research: What books or articles should I write? On what topics, and for which publishing venues? Which invitations to lecture should I accept? Should I agree to serve on the board of this journal or that one? Or consider teaching: which classes should I teach? What texts, ideas, or concepts should I cover? And so on. Wake Forest hired me in part because it trusts my judgment and wants me to use my discretion entrepreneurially to find out the best ways for me to contribute to its mission. When I accepted Wake Forest's offer, I incurred a fiduciary responsibility to do so. And if I do not do this to the best of my ability, I will have failed in this commitment.

Suppose I just do not want to do so, however. Suppose that when I signed my agreement, I thought, in good faith, that I would want to do so, but once I got here I discovered things that I had not anticipated that now incline me to do just the bare minimum. So I reallocate some of my time and energies to other projects that benefit myself but not Wake Forest. This would be a breach of my professional fiduciary responsibility. In this case, according to principle 5, I would have the following choice: either I should rededicate myself, and my time and energies, to fulfilling the mission of Wake Forest it hired me to do; or I should quit and ply my energies elsewhere. To remain on, however, while in breach of my fiduciary responsibility—even if I knew Wake Forest would not notice, even if I knew it would not fire me (I have tenure)—is to engage in an opportunism that exploits Wake Forest and that is inconsistent with my duties as an honorable professional.

Professionalism

We can capture and summarize the duties and obligations of an honorable businessperson in the concept of "professionalism." A business *professional* is one who understands the purpose of business—to create value—and understands its role as part of the institutions that underpin a just and humane society. This is also a person who takes seriously the obligations she undertakes as a business-person and commits to fulfilling them to the best of her ability. The business professional in fact has a dual obligation.[15] First is to the employees, customers, clients, and partners with whom she works: she must at all times strive to fulfill the five principles in the code of business ethics listed above with respect to all these people.

Her second obligation, however, is to business itself *as a profession*. Because she understands business's crucial role in the hierarchy of moral value, she also understands that her society's institutions must be embedded in a proper cul-ture of moral value and personal behavior, and she understands that this culture can be maintained only if the individuals acting in it behave in ways that reflect and reinforce it. That means the business professional must herself behave in those proper ways. This will entail developing a proper business identity for her-self, as well as stewarding the profession of business as a value-creating, honor-able enterprise. The business professional does her job, honorably, in good faith, and to the best of her abilities. If she finds that her present circumstances prevent her from doing so—or if she decides she does not want to do so in her present circumstances—then her professional obligation is to find another place to pur-sue her proper ends.

Conclusion

In this chapter, I have offered a code of business ethics that captures the duties of the individual businessperson and articulates a conception of honorable busi-ness that satisfies the twin objectives of creating value and treating all parties as autonomous agents deserving respect. It further forms a part of, and issues from, the hierarchy of moral value I argued provides a morally justifiable architectonic linking individual action to the just and humane society.

Like law or medicine, business is a profession, and hence it should have a professional code of ethics that reflects its nature and purpose. A firm's mission statement should identify its highest purpose as creating value, while adapting and fleshing out that purpose to reflect how it can use its particular resources, skills, and values to achieve this purpose. But individual businesspeople should also have a code of ethics that begins with recognition that they are moral agents and that others are as well—and thus that captures the mutual respect demanded by that moral agency.

[15] I have benefited from conversations with Matthew Phillips on this point.

I identified five core principles of a code of business ethics for individuals. They do not exhaust businesspeople's obligations, but they are the necessary first steps and should constrain and guide everything else they do, including the positive obligations they have. These principles include the moral mandate to respect others' choices—their opt-out options—though that can have some perhaps surprising implications, including that if others wish not to exchange or partner with us, we must respect their wishes. Fortunately, in a modern market economy like that of the United States, for almost all goods and services there are numerous providers among whom one can choose. So if one does not like the offerings or policies of one provider, one can go elsewhere—and take one's money with one. In that way, one's choices can have a disciplining effect on individual firms.

Taken together, having a proper mission statement for one's firm and adopting the code of business ethics for individual businesspeople imply a conception of professionalism in business. The honorable business professional thereby incorporates into her professional business identity an obligation both to her firm, coworkers, clients, customers, and so on, and to the profession of business itself.

There are, however, numerous criticisms that have been raised against businesses and their practices in a market economy, including that they lead to inequality, unfairness, negative externalities, unfair wages and prices, the manipulation of people's choices and preferences, and an undue focus on making a profit. Does our code of business ethics offer any help or guidance with such worries? We turn to this question in the next chapter.

4

Markets and Morality

Introduction

I have argued that a businessperson acting in accordance with the code of business ethics is behaving professionally, which means he is engaging in honorable business. In this way he is contributing to a system of political economy that both reflects the correct moral way to deal with others—as persons of autonomy and dignity—and encourages cooperative behavior that enables increasing prosperity.

But does this mean that markets, and businesses within markets, are moral? There are many objections that critics have raised to markets and business. These include the worry that markets lead to inequality, that markets are in important respects unfair, that at least some business activity can impose costs on unwilling others, that businesses might pay their workers too little or charge too much, that businesses can induce customers into buying things they do not really need, that businesses in free markets will offer products or services that are dangerous or destructive or otherwise dubious, and that their focus on profits may come at the expense of other worthy goals. Representatives of each of these claims, and more besides, are easy to find. How does, or can, the code of business ethics articulated in the previous chapter address them? We cannot address all of these objections in full detail, but in this chapter let us look at a handful of them and see how the proposed code, embodied in our hierarchy of moral value, might address them.

Inequality

Does business activity in markets lead to material inequality? Yes. Should we worry about that? That depends. In particular, it depends on (1) how the inequality arose and (2) what the condition of the least among us is under conditions of (increasing) inequality.[1] Because people are different, because people's purposes, values, goals, and opportunities are different, because people's skills and abilities are different, and because of sheer luck, people's lives will take different, and unique, trajectories. That means they will have differing outcomes in life, including differing levels of material wealth. The question is whether we should (morally) worry about that. And further: if we should worry about it, what should or can we do about it?

There are many cases of inequality that I argue we should not only not worry about but actually celebrate, because they are reflective of the differences that are part of our individual identities. My best friend from high school is a medical doctor, and he makes a lot more money than I do. Is that unjust? I do not believe so. I could have become a medical doctor, I suppose; in fact, for some time I thought that is what I would become. But in college I had a philosophy course that forever changed my preferences and interests, and hence the course of my life. I knew that going into philosophy would mean a lot less money than if I went into medicine, but that was a tradeoff I was willing to make because I loved philosophy so much. By contrast, my friend also had philosophy courses in college and did quite well, but he chose to give up a potential life in philosophy because he preferred medicine instead. Neither of us was threatened or coerced into choosing our respective fields, and each of us has benefited, according to our respective schedules of value, from the choices we have made. Although I would certainly be happy if I made as much money as he does, I have no grounds for complaint because I knew what I was getting into and made my choices deliberately.

But should I be paid more for what I do? What if I believe that the value I am contributing to society is greater than what my salary represents? I am certainly entitled to believe this, and to try to convince others of it; and—who knows?—I may even be right. But I argue that I may not demand, as a matter of right, to be paid more because others—those who pay my salary—are persons too and their choices must also be respected. If people value my doctor friend's services at a higher rate than they value my philosophy professor's services, I may lament their values and the choices they make on their basis, but I may not impose on them or demand more from them without disrespecting their moral agency, which I must remember is equal to my own. Similarly for anyone else in any other line of work. You may believe you should be paid more, but if others are not voluntarily willing to part with their limited resources at any higher rate, then you have but two choices: you can accept what others are willing to pay you, or you can ply your skills and abilities elsewhere.

[1] See Tomasi 2012 and Piketty 2014.

But is material inequality itself morally unjust?[2] It would not be unjust on a Smithian conception of justice, which, as we saw in chapter 2, entails only protection from injury—specifically, injury in our persons, our property, or our voluntary promises. But should we expand the conception of justice, perhaps calling this new conception "social justice," which would include a prohibition of (suitably extreme) material inequality? Not necessarily. Consider two people, A and B. A has more wealth than B—much more wealth. Let us say that A has one hundred times as much wealth as B. Without knowing anything more about these two people, should we believe that there is something necessarily wrong with a society in which one person can have one hundred times as much wealth as another? Let us further suppose that A did not steal from or defraud anyone to get her wealth; she engaged only in honorable business that created value not only for herself but for others, according to those others' own judgment. This makes it less clear why there would be anything wrong with A having so much more than B.

But if A has this much more than B, does that mean that B's life must be miserable? Perhaps having only one one-hundredth as much as A means that B lives a life of poverty and misery, below the standards of basic human decency. Perhaps B's options in life and opportunities for improvement are far fewer than those of A—which, it seems, would almost certainly have to be the case. Is B, then, owed something? If not from A directly, then perhaps from society? But suppose our A is Bill Gates, who, as of this writing, has a net worth of approximately $90 billion; and our B is Michael Jordan, who, as of this writing, has a net worth of approximately $900 million, or only one one-hundredth of that of Gates. Would this great inequality between Gates and Jordan, and in particular Jordan's extreme relative poverty—relative, that is, to Gates, not relative to the rest of us—entail that he is entitled to some compensation? I suggest the answer is no. Jordan might be worth only a tiny fraction of what Gates is, but he is doing just fine on his own by any reasonable standard. Now, this is an extreme case, but we can extend its reasoning. Consider one C, who is worth only one one-thousandth of Gates; or increase the differential by an order of magnitude and suppose C is worth only one ten-thousandth of Gates. Indeed, increase it by more than yet another order of magnitude and suppose Gates has 180,000 times as much as C. Who is *that* person? That person is me.[3] Even despite that enormous difference between Gates and me, my family and I live in a house with running water, both my wife and I went to college, and our children likely will as well. By any objective global or historical measure, then, we are, despite our

---

[2] See Frankfurt 1998.

[3] Actually, my family and I are not even at that level, but close enough for round numbers.

extreme poverty relative to Gates, still doing very well. We have no reasonable grounds for complaint that we are unable to construct meaningful lives for ourselves, and certainly no grounds for complaint about Gates or Jordan, since their positions do not materially affect ours.

I suggest that this reasoning makes the following general point: the fact that one person has more wealth than another person does not, by itself, justify reasonable complaint or warrant compensatory action. To justify compensation or redistribution, we would need to show not just a difference in wealth between an A and a B, but, in addition, either that A got her wealth through unjust means (violation of person, property, or promise; through threats, force, or fraud; through extraction instead of cooperation) or that B has been prevented from increasing his own wealth through similarly unjust means. But in such cases it would not be the *inequality* that requires rectification but the *injustice*—and that is already addressed by Smithian justice and our code of business ethics.

Unfairness

Sometimes people suffer bad luck. Bad things happen to them through no fault of their own, even when they took due precaution and proceeded with proper deliberation. Similarly, some people just seem to have good luck: good things happen to them, again through no specific agency or choice of their own. In markets and business, some people with good luck might make a lot of money, while people with bad luck do not. If some proportion of the former's success in fact arises through luck, then they cannot claim credit for it; the same holds for people who are relatively unsuccessful in markets and business as a result at least partly of bad luck. If moral credit or blame can attach only to what we deliberately and voluntarily choose, however, then in both of these cases it seems we cannot claim to have deserved the success we enjoyed or the lack of success we suffered.[4] Might this be cause for compensation, or for redistribution of some of the fruits of the success—that is, money—from the former to the latter? Again, not necessarily. In fact, I will make a strong, and controversial, claim: undeserved bad luck and real disappointment do not by themselves, or even together, necessarily require compensation. Let me give an example to illustrate.[5]

Jack and Jill are college seniors who have been dating for some time. Jill is coming to think that she might be in love with Jack; Jack, for his part, also believes he loves Jill. On a Sunday evening, Jack calls Jill and asks her to dinner the next

---

[4] See Anderson 1999; Arneson 2004; and Frank 2016.
[5] I draw here on Otteson 2017.

Saturday evening. She agrees, and he tells her it is going to be *special*. When Jack says that, Jill begins to wonder whether Jack intends to ask her to marry him. She decides that if he does ask her, she intends to say yes. On Monday, Jack goes to a jewelry store and buys an engagement ring because he indeed does intend to ask Jill to marry him. Also on Monday morning, however, Jill is in class; on her way out of class, while happily thinking about the impending Saturday evening date and its potential future ramifications, she gets stopped by . . . Joe. Joe missed what the professor said at the end of class and asks Jill if she could fill him in. When Jill looks up at Joe, their eyes meet, and there is a spark. Joe asks her if she wants to get a coffee; she says yes. They talk and enjoy their conversation. After several hours of talking, they decide to get some dinner. Then they talk, walk around the quad, and talk some more. They eventually realize that they have been talking all night long. The sun is coming up over campus. Joe looks at the sunrise, he looks at Jill, and he says, "Jill, I've never met a person like you before. I can't believe I'm saying this, but, let's get married—right now! Let's elope!" Numerous predictable thoughts whir in Jill's mind, but she replies, "Yes." They agree to elope.

Now think for a moment of poor Jack. Did he suffer undeserved bad luck? Obviously yes: in the very week that he plans to ask his longtime girlfriend to marry him, her meeting a new person whom she suddenly decides to marry is clearly bad luck. Is the disappointment that Jack no doubt feels justified? Again, obviously yes. He and Jill have a history, he loves her, and he had reason to believe they might spend the rest of their lives together. But what can Jack do about it? Can he sue Jill for compensation for the future companionship and affection he expected to get from her but now will not? Can he seek redress for the children he wanted to have with her but now will not? Can he seek reparation for the time, energy, and effort he put into the relationship with her, all of which now has come to an unexpectedly fruitless end? The answers to all of these questions is no. Jack suffered undeserved bad luck and is experiencing a disappointment that I think everyone would agree is justified, but he has no right to Jill. He has no right to her affection, to her love, or to her time. She is a free moral agent, and hence she gets to decide with whom she will spend her time and to whom she will give her affection, even if that means Jack or anyone else is reasonably disappointed.

Is Jack owed something from anyone else? If you are a friend of Jack's, your friendship might require you to console him or offer sympathy. Perhaps you take him out for a beer and talk things over with him. You might introduce him to another potential mate. Any of those extensions of beneficence are acceptable, but what would not be acceptable is to visit some harm, injury, or cost on Jill (or Joe). Does *society* owe Jack something? Should we endorse policy that would require Jill or uninvolved others to compensate Jack? Should we endorse policy that would seek to prevent people like Joe from meeting or speaking to people like Jill? Again, the answer to these questions is clearly no—and for the same reason as that given earlier: Jill is a free person, entitled equally with anyone else to give or withhold her affections to or from whomever she chooses. If she had already entered into a contract (such as marriage) with Jack, or if she had made some promise (express or perhaps even implicit) to Jack, the situation might be different. But in the scenario proposed, no such contract was executed and no such promise made.

I suggest that the same reasoning holds in many other realms of human social life, including in markets and business. Suppose you regularly go to Coffee Shop A (CSA). Then one day Coffee Shop B (CSB) opens up across the street. You discover that you like its offerings better than those of CSA. Perhaps other CSA customers similarly decide they like CSB better; perhaps this change in preference eventually puts CSA out of business. Now, did the owner of CSA suffer undeserved bad luck? Yes: it was unlucky that another coffee shop opened across the street. Is the disappointment of CSA's owner justified? Yes: it seems entirely reasonable that she should be disappointed that her plans for keeping her coffee shop in business indefinitely into the future were dashed. And losing her business will cause significant displacement and difficulty in her life that she did not want or anticipate, which resulted, at least in part, from bad luck she did not seem to deserve. But does she have any rights to press against the owner of CSB or against the customers who have now chosen to stop patronizing her coffee shop? No. Just as Jack has no right to Jill, the owner of CSA has no right to those customers or to their resources, and she has no right to make them choose otherwise than they would on their own—or to visit harm or cost on them if they choose otherwise than she wishes they would. Similarly, the owner of CSB, like Joe, is also a full moral agent and hence entitled to offer his services, just as Joe is free to speak to whomever he chooses. All of them are free moral agents, entitled equally with anyone else to choose with whom to associate or whom to patronize.

I argue that these examples indicate that suffering undeserved bad luck and experiencing justified disappointment do not, even when combined, suffice by themselves to establish that the person is owed compensation. An assumption my argument makes is that all of the persons involved—including not only the disaffected person(s) but also those who made choices leading to the scenario under which the disaffected persons are unlucky and disappointed—are equal moral agents and thus deserve to have their choices respected as much as anyone else's choices.[6] I also assume that there was no contract or promise (explicit or

---

[6] See Rakowski 1991 and Otteson 2006.

implicit) in place that would obligate anyone to act in a way differently from what they chose. If there were such a promise in place, then a disaffected person might be owed compensation—from the affecting parties, if not from anyone else.

The political-economic implication of these examples is that the government should not intervene to protect failing businesses or even industries that are failing because consumers choose to expend their scarce resources in other ways. Subsidies and bailouts, limits on the market to protect firms or industries from competition, as well as tariffs and quotas all constitute either redistribution of wealth or other restrictions on the choices of people that third parties ought not to be entitled to make. They are like forcing Jill or Joe (or other citizens) to compensate Jack for the fact that Jill did not choose him, forcing patrons of Coffee Shop B (or other citizens) to compensate the owner of Coffee Shop A for not choosing to patronize her shop, or forcibly preventing Joe from talking to Jill or Coffee Shop B from opening.

But there is another implication that relates specifically to business ethics: businesspeople and firms should not lobby for such protections or compensation. Asking the government to subsidize their losses or prevent others from either competing with them or patronizing other firms is extractive behavior, and thus violates principle 2 of our code of ethics and the requirement that all transactions be mutually voluntary, mutually beneficial, and positive-sum. These kinds of restrictions would benefit the favored firms or industries, but at others' expense, and thus are disallowed. Now it may be that one is operating in a regime in which such extraction is allowed, perhaps even the norm, and thus one might claim that one must engage in such lobbying even if only for defensive purposes—simply to level the playing field of cronyism, as it were, because everyone else is doing it. I believe that even in such circumstances one should still refrain from engaging in extractive cronyism, but I will not press that point; instead I would concede that possibility and argue merely that one's obligation is not to engage in it unless one has to, and, further, to declare publicly that there should be no such favoritism.[7]

Luck clearly affects all of our lives, in good ways and bad. There is, however, no way to remove all the effects of luck in anyone's life, including everything from chance encounters between people who can help one another to unpredictable changes in the environment or in human society. And although luck

---

[7] An example of what I have in mind is John Allison, former chairman and CEO of BB&T Corporation, which as one of America's largest banks was forced to take a bailout under the 2008 Troubled Asset Relief Program (TARP). Though Allison did not want to and BB&T did not need it, the federal government threatened the survival of BB&T if it did not accept a bailout. So Allison and BB&T accepted it, but Allison made his objections to the existence of such government actions public. See Allison 2012; see also Burns 2009.

will therefore play a role in everybody's relative success in life, it is not clear what we could do about it. What we could do something about, however, is the presence of injustice—harm or injury to one's person, property, or promises, resulting from threats, coercion, or fraud. For that reason I argue that protecting us against such injustice is the right and proper function of our public institutions. Intervening in people's lives in an attempt to rectify good or bad luck is not.

Externalities

Some business practice leads to negative externalities, or the imposition of costs on unwilling others. Pollution is an example, as are nuisances like noise or increased traffic. Some portion of this, within reason, is simply the price we pay for living in a society in which we benefit from honorable business and in which people are allowed to freely conduct their affairs the way they see fit. Perhaps it is a "nuisance" to me that some people dress in ways I disapprove, or listen to music or read books or post things on social media that I do not think they should. Fair enough, but such things do not typically rise to the level of actionable offenses. Otherwise we would be suing or jailing each other continuously. To live with other people, and to benefit from living in a free society, we must make some accommodations for human plurality and diversity.

But in other cases, the costs to us are more significant and do seem to require action. If your business activity is creating serious pollution hazards for me or others, or if it is significantly impeding my ability to live or work peaceably, then you are creating a negative externality that requires remediation. Can our model of "honorable business" accommodate situations like this?

The disappointing news is that in an imperfect world with people who have different and sometimes competing values, there is unfortunately no way to accommodate all of these conflicts to everyone's complete satisfaction. The more hopeful news, however, is that our model provides a guide to address many, though admittedly not all, of them. Here is how. Recall that the prosperity Adam Smith argued that division of labor and markets could provide could be realized only within what he called a "well-governed society," and that he argued that what constituted such a society was institutions that enforce his conception of justice. Of his three "sacred" rules of justice, the second one is that which guards our neighbor's "property and possessions" (TMS, 84). This highlights the crucial role of private property and the critical—indeed, "sacred"—importance of protecting it. A robust set of institutions delineating and protecting private property goes some way toward indicating how our model of honorable business should deal with negative externalities. Many of these externalities are actually violations of property: they damage our property, they impede our peaceful and productive use of our own property, or they prevent us from exchanging or associating with others by using our property. In cases such as these, the externalities would constitute injustices, even on Smith's narrow definition, and thus would give rise to justifiable calls for compensation or restitution.

Nobel laureate Ronald Coase (1960) has offered a now canonical method for adjudicating competing claims about property that would quadrate with our model. Rather than suing one another or asking a court to issue an all-or-nothing judgment in your favor or mine, he suggests that we could bargain. Suppose three private parties have bought land on a large lake. One party wants to open a business that would provide a bed and breakfast and allow patrons to fish the lake. A second party wants to keep the lake and its environs in its pristine, natural state, untouched by human beings. And the third party is a nuclear power plant that wants to use the waters of the lake to cool its reactors. Suppose, for the sake of argument, that these three uses are mutually incompatible—whichever party gets its way will mean the other two parties cannot get their way, which means that the winning party will necessarily impose a high negative externality on the others. How should we decide who should win? One way to decide is to let them sue one another, but that is a long and costly process, potentially with a significant loss of value. And who is to say whether the courts will get it right? Another way to decide might be to poll the members of the surrounding community, or perhaps let them vote on a referendum. But since they have little stake in the outcome—they are not the primary parties who stand to gain or lose by the outcome—we cannot be confident that they will get it right either. It is easy to over- or underestimate costs or benefits when I am not the one paying or receiving them, so the chances that a vote would get things right are small.[8] It is also not clear that having third parties decide would respect the property and interests of the people involved and their rights to do with their property what they choose. So we seem to be at an impasse.

But Coase offers us a way out. Let the parties bargain with each other for the rights to do what they want with their property. We do not know in advance what the outcome of such a bargaining process would be, but as long as transaction costs are low—it is easy for them to speak and negotiate with each other— chances are that for one of the parties, the use to which they want to put the lake will be sufficient for them to offer an acceptably high payment to the others to compensate for the cost of giving up what they ideally wanted to do. So the three parties will start making offers to each other; as long as each of them has the right to say "No, thank you," we can be confident that whatever deal they eventually

---

[8] Voters are also notoriously uninformed about the issues on which they vote, which further questions the likelihood of a vote achieving the best outcome. See Caplan 2008; Somin 2016; and Brennan 2016.

strike will be both mutually voluntary and mutually beneficial. Coase's argument is that whoever wins the negotiation will have discovered what is likely to be the best use of the property, all things considered—in part because other members of the community will necessarily be involved as well: each of them would need to raise capital from bankers, investors, or patrons, whose joint judgment would therefore also contribute to the deliberations. We actually cannot know whether it leads to the best decision, but we would not know what the best decision is anyway. The negotiation Coase recommends would be a mechanism that promises a good, though not infallible, method to discover value.

Thus one principal way to deal with externalities, as well as conflicting claims about what the best use of property is, is to allow directly concerned parties to negotiate a voluntary agreement. Now, this does not always work. Many attempts at such negotiation would, and do, fail. Sometimes that is because of holdouts, who demand far-above-market premiums. Holding out in this way would not violate justice, however, and so should be respected. Yet money has a way of softening people, so we might reasonably expect that the actual number of such cases would be relatively low. Sometimes, however, one party or another will go to the relevant government authorities to try to force another party to comply. Perhaps a company asks for land to be designated as "blighted"; the government then takes possession of the property and transfers it to the party that lobbied the government—perhaps in exchange for payments or campaign contributions.[9] Although this certainly goes on, it would constitute an injustice and should be disallowed. Just because you do not like what I am doing with my property, or you believe (even correctly) that you could make more money with my property if you owned it, does not mean you may therefore take it from me. To think otherwise is to endorse extraction, perhaps the chief overall obstacle to general prosperity. Remember, the purpose of business is to create value—not only for itself but for those with whom it deals. If the others with whom a firm wishes to exchange or transact decline your offer, their opt-out option means they have the right to do so. And our respect for their autonomy and dignity entails that we must respect their decision, even when we disagree with it.[10]

It turns out, however, that in practice people develop all sorts of creative and innovative ways to deal with externalities like this, including in cases of

---

[9] A now-textbook example of this is the 2005 case of *Kelo vs. City of New London*. For an account of this case from the firm who represented plaintiff Susette Kelo, see Institute for Justice, n.d.

[10] Governments in the United States sometimes claim and use a power called "eminent domain" whereby they take private property for public use. Business does not have that power, however. Whether government should have it we leave unaddressed here (but see Epstein 1985 and 1993). My argument is that honorably behaving businesses would not ask government to use the power of eminent domain to benefit them privately.

"commons," or parts of the world to which no one has exclusive property rights. Elinor Ostrom (1990, 2005) won the Nobel Prize in Economics in large part for empirically documenting and providing theoretical models for the many ways different communities have solved such problems, even in what seem like otherwise intractable cases like pollution and overfishing.[11] No solution, or set of solutions, applies to all cases or will perfectly decide all such conflicts. That is one consequence of living in a world of scarce resources, whose uses might serve mutually incompatible ends, and of people with differing conceptions of the good life and differing schedules of value. But I submit that keeping our two main principles of (1) respect for others' autonomy and dignity and (2) seeking ways to create genuine mutual value will provide guidelines that will help us adjudicate many of the difficulties we will continue to face.

Worker Pay and Price Gouging

I group these two together because they both deal with prices, and they raise the question of where prices come from and what their function is in business and markets. In a seminal article, Nobel laureate Friedrich Hayek (1945) asks how we could create a "rational economic order." Before looking at his answer, we first need to know what a "rational economic order" is. By "rational," Hayek does not mean wise, reasonable, or virtuous. Instead he has a functional definition in mind that connects means to ends. On this definition, one is *rational* if one is taking steps that lead to the accomplishment of one's goals, whatever they are; by contrast, one is *irrational* if one's behaviors, actions, or decisions are in conflict with or lead one away from one's goals. No judgment about one's goals themselves is included in this definition, only the relation between one's actions and one's goals. By "economic," Hayek is referring to our resources, and the methods and forms of production by which we turn resources into goods and services. And by "order," Hayek means the pattern of distribution and use of both our resources and our goods and services. Because our resources are scarce, meaning we always want more than we have resources to fulfill, we have to make decisions, sometimes difficult decisions, about how to allocate our resources. And in many cases those decisions will be among mutually incompatible alternatives—if we put those resources here, they cannot go there. Putting these claims together, when Hayek speaks of a "rational economic order," he means that our resources are put in the service of our most important goals first, our second most important goals

---

[11] Ostrom 1990. I discuss environmental sustainability and the "tragedy of the commons" more fully in chapter 8.

second, and so on down the line. Our economic order is, by contrast, irrational if it dedicates resources to lower-valued ends at the expense of dedicating them first to more highly valued ends.

Given these definitions, Hayek asks the big question: how can we achieve a "rational economic order" for our society? One way to do it might be to ask an expert, or group of experts, to make the decisions for us. This, Hayek argues, is unlikely to succeed, however, because the knowledge required to determine good uses of resources—including in particular knowledge of people's preferences, the relevant demographic and other information about our society, and the relevant knowledge of our available resources—is hopelessly scattered in billions of brains. Each of us has some knowledge of our own localized situations, but no one of us has this knowledge about others' situations or about the totality. So the "data" on which a centralized expert would have to make decisions is not centrally aggregated and cannot be so aggregated because it exists only in billions of different people's minds. Yet even if it could be centrally aggregated, it could not be processed in real time. People's preferences change, and the circumstances of our lives—including things like climate and even weather—change constantly, in largely unpredictable ways. Hence Hayek argues that if we had to rely on an expert or group of experts to make all the millions of decisions about allocations of resources for us, the task would be hopeless and doomed to fail. There would be shortages and oversupplies, exactly what we in fact see in large-scale centrally planned economies.

But Hayek offers a different way to approximate the "rational economic order" that we desire, without having to rely on centralized experts: the price mechanism. Hayek argues that real prices, as opposed to aspirational prices, emerge when people say yes: when A and B agree on a price and exchange, that sets a precedent for a price. That price then contains information about what the value of the good or service in question held to the parties to the exchange. When millions of such exchanges take place, prices move up and down, reflecting the constantly changing preferences and situations—and, crucially, the local knowledge—of the people in question. So prices contain the aggregated knowledge of all the buyers and sellers around the world who played some part in the production or consumption of any good or service. But prices also convey suggestions. If gasoline were to suddenly rise to $10 per gallon, I would not need to know the reason it rose—war in the Middle East?—but I would immediately begin to economize on my use of gasoline. If the price of gas went to $1 per gallon, again I would not need to know why, but I would know that I did not need to economize as much. Thus high prices say to consumers: Buy less! Low prices say to consumers: Buy more! And prices give the reverse suggestions to producers and sellers. Low prices say: Produce less! High prices say: Produce more! In this way, what people are able and willing to produce tends toward an equilibrium with what others are able and willing to buy—though in reality a genuine equilibrium is rarely, if ever, reached, in part because of the continuously dynamic nature of the choices people make in response to their constantly changing environments, opportunities, and preferences.

On Hayek's view, then, real prices—that is, prices that emerge on the basis of actual decisions people make in actual situations—contain and are able to reflect the continuously updated and aggregated knowledge of millions, even billions, of people. It is a spontaneously emerging order that is then able to help coordinate the activities of millions, even billions, of people. And prices are able to accomplish this without any person, without any Great Mind,[12] directing them. Although it might appear that prices are set by someone, or that all this rational coordination must be directed by someone, in fact, Hayek argues, the price mechanism operating freely within markets accomplishes this of its own accord. In this it is like a language: people are able to use it to accomplish their ends, it is relatively orderly yet open to constant revision and change and development, and yet no single person or group creates or superintends it. Indeed, if any person or group of persons, however smart or expert, tried to manage prices, they would inevitably fail. It is not a matter of how smart they are; they simply do not have the vast and continuously updated knowledge requisite to do so.

It follows on Hayek's view that there is no such thing as a single correct price. The right price of any good or service is whatever the relevant parties agree to. And any given good or service might have indefinitely many prices, all indexed to specific choosers and reflecting their differing respective schedules of value. Centuries ago, however, St. Thomas Aquinas argued by contrast that there was such a thing as "just price," by which he meant a price at which a good or service ought, morally, to be bought or sold.[13] Deviation from this "just price," even on the basis of mutually voluntary decisions, was therefore an injustice, warranting rectification or correction from third parties. And many people still today speak of unjust prices, claiming that some people should be paid more (minimum-wage workers, for example)[14] or less (CEOs, for example)[15]. Some also claim that some prices are too high (price "gouging," for example), or too low ("predatory" pricing, for example). How does Hayek's argument help us address these concerns?

The first way is by arguing that there is no single "correct" price.[16] Unless government mandates specific prices, prices otherwise simply emerge and change

---

[12] See Otteson 2010.

[13] See Aquinas 2002.

[14] See, for example, Coakley and Kates 2013.

[15] See, for example, Gavett 2014. For evidence that executive compensation correlates with firm performance, see Hall and Liebman 1998.

[16] See Zwolinski 2008.

according to the choices people make. So to claim that a price is unjust is to claim in essence that people are making mistakes. But how is a third party to know whether others are making mistakes? Without knowing others' schedules of value, without knowing the opportunities, purposes, goals, and resources they have, a third party is unable to know whether others are making wise choices or not. We might know whether we ourselves would, or should, make similar choices, but because others are not us, what is right for us might well not hold for them. If we decide nevertheless to interpose our own judgment into others' voluntary agreements, then, it is presumptuous: we presume either that we know their situation, possibly better than they do; that our own judgment is sounder than theirs; or both. But Adam Smith's local knowledge argument suggests that we should be cautious when making such assumptions. Smith, in fact, calls it "folly and presumption" (WN, 456).

My larger argument about the proper code of business ethics—specifically, principle 4—suggests another reason to be wary of intervening in others' voluntary agreements: it is none of our business. They are full moral agents, equal in this regard to us and anyone else, which means that we must respect their choices. Even when we disagree with their choices, and even when we are right and they are wrong, they are still entitled to make the choices they believe best in their own situations. So if someone wants to work for a wage we think is too low, if someone wants to buy something at a price we think is too high, or if someone wants to offer a good or service at a price we think is too low or too high, we may remonstrate with them or try to talk them out of it. But if they wish to proceed nonetheless, we must, out of respect for their equal moral agency—and, indeed, out of respect for justice—respect their choices. We do not have to support their choices, but we may not threaten or coerce them into doing something other than what they, along with willing others, decide to do.

Manipulating Choice or Inducing Desires

Some critics of business and markets hold a rather dim view of marketing. They view it as more or less manipulation, perhaps even tantamount to lying.[17] The whole point of marketing is to get people to buy a good or service, or to patronize a business, that they otherwise might not. And in many cases, marketing aims to generate in people desires for goods or services that they would not have had if they had not been exposed to the marketing. Good marketers are very good, in fact, at figuring out just what to say, or how to frame things, so that people go

[17] See, for example, Schor 1999 and 2004.

ahead and buy—and they, as well as the firms for which they work, may seem not to care about whether a consumer actually needs or would benefit from buying; they just want us to buy. Is this moral?

If marketers lie or defraud customers or consumers, then that is clearly immoral, and is ruled out by principle 3 of our code of business ethics. And of course there are unscrupulous marketers, just as there are unscrupulous people in all walks of life. I argued earlier, however, that trying to persuade someone, or giving someone reasons to make one choice rather than another, is acceptable. Indeed, as long as a potential customer's opt-out option is respected, trying to convince her is a way of showing her respect. You make the best case you can, but as long as you respect her right to say, "No, thank you" and go elsewhere, you have not acted unjustly. But our hierarchy of moral value indicates a further requirement: your goal should be to create genuine value not only for yourself but for your (potential) customers as well. You have to think about them, about their needs and preferences, and come up with ways to address them. In this way, honorable marketing conceives of itself as a "problem-solver."[18] A good marketer is an extension of a good entrepreneur: a keen observer of human life, looking for problems or obstacles people have to achieving their goals, and then trying to find ways to remove those problems or obstacles. Once an entrepreneur has an idea, the marketer's job is to communicate to people how the idea might solve a problem they have. If the marketer uses her tools of persuasion to get you to see that you are facing an obstacle—which we often do not realize until it is pointed out—and to get you to see how her product can help you overcome that obstacle, then the marketer is acting honorably and creating, or attempting to create, value for you.

Does marketing sometimes actually generate desires and preferences, instead of merely trying to satisfy our preexisting desires and preferences? Absolutely. Who knew we needed an iPod or a smartphone before they existed? Who knew we needed Facebook or Instagram before they existed? Who knew we wanted washing machines or televisions or air conditioning or cars or planes or Air Jordans before they existed? No one had a desire for these things, or any number of things you and I currently own and use, before they existed. So they created new desires for them, but there is nothing wrong with that—indeed, these are among the great contributions to our lives that entrepreneurs and marketers, working honorably, have provided for us. And thank goodness. One day soon you may have a desire to purchase a self-driving car or a fully autonomous robot or an artificial replacement body, and marketers will help entrepreneurs bring them to your attention so that you can find out about them and then buy them.

---

[18] I thank Michelle Steward for helping me understand this insight. See also Bridges 2017.

The real worry about marketing, then, beyond lying and deception, is that marketers might get us to buy things that actually are not valuable to us and that do not create value. There are, for example, products and services provided in markets that many people believe are dangerous or immoral. Cigarettes, drugs, wingsuits, guns, and motorcycles might be examples of the former; prostitution, body parts, pornography, and some kinds of music and reading material might be examples of the latter.[19] These worries raise actually two related questions. First, what limits, if any, should we place on markets or business in the production of such goods and services—in other words, what is government's duty here? Second, what should you and I, as individuals, or as individuals involved in or dealing with business, do in the presence of the production of such goods and services? Given my argument that the primary role of government is to provide institutions that protect justice, the answer to the first question seems clear: the government should do nothing. The government's principal job is to protect justice, that is, to protect our persons, property, and promises against threats, force, and fraud. As long as these goods and services are offered to willing consumers and are bought and sold via mutually voluntary transactions, the government should have nothing more to do with them. And given the local knowledge argument, legislators and regulators are not in a good position to know whether individuals whom they do not know and about whose situations they know little or nothing are making good decisions.

But it seems likely that in markets there would be businesses that would offer goods and services of which we, or some of us, might disapprove, and people might be inclined to accept offers and enter into agreements that we, or some of us, might think they should not. So what recourse is left to us in the face of such cases? Here it is useful to introduce a distinction that Albert Jay Nock (1994) made between "social power" and "political power." Political power is coercive power: it is the power of law, legislation, and regulation that forbids or mandates action. Social power, by contrast, is the power of persuasion: it is the authority of judgment, suasion, and recommendation that encourages or discourages action. Nock argued that the more areas of human life we give to political power, the less there is left for social power, and thus the weaker our social power becomes. This, he thought, had deleterious consequences because it is social power, and the force of our moral characters, that gave us what he called "moral fibre" (1991, 323).

The relevance of Nock's argument here is that we often underestimate the power that moral commendation or condemnation can have in influencing others' behavior. As we have seen, Aristotle and Adam Smith agree. In cases that

---

[19] See Ubel 2009; Satz 2010; Sandel 2012; and Conly 2013.

fall outside the scope of justice, we should call upon our social power. If a firm is offering for sale a good or service that we believe it should not, the first thing to do is not to ask the government to prohibit, regulate, or punish the firm but instead not patronize that business ourselves. But the second thing we can do is discourage others from patronizing the business as well. If a firm is offering terms of employment that we believe are unacceptable, rather than asking the government to intervene, we should instead not work with that business. If we feel strongly enough about it, we should encourage others not to as well. If others do not heed our suggestions, we must respect their choices; but that does not mean we should not voice our disapproval. Indeed, it is precisely through this process of offering and listening to one another's moral sentiments that we develop our own moral judgment and contribute to our community's shared moral consensus. This is now much easier than it once was, owing to the ease of digital communication. Social media platforms like Twitter and many others have greatly increased the potency of expressing one's judgment about what others are doing. So one should not too hastily discount the effectiveness of public criticism—especially today.

Profit and Corporate Social Responsibility

If there is nothing inherently wrong with firms trying to find creative solutions to problems, or trying creatively to get us to see how they can solve problems for us, what should be the primary aim of a firm? I have argued that it should be to create value, but how exactly do we know if a firm is creating value? Can we measure value? Nobel laureate Milton Friedman (1970) argued that the central purpose of a business is to increase its profits, within the bounds of law and morality. In taking this position, Friedman was opposing claims that have become even more prevalent today that a business should concern itself not, or not only, with *shareholders* but with *stakeholders*. In Friedman's view, the CEO of a company is an agent of the owners, or principals, of the company, which in the case of publicly traded companies is its shareholders. For Friedman, this means that the CEO has a fiduciary responsibility to do what she is hired to do, which is typically to guide the company to higher profitability and higher returns to the shareholders.[20] Why do people invest in a company? Usually it is to see the value of their investment increase. So Friedman argues that a CEO must dedicate her professional activities to increasing the profits of the company. If the CEO personally

---

[20] Jensen 2001 famously claimed that CEOs and firms have an obligation to maximize profit. See also Jensen and Meckling 1976 and Primeaux and Stieber 1995; for a differing view, see Hussain 2012.

believes that investment in the community, or giving to charity, are good things in themselves to do, she might be right, but she must do it on her own time and with her own money—not on company time or with company money.

Corporate Social Responsibility

In the last forty years or so, however, an alternative conception of a firm's primary aim has emerged and even gained prominence. This is a concept called "corporate social responsibility" (CSR), which holds that a firm should concern itself not only with profit but also with being responsible stewards of the community. This might include everything from hiring a racially diverse workforce to engaging in "fair trade" to protecting the environment.[21] This is connected to what is called a "stakeholder" view, according to which firms are called on to strive to benefit all people who have a "stake" in the success of the company, which might include the local community, the state, the country, even the world.

Almost all companies today engage in CSR-related activities. A perhaps cynical view might hold that they do so only because they believe it will ultimately lead to higher profits. If businesses know that consumers are concerned about such matters, then it is simply good business to engage in them—to give the customers what they want, thus to have more customers, and thus to increase profits. And many articles and studies supporting CSR do so on the basis of the increased profitability to which it can lead, given the current consumer taste for such activities.[22] For Friedman's part, he has no objection to businesses portraying themselves as committed to CSR in order to increase profits, though there might seem something disingenuous about this. In order to get public credit for their CSR-related activities, businesses have to claim that engaging in CSR is done for its own sake—because it is the right thing to do. But if they are in fact engaging in CSR only because they want thereby to increase profits, then it might seem that they are not being honest about their true aims and motives. For consider what is being suggested: you can make more money if you engage in CSR. If the motivation to engage in CSR is ultimately the increase in shareholder value to which it can lead, however, then it is hard to see how CSR is in this way any different from what we might simply call "good business practice." Suppose getting employees uniforms or better computers would lead to increased productivity; then engaging in such expenditures would, or might, be justified because

---

[21] The literature here is vast. For recent overviews and defenses of CSR on the basis of its capacity to increase profits, see Chandler 2016 and Malecki 2018. For a list of indices that rate companies on their commitment to "corporate social responsibility," as well as a list of activities included in such indices, see Warsaw Stock Exchange 2010 and Business in the Community 2016.

[22] See, for example, Haque 2011.

it constitutes a greater return on investment. If engaging in CSR also leads to a greater return on resources, then that sounds like just another matter for efficiency and cost-benefit analysis. In this way, however, CSR activity would not seem to have any separate or independent moral value—which is what people *outside* the business world tend to have in mind when they think of CSR.

Principle 3 of our code of business ethics states that we should refrain from fraud and deception. If we are inducing people into buying our goods or services or into working or partnering with us by claiming a principled commitment to CSR, when in fact we are engaging in CSR only because we want more business, then we are acting deceptively and perhaps even fraudulently. We should instead be forthright about our motives. If we have understood our hierarchy of moral value correctly, we can do so with justified pride: yes, we are seeking profit;[23] but we commit to doing so only by creating value for others at the same time. In some circumstances, that might mean that we should engage in community or other charity; in some cases that means that we should dedicate more resources to research and development, company infrastructure, or increased wages or benefits; in still other cases, that might mean we should plow our earnings into returns for shareholders. Sometimes a combination of these will be called for. But the right choice of actions with our resources will be (*a*) best known by the individuals involved and (*b*) in the service of enabling the creation of ever more value.

Profit

The word "profit" often has a negative connotation, and "profit-seeker" is usually an epithet of abuse. Part of the reason for this is its association with the vice of greed. The character Gordon Gekko in the 1987 movie *Wall Street* told us— repeatedly, no less—that "greed is good." Most of us recoiled in response because greed is a vice, not a virtue. The greedy person not only might be insatiable— which is almost always a bad thing[24]—but also makes the mistake of confusing a means to an end for the end itself. Money is a means to many ends, but it is a tool, and it is valuable only insofar as it is put to good ends. The greedy person, however, comes to believe that money is an end in itself, and from there begins to believe that money represents the only scale of value that matters. Hence he

---

[23] See Rose 2000.

[24] The ancient Greek word for this vice was *pleonexia*, which both Plato and Aristotle connected with injustice. Aristotle identifies it with not just wanting ever more, but wanting it unfairly or at others' expense. See Aristotle 2000, book 5, chap. 1. For commentary, see Miller 1997 (who translates *pleonexia* as "excessive possessiveness") and Kraut 2002 (who defines it as "a combination of spite, envy, and greediness for profit").

always wants more of it, and he may even come to want others to have less of it. This is both a moral and an intellectual mistake. The intellectual mistake is to confuse the means (money) for the end it should serve (eudaimonia). The moral mistake is to deny or disparage all of the other virtues and values in life that also go into a eudaimonic life—everything from truth and beauty to love and sacrifice.

So profit is often viewed with suspicion because of its association with greed. Another reason, I think, is because people often think of profit as constituting benefit to one person or group of people *at the expense of others*. In other words, it is seen as extractive and zero-sum. If it is sought and achieved only according to our code of business ethics, however, it is instead cooperative and positive-sum—the result of mutually voluntary and mutual beneficial transactions. When business is conducted honorably, its profit is thus honorable profit and an indicator of the extent to which a firm is providing value to its customers. In this way, I would like to suggest, honorable profit already engages in CSR. It is the creation of wealth for the firm, including its owners and employees, for its customers and clients, for its partners and associates, and for the families and communities of all of these groups. The money a firm or a CEO has does not stay locked in a vault or buried in the CEO's backyard but is instead spent, saved, and invested to enable yet further satisfaction of ends. These can combine to create a virtuous multiplier effect that results from Adam Smith's invisible hand, and its beneficial effects spread far beyond the CEO herself or the firm itself.[25]

To further illustrate the way firms might contribute to CSR, consider an argument made by the nineteenth-century political economist Frédéric Bastiat (1801–1850). Bastiat distinguished between the effects of economic decisions that are "seen" and those that are "unseen."[26] His specific target in drawing this distinction was the "unseen" costs involved when we, or when circumstances, force people to spend resources in directions they otherwise would not have. His now famous example is that of a boy who throws a rock through a shopkeeper's window pane. Bastiat said that many people fallaciously believe this provides a boost to the economy, because the shopkeeper must now buy a window from the glazier, giving the glazier new business he otherwise would not have had. The fallacy, however, as Bastiat points out—what is now in fact called the broken window fallacy—is that the new business to the glazier is "what is seen"; on the other hand, "what is not seen" is what the shopkeeper would have done with that money otherwise. Perhaps, Bastiat suggests, he wanted to buy a new pair

[25] Hume (1754) 1985b argued that the benefits to others spread widely: "The encrease of riches and commerce in any one nation, instead of hurting, commonly promotes the riches and commerce of all its neighbours" (328).

[26] Bastiat (1850) 2017.

of shoes or new books for his library. The value to the shopkeeper of the new shoes or books is now lost, and that loss must be reckoned against the value of the new windowpane. As Bastiat explains, however, the new shoes or books represent even higher value to the shopkeeper than a new windowpane. We know this because the shopkeeper could have already bought a new pane for his shop if he had wanted to, but he wanted instead to buy the shoes or books. The boy breaking his window forces him to spend those resources instead on something he valued less—even if we can suppose it does have some value to him—rather than on something he valued more highly. That is the "unseen" loss.

But there is a loss to the community as well. If the window had not been broken, then society would have had *both* a window *and* a new pair of shoes or books; once the window is broken, we now have only the (replacement) window. Bastiat concludes this from his discussion: "Destruction is not profitable" ([1850] 2017, 406). Even if we can replace or rebuild, and even if the replacements or rebuilding are of better quality than what we had before, it remains the case that what was destroyed was lost, and all the value it provided was lost as well.[27]

This is an important, even crucial, lesson in opportunity cost, and in the necessity of estimating opportunity cost when contemplating intervening to redirect resources to places other than wherever they would otherwise have gone. But Bastiat's lesson applies to the discussion of profit and CSR as well. What is the best use of a firm's resources? This is often extremely difficult to know—which perhaps helps explain not only the extremely high turnover rate among CEOs but also the high failure rate of businesses generally.[28] And this is when firms and CEOs are singularly focused only on their own relatively narrow ends of succeeding in a field that they know intimately well. If we were to charge firms and CEOs with the additional task of superintending the betterment of society more generally, this would be to set them up for almost certain failure. For consider: the betterment of society is a broad and vague goal, with many different elements and conflicting conceptions; there are indefinitely many ways that we might achieve it, yet no clear guidance for which to choose or how to choose among competing, and often mutually inconsistent, means and ends; and in any case a company could achieve it only if it was already otherwise profitable—for otherwise it would have no resources to reallocate. The inevitable and unfortunate limits of human knowledge arise again to hamper our best intentions.[29]

---

[27] Many today continue to succumb to the broken window fallacy—even Nobel Prize–winning economists. See, e.g., Krugman 2001.

[28] Some 80 percent of new businesses fail within eighteen months; see Wagner 2013. See also Ormerod 2005.

[29] As Popper famously said in his discussion of social science, "Our ignorance is sobering and boundless" (1976, 87).

This depressing conclusion follows, however, only if we assume that the only way a firm could achieve it is by making some *centralized* decisions about how to allocate its assets. What if instead we applied the Hayekian insight that *decentralized* decision-making is able to exploit local knowledge in a way that centralized decision-making cannot? Based on Hayek's claim, a firm could reason that a perhaps better way to achieve social betterment would be to put as many resources in the hands of as many people as possible, to be deployed as the individuals themselves respectively judged best. They would then use their local knowledge to put those increasing resources in directions that could generate benefit to themselves, their families, and their communities, according to their individual knowledge and judgment.

This, in effect, is what a business seeking honorable profit does. If it uses its profit to pay its workers more, to pay dividends to its shareholders, or to lower its prices, in all of these cases it is putting more resources into the hands of those many individuals—and leaves it to them to dedicate those new resources to the places they judge most worthy. The benefit that would accrue to not only those individuals but to society more generally is like Bastiat's "unseen": it is part of the benefit created by a successful firm that does not show up on its balance sheet. Because the firm does not know to what uses its employees, investors, and customers put these resources, they are "unseen." But we know they exist. Take as an example a company like Walmart.[30] It employs 2.2 million people worldwide, it has millions of shareholders, and in 2017 it had revenues of $486 billion and net profits of $13.6 billion. Now consider: How many people has Walmart enabled to afford things they otherwise would not have been able to afford, freeing up their limited resources to afford yet other things? How many thousands of recent immigrants, poor people, and young workers has it employed and given a first chance to? How many people have been able to go, or send their children, to college with the revenue created by Walmart? And how many billions of dollars in taxes did Walmart and its employees and its customers pay? Perhaps you do not shop at Walmart; perhaps you do not invest in it, or perhaps you disapprove of some of its policies, offerings, or practices. Fair enough. But when evaluating this, or any other business, we tend to focus only on the negative, and we often fail to consider the many and extensive benefits—including the "unseen" benefits—that businesses like Walmart provide not only to those directly involved but those indirectly affected as well.

Many of today's firms take it as part of their explicit mission to contribute to charitable projects they consider worthwhile—think of TOMS Shoes, for example, which is a for-profit company that donates a pair of shoes to an impoverished

---

[30] See Vedder and Cox 2006.

child for every pair of shoes it sells;[31] or of various "fair trade" coffee companies. Still others, like Grameen Bank, founded by 2006 Nobel Peace Prize winner Muhammad Yunus, operate on a business plan that is based on what Yunus calls "social business"—or the idea that profit is sought but only to expand its ability to add value to the community.[32] As long as all of these firms are open about their aims, and about whatever tradeoffs they make that might reduce profit in the service of CSR-oriented activities, my argument has no objection to what they do. On the contrary. But there is not only one way to create value in the world, and it is not only those firms that explicitly take as part of their missions to engage in CSR that do so. All firms engaging in honorable business do.

But What About ... ?

Does this mean, however, that all business activity is good, or that all people in business behave honorably? No. Does it mean markets never misallocate resources, or that they always produce the best possible results from our scarce resources? Again, no.[33] Does it even mean that all people who engage in business only honorably, as defined here, always create value? No, not even that is true. Human beings are too flawed, too limited in their knowledge, too subject to biases and prejudices, and too susceptible to opportunism to justify any such rosy claims. But humans have these limitations and flaws in all walks of life, not only in business. All of us make good-faith mistakes, and there will always be some who engage in bad-faith behavior as well. Given that, perhaps the best we can hope for from a system of political economy is to have institutions that minimize the damage that flawed and bad actors can cause, and that maximize the benefit to themselves and others that even such actors can create, including despite themselves. Political economy deals in a world of second-bests: it does not focus on what the ideally best form of society is or on how it would benefit us if ideally wise and good people populated it. Instead, it surveys human nature, human history, and the human condition as it actually finds them, and asks what can be hoped for from so limited and coarse a clay as is humanity. It seeks, then, not the ideally best, but rather the better among actually possible alternatives. Perhaps, indeed, the most that can be hoped for is simply the least bad among the actually possible alternatives.

---

[31] Some have criticized the TOMS business plan, however, on the grounds that it displaces local footwear production and depresses local markets; see, for example, Wydick, Janet, and Katz 2016.

[32] See Yunus 2017.

[33] For contrasting views on market failure, see Simpson 2005 and Heath 2014.

Given these rather humbler aims, the political economist is not as susceptible as, say, a philosopher might be, to having problems pointed out. The ancient Greek philosopher Plato (428–328 BC), for example, articulated in his *Republic* the structure of the ideally conceived city-state. It was headed by those few superhumans—Plato called them "philosophers," or "lovers of wisdom"—who could apprehend the Form, or perfect conception, of the Good, and who, as "philosopher-kings," arranged all the other parts of society so that they would achieve this conception of the Good (Plato 1992). However beautiful Plato's vision might be, because it aims at theoretical completeness, it is what we might call a "fragile" conception: even a single omission or problem could defeat the entire philosophical edifice. By contrast, the political economist—for example, Adam Smith—sets his sights rather lower, but in so doing is able to generate not a fragile but a "robust" conception.[34] Smith discharges the philosopher-kings from a duty that, as he says, "could safely be trusted, not only to no single person, but to no council or senate whatever" (WN, 456) and instead offers a vision of society that is practical and mutually beneficial. Even if it is not ideally perfect, it might be "the best that the people can bear" (TMS, 233).

Although the Platonic system might realize ideal goodness in its theoretical conception, the Smithian system, by contrast, expects and anticipates that mistakes will be made—both by its leaders and by its citizens. Instead of constructing a vision of political economy that could succeed only if administered by people with more knowledge and better morals than average human beings,[35] the Smithian aim is instead to minimize the effects of these inevitable mistakes. Smith proposes to accomplish this principally by reducing the scope of any individual decision-maker's authority mainly to himself, and by maximizing the benefits of decentralized experiment, innovation, and productive entrepreneurship by foreclosing extractive routes to benefit and thereby leaving only cooperative routes. If—or, rather, when—an individual makes a mistake regarding the proper allocation of resources under Smithian institutions, the negative consequences that result tend to redound only on herself; she is thereby encouraged to learn from her mistake, but limiting the scope of the consequences to her means she does not jeopardize the institutions themselves. By contrast, the centralized nature of the Platonic system means that if—or, rather, when—its decision-makers make mistakes, their consequences propagate throughout the system, because all of it depends on their judgments. In such a case, a misjudgment can jeopardize the institutions themselves, their fragility making them

---

[34] See Paganelli 2006 and Pennington 2011.
[35] This would be an example of the "great mind fallacy." See Otteson 2010.

more susceptible to systemic failure than the more robust decentralized system of Smithian political economy.

In a similar way, honorable business as we have described it proceeds on the basis of decentralized decision-making and entrepreneurial innovation under risk and uncertainty. It will make mistakes, but because the negative consequences of those mistakes tend to be limited to the individuals, entrepreneurs, and firms themselves, they absorb and learn from the losses without endangering society's overall generation of prosperity itself. Honorable business will not achieve perfect deployment and utilization of all resources and will never be able to procure for everyone everything they want. There will be disappointments, failures, and mistakes. But what it can hope to accomplish is steady improvements and gains, which are enabled by the decentralized process of entrepreneurial experiment and trial and error that sees its goal as creating value.

Thus the project of political economy, of which our conception of honorable business is a part, is more robust than ideal theory.[36] Both its theoretical recommendations and its practical applications allow for and hence can withstand many of the problems that might arise. I believe that that is a strong argument in favor of political economy and the approach to business ethics we have taken. But note that I said it can withstand "many" of the problems that might arise—in other words, not all of them. That provokes the following question: What *would* defeat the Smithian political-economic methodology, and the conception of honorable business I have defended—either in theory or in practice? Are there recurring problems facing honorable business in markets that it cannot plausibly address, or that it might even make worse? We shall turn our attention to this question in subsequent chapters.

Conclusion

In this chapter, I have taken a first pass at raising and addressing several potential worries about markets and the conception of honorable business I have defended. The worries included inequality, unfairness, externalities, low worker pay and price gouging, manipulation of consumer choice, and profit-seeking. I argued that the conception of honorable business, along with the code of business ethics articulated in the previous chapter, provides tools to understand and address these worries. Moreover, I have discussed corporate social responsibility and argued that honorable business and honorable profit-seeking are plausible ways to address it as well. And I argued that the public institutions of which

---

[36] See Schmidtz 2011a and Gaus 2016.

honorable business forms a part are relatively more robust, and thus relatively more able to withstand both shocks and inevitable human misjudgment, than are other sets of institutions—while still allowing scope for entrepreneurial experiment that can lead to discovery of better ways to use our resources and improve people's lives.

It is now time to complete the circle of my argument about how honorable business can lead to both morality and prosperity, to which we turn in the next chapter.

5

From Business to a Just
and Humane Society

Introduction

We discussed in chapter 2 the spectacular growth in worldwide prosperity that has occurred since 1800, and we there raised the question of why this growth happened, specifically when and where it did. Why did it not happen earlier or in some other place? If anatomically modern human beings have been on earth for tens, even hundreds, of thousands of years, why did growth in prosperity not occur until so relatively late in human history? And why did it begin primarily in places like Holland and in Britain, as opposed to China or Egypt or Italy or South America? Why did the Industrial Revolution begin when and where it did, as opposed to somewhere else or at some other time?

Suppose you were transported back in time to AD 1000, without any knowledge of humanity's subsequent history, and were asked to survey the world at that time and predict where an unprecedented, substantial, and sustained growth in overall prosperity would occur. What would be the likeliest possibility? It certainly would not be Britain, which was relatively poor in natural resources and had a small population riven by violence and internecine battles for warlord supremacy. It would not be Scandinavia, which at that time was chiefly characterized by the raiding and pillaging of the Vikings. It would probably also not be North America, which was a large but sparsely populated land with small, mainly nomadic hunter-gatherer tribes. There would have been instead two other clear, leading candidates: the Islamic world centered in Baghdad, and the Song Dynasty of China. The Islamic world at the time was in its golden age, flourishing in philosophy, science, literature, and commerce. And the China of the Song Dynasty was also flourishing, with arts, literature, and philosophy, a standing navy, and gunpowder. Both communities also had large populations and claimed control over large territories.[1]

And yet in neither case was there a sustained growth in general prosperity. In fact, in both cases there was hardly a blip in overall wealth. Some few people and families got very wealthy indeed, but their general populations benefited little from the wealth of their caliphs and emperors. In neither case was there an Industrial Revolution, and in neither case were their considerable advances in science and technology translated into anything like the mass flourishing that began in northwestern Europe around 1800 and has continued to this day and spread to many other parts of the world. The Asian gross domestic per capita in year 1 was $456.[2] In year 1000, it was essentially unchanged at $465. By 1500 it had risen to $568, but by 1870 it had actually regressed slightly to $556. Thus in the span of nineteen centuries, Asia had grown in per capita GDP only about $100, and the golden age of the Islamic world and the Song and other dynasties made virtually no difference.

Per capita GDP in Western Europe in year 1 was $576, about where Asia was at the end of the nineteenth century. Western Europe itself saw a regression by year 1000, retreating to $427. In 1500, it had risen to $771. By 1820, however, it had risen to $1,202 and had begun its steady march upward. Just fifty years later, it had risen to $1,960, while its offshoots, including America, had risen even higher, to $2,419. By 2003, western Europe and its offshoots, including America, stood at $23,710. Asia in 2003 stood at $4,343—a tremendous, eightfold real increase from just a century earlier, but yet nothing like what the Western world enjoyed. What we in fact have seen in human history was a relatively consistent, and consistently low, average of about $1–$3 per person per day throughout the entire span for which we have data. There was a great deal of average material equality throughout the world throughout human history, though people were equally poor—indeed, in real terms they were at or below the threshold of "absolute poverty" set by the United Nations today. And then, something began to change. Slowly at first, and mostly localized in northwestern Europe; but then it began to pick up steam and spread to other parts of Europe and to the Americas, and now, today, is at far higher levels than ever seen before, enriching the lives of far more people than ever before.

Deirdre McCloskey (2016a) calls this the "Great Enrichment," and she documents how humanity survived on approximately $3 per person per day (in contemporary dollars) for all of its history, until the Great Enrichment began to take place around 1800. Today the average American enjoys approximately $157 per

---

[1] See Mokyr 1992; Landes 1999; and Macfarlane 2000.
[2] This data comes from Maddison 2007. All figures are in constant 1990 international dollars.

day; the worldwide average is approximately $45 per person per day. This is a real and substantial, and again historically unprecedented, increase that has benefited billions of people. Tragically, there are still people today who are living at humanity's historical norms of poverty, so there is much work to do. But the good, indeed great, news is that the proportion of people living at those levels has now reached all-time lows: In 1900, the proportion of people worldwide living at the $1–$3 per person per day level was approximately 90 percent; today it stands at about 5 percent—and it is falling rapidly.[3] In 1980, 90 percent of all Chinese lived at the levels of absolute poverty; today, only 10 percent do. So in less than forty years, over 1 billion people in China alone have risen out of poverty.[4] In just the next decade or so we may well see the number of people living at absolute poverty decrease to *zero*.[5] This is indeed one of the most important and significant achievements in all of human history, though a story that somehow many of us do not know.

These facts raise several pressing questions. First and foremost, what exactly led to the Great Enrichment? Second, how can we enable yet others to partake in its unprecedented prosperity? And third, what role has honorable business in markets played? The miseries attendant on our historical levels of poverty, as well as the blessings enabled by our current and increasing levels of wealth, join, moreover, to indicate a moral mandate.[6] These are not merely academic questions of historical curiosity. People's survival, not to mention their chances of constructing lives of meaning and purpose, can depend on the political-economic institutions their countries adopt.

The Story of Prosperity

What is required for prosperity is principally two kinds of things: the right public institutions and the right personal attitudes or principles. The right public institutions include in particular institutions protecting what Adam Smith called "justice": protecting the persons, the property and possessions, and the voluntary promises and contracts of every member of the society. Institutions that protect these things presume that the property and possessions are honestly, or "justly," acquired—that is, without the use of threats or force. In other words, they are acquired only through mutually voluntary and thus mutually beneficial

---

[3] See Chandy and Gertz 2011; German 2015; and Tupy 2017.

[4] See Coase and Wang 2012 and Donaldson 2017.

[5] See Yunus 2017.

[6] As Rosling, Rosling, and Rönnlund put it, we have a "moral imperative to help people escape from the misery and indignity of extreme poverty" (2018, 91).

transactions.[7] They also presume that the promises made and contracts entered into are also the result of honest, or "just," agreement—that is, only when there was no fraud and when all parties enjoyed an opt-out option. It may be that some of the parties to a voluntary agreement do not have many other options, or that their other options are all much worse (or even very bad); it may also be the case that we can imagine hypothetical agreements they might make that would be better, even much better, than the agreements they actually make. Even in such cases, however, the fact that they voluntarily agreed indicates both that they did in fact enjoy an opt-out option and that they believed the option they chose is an improvement over whatever other options they had. Though we may worry about, for example, the poor having few options and thus accepting agreements that, though voluntary, are not as good as we would wish for them or are perhaps even exploitive, the good news is that this will not be their only chance to strike an agreement.[8] It will be the first of what is likely to be many, with each subsequent opportunity—one hopes and expects, especially if they live in a Smithian "well-governed society"—better than the previous. One of the things that the growing prosperity enabled by Smithian institutions provides is more options for people: options about where or from whom to buy, where or for whom to work, and so on. Adding more options to people's choice sets almost always improves their situations, whatever their conditions; and in any case it does not worsen it.

The other requirement is the members of the society possessing the right two kinds of attitudes: (1) to see it as a necessary requirement of any exchange, transaction, or association that it constitute the creation of positive (if not necessarily equal) value for all concerned; and (2) to treat all persons with whom they might exchange, transact, or associate as full, equal, and autonomous moral agents of dignity deserving respect. The first set of attitudes entails that we may seek to better our own conditions, but only if we thereby simultaneously better the conditions of others—as judged by those others. The second set entails that we respect the choices others make and that we seek to exchange, transact, or associate with others only by making offers that they are free to decline if they so choose. Together, these attitudes require us to concern ourselves with others' well-being sufficiently to effectuate an exchange, though they do not require us to sacrifice ourselves for the sake of others or to demand that others sacrifice themselves for our sake. These attitudes apply primarily in contexts of strangers dealing with one another, or with people who have no particular personal relationships that might require other kinds of considerations. With family

---

[7] See Munger 2011, which suggests that perhaps such exchanges should be not just voluntary but "euvoluntary."

[8] For related and instructive discussions of sweatshops, see Zwolinski 2007 and Powell 2014.

members or friends, we might well, out of familial love or friendship, be required to make sacrifices of ourselves for their benefits. There might even be special cases of exigency when we are required to help strangers—as, for example, if we happen upon an injured person.[9] But when dealing either with people we do not know or with whom we have no personal relationships—as is the case typically in markets and business—and in cases when we are exchanging, transacting, or associating for mutual benefit, the requirement is for us to find win-win scenarios, judging for ourselves what counts as a "win" for us and allowing others to judge what counts as a "win" for them.

As Smith articulated, the proper institutions of a "well-governed society" include a government that protects against injustice arising either from foreign or domestic threats. This means we will need a military, as well as police and courts. Beyond that, the government will do little—only what is required by demonstration that a proposed governmental activity is both (1) unable to be provided by private enterprise and initiative and (2) conducive to the betterment of the entire society and not simply of one group at the expense of another group. This latter duty of government is open-ended, though the two necessary criteria establish a high threshold and put the burden of proof on the person proposing the new activity of government. It should also be noted that what putative duties of government would qualify on these two criteria might change over time, in particular as the society advances in prosperity.

As we saw in chapters 2 and 3, the members of a Smithian "well-governed society" should seek to apply their time, talent, and treasure in the service of discovering ways to better both their own and others' conditions. That means they will seek to engage in business activity that is honorable—taking responsibility for their own actions, never proceeding on the basis of threats or force or fraud, never unjustly exploiting others, respecting the dignity and autonomy of all with whom they associate, and honoring both the letter and spirit of all promises and obligations they freely undertake. They have the additional obligation, however, not only to be honorable businesspeople but to steward the profession of honorable business in that context. This means they respect the institutions of a just and humane society and the proper purpose of business. They adopt and internalize a code of business ethics that they demand of themselves through the force of their own characters, even when faced with "golden opportunities" in which they could benefit themselves by breaking their code and when they are certain they would not be caught. Moreover, they model and represent their professionalism to others, and they demand, by force of their example and by their personal commitments, that others adopt a similar code of honorable business.

---

[9] See Otteson 2000; Cullity 2004; and Singer 2009.

Individuals who decide and commit themselves to engaging in honorable business need, as we have seen, institutions to support them. But those institutions include not just formal public institutions, but also cultural ones as well. In particular, they need the support of a widespread consensus about not only what honorable business is but also why it is praiseworthy. They need a culture that celebrates, instead of deprecating, mutually voluntary and mutually beneficial exchanges, that celebrates, instead of deprecating, increasing prosperity, and that understands the generally beneficial effects of honest commerce and honest profit. Their culture must also not be immediately suspicious of inequalities in wealth.

This last requirement needs elaboration and justification. As the history of human prosperity, as well as the results of numerous historical experiments in differing systems of political economy, seems to have shown, we face an unfortunate choice between general prosperity and equality. For most of human history, people were relatively equal in levels of wealth, but they were equally poor. During the only time in history that substantial numbers of human beings were able to rise out of poverty—namely, since around 1800—what enabled this rise also led to inequality. Now, people measure inequality differently, and the economic literature is filled with competing, and sometimes contentious, debates about exactly what kinds of inequality matter most, how exactly to measure it, and so on.[10] Let us sidestep those debates, however, and simply concede, for the sake of argument, that business and markets lead to material inequality. What presents us with an uncomfortable dilemma is that the clear lesson from human economic history seems to be that the only way we have ever discovered to enable substantial numbers of people to rise out of poverty is a set of political-economic and cultural institutions that also engender inequality.

Equality, by contrast, has historically correlated with low levels of prosperity. Indeed, as Scheidel (2017) has recently shown, the central causes of reductions in inequality, or the great causes of equality—what Scheidel calls the "Four Horsemen" of leveling—are war, violent revolutions, state collapse, and catastrophic plagues. All of these are combated by having a government that protects justice and by the increasing prosperity such a society fosters. This suggests that we face this stark choice: we can combat poverty, by increasing general prosperity; or we can combat inequality, but by extraction and coercion, which leads to poverty. If you could eradicate either poverty or inequality, but not both, which would you choose? I suggest that poverty is more deserving of our concern. Poverty is the cause of far greater misery, and what keeps people in poverty— Scheidel's "Four Horsemen"—are far more destructive than inequality. This

[10] See Sen 1995 and 2000 and Nussbaum 2013.

is especially true if the institutions enabling mass flourishing actually benefit everyone, including especially the least among us, even if it does not benefit everyone equally. And that has actually been the case in the over two centuries since Smith published his *Wealth of Nations* for the people lucky enough to have been members of those countries that adopted his prescriptions.[11]

McCloskey argues that a change in attitudes about what constitutes moral ways to associate with others, and the cultural changes to which that led, are what have in fact effectuated this Great Enrichment. In three massive and impressively documented books (McCloskey 2006, 2010, and 2016a), she has painstakingly laid out the case that it was in fact primarily a change in attitude, not in institutions, that launched the trajectories from which we now benefit. In particular, she argues that it was a change in our beliefs and attitudes about what she calls the "bourgeois virtues"—including things like honesty, fair-dealing, industriousness, perseverance, prudence, and punctuality—that led to changes in formal institutions that in turn buttressed and enforced these changing attitudes. While formerly such virtues were in fact considered vices—think, for example, of the way philosophers, priests, artists, and writers (what McCloskey calls the "clerisy") have portrayed merchants[12]— in the seventeenth and eighteenth centuries, particularly in northwestern Europe, those attitudes began to change. People came to see what I have called honorable business first as not necessarily vicious, then as morally neutral, then as morally praiseworthy. As this change in attitude spread, along with it came changes in our institutions. There ensued a transition from finding virtue in extraction and praising the great "heroes" who raped, pillaged, and plundered, to finding vice in such activities and instead finding virtue in peaceful cooperation and mutual betterment. And as the prosperity has increased to which this change in attitudes and thus institutions led, similar changes spread to other parts of the world, enabling yet further increases in prosperity. Like the miracle of compounding interest, this led to exponential growth, generating the unprecedented prosperity we see in the world today.

As plausible as McCloskey's account seems, not everyone accepts it. Some contemporary scholars think institutions themselves were both necessary and

---

[11] There is, however, some evidence that global inequality has actually been decreasing as global wealth has been increasing—following an inverted U or "Kuznets" curve—especially in places like China and India. See, e.g., Cowen 2013 and 2017 and McCloskey 2016a. So perhaps we *can* address both poverty and inequality, but the evidence suggests we should address them in that order because the nonviolent and productive way to reduce inequality is by increasing overall prosperity. I thank Maria Pia Paganelli for discussion on this point.

[12] Consider also Mandeville (1714) 1988, who argued that the "public benefits" of our actions arise in fact from "private vices"—that is, that all professions, including business, that generate benefit for others do so only on the basis of individual selfishness.

sufficient, and so tend to discount the role of a change in attitudes.[13] Others, like Jared Diamond (1999) for example, argue for a kind of geographic and demographic determinism, significantly discounting the role of human agency. Still others, like Joel Mokyr (1992),[14] credit principally technological innovation and the growth of scientific knowledge for the growth patterns we have seen. I find McCloskey's argument more plausible. Institutions do not arise on their own or enforce themselves, so it seems that for them to function as they are intended by theorists they require the widespread support of their citizens—which seems to return us to human agency, attitudes, and hence culture.[15] Similarly, while geography and demographics certainly affect prosperity, the geographical and demographic constraints and opportunities faced by human beings have been in place for a long time—which means they would not explain why prosperity began to increase when it did as opposed to some other time. In any case, whether McCloskey's explanation turns out to be historically correct or not, it is at least plausible, and it comports with the Smithian story. Smith's argument would account for and theoretically predict exactly the prosperity we have seen, and McCloskey's argument about changing culture complements it in ways incorporated by and consistent with the account we have given of honorable business.

The Smithian prediction is that a society so constituted with the right institutions and with members possessing the right characters will see increasing wealth. In fact, the Smithian argument is that there is no upward bound on the wealth—and genuine prosperity—that such a society could generate and enjoy. Even a lone country with these characteristics, surrounded by other countries engaging in extraction, cronyism, corruption, and so on would still soon outpace the others in prosperity. And it would then become an example to those other countries, as well as a beacon welcoming honorable business and honorable businesspeople from other countries. In this way it would place competitive pressures on other countries to give up their extractive ways, on pain of losing people or resources or both, and thus incentivize them to reform their institutions and attitudes to encourage cooperative and mutually beneficial interactions.

---

[13] See, for example, North 1982 and 1990; Rosenberg and Birdzell 1987; and North, Wallis, and Weingast 2009. For other instructive accounts of the growth of wealth that take various positions, see Landes 1999; Macfarlane 2000; Beinhocker 2007; Singer 2009; Deaton 2013; and Morris 2013.

[14] See also Mokyr 2016.

[15] See Rose 2019. See also Maine 1861, who famously distinguished between a "status" society and a "contract" society, and suggested that human progress coincided with the switch from the former to the latter. See also Oman 2016.

Is Money All That Matters?

That is the summary of my argument about the nature of honorable business, about the institutional and cultural requirements for it, and about the predictions it makes regarding the effects on prosperity of any country adopting it. It is also our account of the actual historical trajectory that worldwide wealth has experienced over the last approximately two centuries. Thus it would seem to enjoy not only theoretical coherence but also substantial empirical support as well. Moreover, the Smithian argument gives us an explanation for why those places in the world today that have not yet enjoyed increasing generalized prosperity have not. The prediction would be that such countries either do not sufficiently protect justice, or they are marked by an excessive reliance on centralized economic decision-making, or both. Either of these, and especially both of them, would retard growth, whatever other virtues they are intended to serve. If one surveys the world today, and compares those that have experienced the highest levels of prosperity to those that are still at humanity's historical norms of poverty—and all the countries in between—one finds further corroboration of the Smithian theory. Compare, for example, mainland China to Hong Kong, North to South Korea, or Venezuela to Chile. Or compare the countries of western Europe to those of sub-Saharan Africa. Or Israel to the rest of the Middle East. It is readily apparent which in those comparisons come closer to approximating Smithian recommendations, and just as readily apparent which are more prosperous. And the comparison is all the more telling when one compares the poorest segments of each respective country. The poorest 10 percent of those countries that most closely approximate Smithian recommendations are, in real terms, an order of magnitude more prosperous than the poorest 10 percent of those countries furthest away from Smith.

An objection one might raise in response to these claims, however, is that it all seems to concern money—as if money were the only thing that mattered in life. Is money all that matters? I hope my answer is both obvious and uncontroversial: no, of course money is not all that matters. But that does not mean money is unimportant. Recall Smith's definition of wealth: it is the means to achieve our ends, whatever they are. What increasing wealth can do is enable us to satisfy our more basic and pressing needs, and thereby enable us to turn our attention to the satisfaction of those higher ends that can begin to constitute not mere subsistence but flourishing. If I am so poor that I do not know whether I can eat today, or whether my children can eat today, or, as Smith puts it in the introduction to *The Wealth of Nations* (WN, 10), if I am faced with the horrifying prospect of having to decide which of my children to expose so that my other children might survive—and let us be clear: these are in fact the kinds of decisions that have faced humanity throughout most of its existence, and that still face some yet today—then there is no space in my life for thinking about the good life or contemplating justice and virtue, for wondering which college my children will attend, for writing a novel or leaning to play the piano or reading (or writing) a book like this one. These elements of a life of meaning and purpose, or whatever other elements a eudaimonic life might require, become possible only above a certain threshold of wealth. And as our wealth increases, we are then liberated to turn our attention to ever more of our higher ends and purposes.[16]

Smith writes: "But when by the improvement and cultivation of land the labour of one family can provide food for two, the labour of half the society becomes sufficient to provide for the whole. The other half, therefore, or at least the greater part of them, can be employed in providing other things, or in satisfying the other wants and fancies of mankind" (WN, 180). This constitutes, again, part of the moral mandate that motivated Smith's investigations and our own today: as long as there are still people at or below the minimum thresholds of absolute poverty, and as long as there are still people who, while above that threshold, nevertheless do not yet have sufficient wealth to enable the eudaimonic lives to which they aspire and that constitute the fulfillment of their humanity and identities, I believe we are under a moral obligation to do what we can to help create increasing prosperity. Poverty may be, in some sense, the natural state of humanity; but, as Smith predicted and as subsequent history has shown, it is not our destiny. Those of us lucky and privileged to be in a position to contribute to the generation of prosperity and thence enable more people to have the means to construct for themselves eudaimonic lives of meaning and purpose are under a moral obligation to do so.

In the context of business, and the ethics of business with which we are here concerned, I believe this means we are under an obligation to undertake to use our resources—our time, talent, and treasure—to positively seek out ways to create value, both for ourselves and others. We must do so honorably, by following the code of business ethics, and not waste or squander our limited resources, or prevent others from using their own limited resources, to improve their situations. If we do it right, we will benefit ourselves only by benefiting others. In this way, our individual actions as honorable business professionals can, and should, contribute to the just and humane society each of us wants and deserves.

---

[16] Empirical evidence suggests a correlation between wealth and happiness, with an even more pronounced effect on the poor. See Kahneman and Deaton 2010; Layard 2011; Stevenson and Wolfers 2013; Badhwar 2014; Lyubomirsky 2014; and Graham 2017.

The Just and Humane Society

The highest level of our hierarchy of moral value is a "just and humane society." You may recall that when I first introduced this notion in chapter 2, I did not define what a "just and humane society" (JHS) was. Part of the reason for not doing so at that point was to leave the concept sufficiently open to allow for a wide variety of differing conceptions, in an effort to enable us to discuss the other elements of the hierarchy without stalling the development of the argument in disagreements that, at that point in the argument, were unnecessary. But now that I have fleshed out the other elements of the hierarchy, I need to specify more clearly what constitutes a JHS. Additionally, if we are to evaluate whether the elements lower in the hierarchy make sense and cohere with one another in a reasonable way, we have to complete the chain linking them all the way to the top. Recall that Aristotle argued that a rationally ordered moral life is one in which one's daily activities served one's proximate ends, which in turn served one's intermediate ends, which themselves in turn serve our final or ultimate end. Aristotle called the ultimate end for human beings eudaimonia, and a rationally ordered moral life is one in which each individual has come to some understanding of what a eudaimonic life would be for him, and then orders the rest of his life to achieve it. To know, then, whether what we are doing today is right for us, we have to know what kind of life we will have led such that at the end of it, we can look back and justifiably believe we led a life worth having been led. Similarly with business: in order to justify our daily actions as business professionals, we need to understand their connection to the ultimate end those actions serve, which is contributing to a JHS. So we need to know what a JHS is.

As I argued in chapter 1, human beings are purposive creatures. That means that they have purposes, of course, but it means more than only that. Human beings also have the capacity to deliberate on their ends, to change or modify them, and to construct rational plans for their lives to achieve their ends. They also have the freedom, or autonomy, to make choices: they can opt for this purpose or that, decide to do this or that. This capacity for autonomous choice is precisely what makes them moral agents: their ability to freely choose to act or not means they can be held responsible—*morally* responsible—for their actions. When they choose well, the positive consequences of their actions reward them for their good choices. And when we let them enjoy the good fruits of their good decisions, this is not only a fitting and proper reward for having chosen well but also the feedback they need to encourage them to make similarly good choices in the future. On the other hand, when they choose badly, the negative consequences of their decisions should also redound upon them. Although this is the painful part of being free and responsible people, it is just as proper, and just as necessary, for us to experience the negative consequences of our bad choices as it is for us to experience the positive consequences of our good choices. Experiencing both is necessary for us to develop judgment. Judgment is a skill, and, like other skills, it needs to be practiced to develop, and it must be practiced under correction. To develop good judgment, each of us must go through the sometimes rewarding and sometimes unpleasant process of making decisions, experiencing their consequences, and then honing our judgment in the right ways.

A JHS is one in which all people respect the rules of justice with respect to one another—no one injures or interferes with others in their persons, property, or promises—and people actively deploy their resources in the pursuit of cooperative relations with others that lead to their mutual benefit. What constitutes "benefit" is left largely to the individuals themselves, as their judgment about what constitutes a eudaimonic life for themselves indicates. But this does not entail a conception of life as lonely individuals or solipsistic islands. Because human beings are a naturally social species, because they seek mutual sympathy of sentiments with others, and because their natural limitations entails that they need to cooperate with others to achieve their ends, the result will be mutual seeking of productive, cooperative ventures aimed at mutual betterment. In this way, we are all encouraged to find ways to contribute to one another's pursuit of eudaimonia, of lives that each of us believes are worth living and having been led. Now, this often goes wrong because we often make mistakes. And the temptation to engage in extraction can call to us like a siren song. Hume ([1741] 1985) went so far as to argue that, for that reason, "it is [. . .] a just *political* maxim, *that every man must be supposed a knave*," though he allowed that "at the same time, it appears somewhat strange, that a maxim should be true in *politics*, which is false in *fact*" (42–43). But both history and theory suggest that the JHS envisioned here is the one that stands the best chance of allowing individuals to construct lives of meaning and purpose, in cooperation with willing others, and at the same time grants to us the liberty to be the captains of our own lives and the respect of being held accountable for the choices we make.

The Tyranny of Choice?

Some contemporary critics call this argument into question, however, by claiming that if we know that people are likely to make bad decisions, then at least sometimes it is unnecessary, and perhaps even cruel, to give them the freedom to do so. Thaler and Sunstein (2009), for example, argue that modern behavioral economics has discovered that people make in fact many, and even systematic, mistakes in their reasoning. For that reason, Thaler and Sunstein advocate what they call "libertarian paternalism," which calls on legislators or regulators to "nudge" people in the right directions by framing the options they face so that people are directed—sometimes subtly, sometimes not so subtly—to choose (the libertarian part) those actions or behaviors that we know they should (the paternalistic part). Thaler and Sunstein recognize the importance of allowing people still to make their own choices, but they argue that our goal should be to help people make the choices they would make if they "had paid full attention and possessed complete information, unlimited cognitive abilities, and complete self-control" (2009, 5).[17] This seems a rather high standard, and Thaler and Sunstein acknowledge that legislators and regulators will not always be in a position to know which decisions for specific individuals might meet it. But they claim that in many cases legislators and regulators do know, and when they do, they should act as "choice architects" to make us more likely to make the right choices. They suggest everything from requiring cafeterias to rearrange their food offerings so that people are more likely to select fruits and vegetables than fried foods or desserts, to requiring employers to arrange the default settings for retirement and savings accounts so that people are more likely to save more.

Others have taken the Thaler and Sunstein argument further, asserting that we should abandon the "libertarian" part of "libertarian paternalism" altogether. Peter Ubel (2009), for example, claims that an argument for markets and choice is viable only if we do not actually know what decisions are good (or bad) for people. Perhaps in the eighteenth century, when Adam Smith was writing, we did not know what foods, for example, people should or should not eat. In that case, allowing people to experiment by making free choices might have been justifiable. No more, however. According to Ubel, the sciences of health and nutrition have advanced to the point where we actually do know a great deal about healthy and unhealthy lifestyles. Given that, why should we allow people the "freedom to choose" when we know that at least some of their choices will be bad for them? Sarah Conly (2013) argues that we should abandon the idea of autonomy altogether. She considers it a relic of a prescientific age, before the modern sciences of psychology, medicine, and nutrition. Moreover, she argues that it is based on the false assumption that people actually know what is best for them. I am not a psychologist, a doctor, or a nutritionist, so how could I possibly know what the healthy choices are that I should make? She hence invites and welcomes instruction from experts in these fields and in many others (like finance and education) and calls on legislators or regulators to constrain our

[17] See also Thaler 2015. For criticism, see Rizzo 2007 and White 2013 and 2017.

choices—even, if necessary, against our will and contravening our overt expressions of preference—so that we are required to make the right choices.[18]

A complementary argument comes from Barry Schwartz (2016). Schwartz argues that having more choices can paralyze us. Being confronted with, for example, dozens of choices among different kinds of toothpaste, blue jeans, potato chips, or chocolate (his examples) can induce anxiety and worry. It can be a bewildering array, and how are we to know whether the one we choose is the best choice? Schwartz presents evidence purporting to suggest that perhaps the main results of allowing unlimited choice are an unpleasant feeling of anxiety, a paralyzing inability to make a choice, and, once we do make a choice, a residual feeling of regret or remorse resulting from uncertainty over whether we chose well. If we add to this the fact that marketing harangues us, trying to induce us to choose this product or that one—in many cases, Schwartz argues, with no real difference among the various products or no significant difference in their utility to us—the result is that markets and business lead to the proliferation of pointless but psychologically costly options.

These arguments call into question the importance I have argued autonomy and responsibility have for us. And they offer a competing vision of a JHS. The Aristotelian and Smithian vision of a JHS for which I have been arguing is one in which people are enabled and encouraged to seek ways to create benefit for themselves and others, as a result of free choice and being held responsible for their free choices. By contrast, the vision endorsed by Thaler and Sunstein, Ubel, Conly, and Schwartz is one in which people do not confront the perhaps unsettling responsibility of making decisions for their own lives, the risks and uncertainties involved in captaining one's own life, or the pain or discomfort resulting from having made bad decisions. In their world, we are nudged away or forbidden from making bad choices, and instead our actions—whether by voluntary choice or not—are in the service of the healthy, safe, and secure life they believe is best for us. Their world would not only provide little scope for individual liberty and responsibility, which they acknowledge; but it would also restrict the operation of business, markets, and entrepreneurship, which they tend to overlook. Much of business activity in markets comprises constant efforts to discover new and—one hopes—better ways to allocate resources, to satisfy more of people's changing needs and preferences and, in turn, allow them to improve their conditions. But some of this continually searching activity will issue in innovations that will not, in fact, improve people's conditions. As we have seen, the large majority of innovative ideas and new business ventures fail,

---

[18] Conly 2015 goes yet further: she calls for government restriction on the number of children people may have.

which means lost resources and perhaps other costs (including psychological) along the way. The same is probably true for the majority of individual decisions that people make: though some of them will turn out well, many of them will not, entailing pain, discomfort, and loss.

I have argued, however, that the pain from having chosen badly is, though unpleasant, nevertheless a necessary part of the process of developing judgment. I would go further: failure, and the experiencing of the consequences of having failed, is an indispensable part of developing the judgment that characterizes the agency of a morally mature person of dignity. We cannot develop good judgment if we do not practice it, and practicing necessarily means sometimes failing—in moral judgment just as in learning to play the piano or shoot a jump shot. We could indeed prevent the pain associated with failure by not trying at all—by not attempting new things and by not taking risks. But what we would thereby give up is our liberty, responsibility, and moral judgment—as well as all the innovations that constitute our increasing prosperity. We could prevent the loss and failure involved with most business ventures by either preventing new businesses from starting or by subsidizing any losses of those that currently exist. The "seen" benefit, using Frédéric Bastiat's language, from that would be fewer failures and less risk of loss; but the "unseen" cost of that is all the potential contributions to our prosperity never realized from innovations that were never created. The Thaler and Sunstein, Ubel, Conly, and Schwartz vision of the world makes little room for entrepreneurship, for innovation, or for honorable business that includes seeking new ways to cooperate, exchange, transact, partner, and associate, and thus trades security off against increasing prosperity.

Is the tradeoff worth it? One way to address this question is to ask whether we would be content with our current state of science, technology, and prosperity. Would we be willing not to have any more innovations? No new medicines or treatments or drugs; no new phones, computers, or apps; no new companies or products or services? Consider these questions from a slightly different angle. At what point would we be willing to say, "Now we have enough—we do not need any more innovation"? Thaler and Sunstein's *Nudge* and Ubel's *Free Market Madness* both came out in early 2009, before the launch of, for example, Uber and Lyft. Conly's *Against Autonomy* came out in 2013, before artificial embryos, zero-carbon natural gas, "genetic fortune telling," and the internet of things.[19] If we had adopted their recommendations when they made them, we would be without those things—and many others—not to mention the further and potentially pathbreaking future possibilities of gene therapy, nanotechnology, 3D printing, and on and on. Thank goodness people did not take their advice.

---

[19] See MIT's annual list of technological innovations by year for further examples (MIT 2018).

Imagine how much poorer our lives would be if someone had decided in, say, the year of your birth, that at that point we already had enough. How many of the goods, services, and technologies that we currently enjoy would we no longer have?

Zookeepers and Regulators

In addition to the material increases in wealth we would have to forgo if we eliminated autonomous choice and experimentation, I would also argue that we give up part of our humanity. Consider on this point Rainer Maria Rilke's arresting poem "The Panther" (1907), which tells of a powerful and beautiful panther that, once free, is now caged in a zoo and thus now sees the world from behind bars, indeed behind "a thousand bars." As Rilke tells us, the great cat's beauty and power rapidly decline—not because he grows older, but because his *spirit* is caged and thus defeated. Sooner than one could expect the panther is, though alive, truly dead, because behind the bars he is no longer really a panther.

The panther's well-intended zookeepers will rightly point out that in the wild his life is full of dangers. Nature can be parsimonious and unforgiving—nature is, in Tennyson's memorable phrasing, "red in tooth and claw"—whereas the zookeepers are benevolent and protective. We can further assume that they are trained in the most modern techniques of animal husbandry, zoology, veterinary medicine, and so on, and that they are committed to humane treatment of animals. So although behind the bars the panther is not free, he is at least safe, comfortable, healthy, and secure. On that basis, the zookeepers may argue that they have made a better life for the panther than he would have had in the wild, and they have a point. But as Rilke's poem dramatically illustrates, the pampered and protected panther is still a *caged* panther—and, in a deep sense, is no longer really a panther at all. It is part of the panther's nature to be free and wild, not just fed and inoculated. Without his freedom, he is a shadow of his true self; as Rilke puts it, even if his literal heart continues to beat, his true "heart ceases to be."

Still, since the panther is not a moral agent, perhaps one is not inclined to value his freedom very highly, and so one is inclined to think that what we might call a *zookeeper morality* is acceptable for him. I disagree, but I am willing to concede the point. However: human beings *are* moral agents. Therefore the zookeeper morality is unacceptable for them. Living free is indeed uncertain and sometimes dangerous, and it does involve both success and failure. But both one's successes and one's failures are one's own. They are part of our identities, and I argue that it constitutes the true dignity of humanity to fully exercise all its abilities in striving and contending, in taking risks, and sometimes succeeding and sometimes failing.[20] President Calvin Coolidge said this in 1923:

> Unless [...] people struggle to help themselves, no one else will or can help them. It is out of such struggle that there comes the strongest evidence of their true independence and nobility, and there is struck off a rough and incomplete economic justice, and there develops a strong and rugged [...] character. It represents a spirit for which there could be no substitute. It justifies the claim that they are worthy to be free. (Coolidge 2001, 242)

Human beings, I contend, are capable of being "worthy to be free." Human beings become noble, and I would suggest even morally beautiful, by the vigorous use of their faculties, and they become dignified when their lives are their own, when all the forced care and protection of others is taken away, and the bars are thrown open.

One of the best-selling books in British history is Samuel Smiles's *Self-Help* ([1859] 1996). It is based on lectures he delivered to young men in Scotland giving them advice on how to be successful in life. He based his advice on particular examples of great figures, mostly in British history, and the trials, tribulations, and challenges they often had to overcome before they achieved their great innovations. He discusses figures like Josiah Wedgwood (1730–1795), the abolitionist and potter who overcame multiple failures and great odds on the path to inventing the china for which he is famous today; and John James Audubon (1785–1851), the American ornithologist after whom the Audubon Society is named. One particular episode from Audubon's life is worth recounting. Here is Smiles quoting from Audubon himself:

> "An accident," he [Audubon] says, "which happened to two hundred of my original drawings, nearly put a stop to my researches in ornithology. I shall relate it, merely to show how far enthusiasm—for by no other name can I call my perseverance—may enable the preserver of nature to surmount the most disheartening difficulties. I left the village of Henderson, in Kentucky, situated on the banks of the Ohio, where I resided for several years, to proceed to Philadelphia on business. I looked to my drawings before my departure, placed them carefully in

---

[20] See Bobadilla-Suarez, Sunstein, and Sharot 2017, which provides evidence of the intrinsic value of making autonomous choices.

a wooden box, and gave them in charge of a relative, with injunctions to see that no injury should happen to them. My absence was of several months; and when I returned, after having enjoyed the pleasures of home for a few days, I inquired after my box, and what I was pleased to call my treasure. The box was produced and opened; but, reader, feel for me,—a pair of Norway rats had taken possession of the whole, and reared a young family among the gnawed bits of paper, which, but a month previous, represented nearly a thousand inhabitants of air! The burning heat which instantly rushed through my brain was too great to be endured without affecting my whole nervous system. I slept for several nights, and the days passed like days of oblivion,—until the animal powers being recalled into action, through the strength of my constitution, I took up my gun, my note-book, and my pencils, and went forth to the woods as gayly as if nothing had happened. I felt pleased that I might now make better drawings than before; and, ere a period not exceeding three years had elapsed, my portfolio was again filled." (Smiles [1859] 1996, 61)

Smiles tells similar stories about many other giants in their fields, highlighting the perseverance, industry, and concentrated application they required to reach the achievements for which they are now known. Smiles's conclusion:

"Heaven helps those who help themselves," is a well-tried maxim, embodying in a small compass the results of vast human experience. The spirit of self-help is the root of all genuine growth in the individual; and, exhibited in the lives of many, it constitutes the true source of national vigor and strength. Help from without is often enfeebling in its effects, but help from within invariably invigorates. Whatever is done *for* men or classes, to a certain extent takes away the stimulus and necessity of doing for themselves; and where men are subjected to over-guidance and over-government, the inevitable tendency is to render them comparatively helpless. (Smiles [1859] 1996, 1)

This constitutes both an economic and moral response to Thaler and Sunstein, to Ubel, to Conly, and to Schwartz. The economic response is that the zookeeper morality they recommend prevents people from taking the risks and achieving the innovations they are capable of that can improve the lives of the rest of us. The prosperity we enjoy today—not just in money but in Smith's fuller sense of genuine wealth—is not possible without the entrepreneurial risks that innovators take.[21] These ventures, because they are risky, often fail; but when they succeed, they improve the lives of others in multiple and manifold ways. And the people who will succeed, as well as the ways in which they will succeed and the ways in which their success will not only benefit others but lead to yet further successes, are often unpredictable and thus cannot be planned even by the most intelligent experts. As Matt Ridley (2016) has argued, almost all of the progress in human life has proceeded via a process of unplanned evolution, by innovators finding new ways to build on what others have done in an organic march toward ever more prosperity.

I would like to suggest a further reply to what I have called the zookeeper morality, one that is moral rather than economic: the freedom to choose is valuable in itself. It is a constituent part of our identities as full moral agents. The acts of deliberating, of making a choice, and of acting on one's choice marks us out as distinctively human, as being distinct from other creatures. We are project-creators and, as Loren Lomasky puts it, project-pursuers.[22] We are also choosers and learners, capable of conceiving of ourselves, and of treating others, as specifically moral agents capable of assuming and exhibiting a moral dignity we would not otherwise have. Thus even if we know that we will make mistakes, even if third-party experts can predict at least some kinds of the mistakes we are likely to make, and even if we ourselves would acknowledge after the fact that we had made a mistake and that a third party might have been right: even granting all of this, it is still valuable, even necessary, for us to make decisions for ourselves. That does not mean we should not consult the advice of others, of course. On the contrary, good judgment will indicate that we should routinely solicit the advice of people expert in fields other than our own—everything from medical professionals to financial advisers—but the decision about whether to act on their advice, even whether to solicit their advice in the first place (and whose advice to solicit), must remain ours. There is no other way for us to develop good judgment, and no other way to embrace our identity as free and responsible creatures.

This argument bears importantly on the proper regulatory role of government. It does not entail that all regulations are bad, or that no regulation can ever be warranted. But it does imply that a high threshold must be met before instituting a regulation. It is not enough to claim that it might lead to a good result, or that it might lead to a result that the person proposing it would prefer to whatever would otherwise happen. Regulations by their nature go beyond Smithian justice—the "three Ps" of person, property, and promise—because breaches of them would already be covered by the protections of justice and would thus

---

[21] See Isaacson 2015.
[22] See Lomasky 1990 and 2016.

require no additional protection. Regulations instead apply to otherwise voluntary exchanges or partnerships whose nature or consequences are disfavored. To be consistent with respecting others' equal moral agency, however, such regulations would have to be limited to cases that involve imminent danger or whose negative consequences could not be known or foreseen by the parties to them. Because of the paramount importance of respecting people's moral agency, however, the latter case would itself have to involve not just negative consequences but large, even potentially catastrophic, negative consequences—if not to the persons directly involved, then to uninvolved others.[23] Having different preferences, different risk tolerances, different hierarchies of value, or even a combination of these would not by itself justify regulatory intervention. The good news, however, is that governments that protect the Smithian "three Ps" and have a light regulatory apparatus that acts only when this high threshold is met have historically engendered substantially growing overall wealth, along with all the ancillary benefits—both material and nonmaterial—that that entails.[24]

Deontology, Utility, or Virtue?

One final question remains for us to address in this chapter: Is this defense of the institutions and attitudes necessary for prosperity, and the conception of moral agency and obligation implied by our hierarchy of moral purpose, based on deontological, utilitarian, or virtue-based considerations? Recall from the introduction that many books about and courses on business ethics begin with delineating these theories and ask readers or students to assess a variety of specific cases from each of these perspectives. As I argued in chapter 1, I have my doubts about the benefits of beginning a discussion of business ethics with a discussion of competing theories of ethics—or of metaethics, that is, theories not only about *what* it is right to do but *why* what is right is right. Instead, I have argued, we should first consider the proper purpose of business, and what the honorable businessperson's obligations are, given that purpose. But at this stage of the argument, the reader may well, and rightly, wonder what connection it bears to these theories. The answer is that it relates to, and draws on, all of them—but in different ways, and at different stages, as it were, in the argument.

---

[23] See R. S. Taylor 2017.

[24] The history of Hong Kong after the Second World War is one spectacular example, but there are many others. On Hong Kong, see Monnery 2017; for discussion of many countries' historical trajectories under varying regulatory and institutional systems of political economy, see Otteson 2014. I discuss regulation further in chapter 6.

Begin with deontology. Deontological systems of ethics are marked by their reliance on rules, typically rules about what one may not do and then also what one must do. And though different deontologists will propose different rules, all of them are typically characterized by conceiving of these rules as mandates: "Do *x*" or "Do not do *x*." Immanuel Kant (1724–1804), perhaps the archetype of the deontological philosopher, identified a single rule for morality, which he called the "categorical imperative" (Kant [1785] 1981). By calling his moral imperative "categorical," Kant meant to distinguish it from what he called "hypothetical" imperatives. Hypothetical imperatives take the form of "If you want *x*, then do *y*." An imperative of this form is "hypothetical" because it depends on whether you in fact want *x*: if you do, then you should do *y*; if you do not, however, then this imperative does not apply to you. Such imperatives do not by themselves take a position on whether you should want *x*; they leave that to you. Categorical imperatives, by contrast, admit of no exceptions and are intended to apply regardless of an individual's wants or desires—hence the term *categorical.* "Thou shalt not steal" is a categorical imperative; "If you want people to trust you, you should keep your word" is a hypothetical imperative.

Our argument about the kind of moral attitudes necessary to foster a culture that encourages prosperity requires that people treat at least some of the moral rules—including in particular the prohibitions on injustice and the planks of our code of business ethics—as categorical imperatives. If they instead treat them as hypothetical, they will end up undermining the very support that the principles can provide for successful cooperation with others. I will be far more inclined to trust and thus cooperate with you if I think your commitment to abjuring injustice and opportunism is a principled one, one by which you abide no matter what. If, by contrast, I think that you view your commitments as merely hypothetical—commitments, in other words, that might be overridden if, in a particular case, you think there is greater benefit to be had for you if you violate them—then I would be far less inclined to trust and thus cooperate with you. The more of us who take a consequentialist approach, rather than a principled or deontological approach, to our dealings with others, the more potential cooperation we therefore forsake, and the less overall prosperity we will enjoy. So our commitment to these codes of ethics must be principled—as a deontological theory would hold.

Yet my argument relies heavily on virtue ethics as well. Virtue ethicists, from Aristotle on down, have held that the moral life is the one marked by adherence to specific virtues—courage, justice, temperance, and wisdom, for example—and that the moral person is the one whose life is characterized by routine, even habitual, exhibition of these virtues.[25] As I have argued, however, one crucial aspect of the required moral attitude is that we must adhere to proper behavior even when

---

[25] See Miller 2014.

others are not looking. Thus others must believe that even when we are confronted with "golden opportunities" we will not exploit them and will instead adhere to our principles. How do we assure others that we are such people, and how in fact do we become such people? By internalizing these rules, and our commitments to following them, as parts of our general moral character. They must be woven into the fabric of who we are as constitutive elements of our personality, just as integrated into our identities as, for example, the language we speak. We speak our native tongue without thinking about speaking our native tongue. It is the instinctive medium in which we think and speak, so much so that it requires great and concerted effort to learn a new language, or to get ourselves to think and speak in one. The same should be true of our moral principles. They should be instinctive, and guide our actions as a matter of course and not as a result of conscious—and thus slow and uncertain—deliberation.[26] When we reach this stage, our actions become both extensions and representations of our virtuous character.

But what is the ultimate reason we want the particular institutions, the particular moral rules, and the particular attitudes toward our moral principles for which I have argued? If we keep asking "Why?"—as we should—we eventually get to the final or ultimate reason, to that consideration that is valuable in itself and for no further reason, a consideration for which we do everything else we do but that we seek only for its own sake. I argued in chapter 1, following Aristotle, that this final end or purpose in an individual human life is eudaimonia. But what is the final end or purpose that our public institutions, both formal and informal, should serve? It is the same: eudaimonia. That is, our formal and informal institutions should enable and encourage people to seek and achieve eudaimonic lives. This, ultimately, is why we have spent so much time discussing Aristotle.[27]

Yet I have further argued that while wealth is not equivalent to the eudaimonic life it nevertheless enables it. In this way, then, my argument resembles a utilitarian one. If we define "utility" as "conducing to eudaimonia,"[28] then I can reframe the argument in the following way. I advocate for these particular institutions, codes of behavior, and attitudes because they conduce to our utility—so defined. It is a consequentialist argument insofar as it claims that

[26] For a discussion of these two different types of reasoning, see Kahneman 2013. See also Pinker 2002, chap. 3.

[27] Adam Smith writes, "All constitutions of government, however, are valued only in proportion as they tend to promote the happiness of those who live under them. This is their sole use and end" (TMS, 185).

[28] I note that this is different from the way most contemporary economists define "utility." Today, "utility" is typically taken to mean the satisfaction of preferences, whatever they are. By connecting "utility" to eudaimonia, I distinguish among preferences that would take us away from or interfere with our pursuit of the truly happy life connected to virtue, and those that lead us toward that ultimate end. For further discussion, see Russell 2012 and LeBar 2013.

these institutions, codes, and attitudes will likely have the desired effects of prosperity, thus a just and humane society, and thus eudaimonia. They would not, however, guarantee eudaimonia, since human life is filled with failures, vagaries, and unpredictable surprises that can interfere with our pursuit. That is why good judgment is so important—we must rely on it to help us navigate these obstacles as they arise in our lives. Nonetheless, my claim is that these will give us the best chance of achieving the necessary elements enabling eudaimonia, and that historical and empirical evidence substantiates this claim.

The overall argument relies, then, on deontological, virtue-based, and utilitarian considerations, in different ways and at different stages. Deontological: I have offered rules—both for institutions and for our individual behavior within those institutions—that we must follow as a matter of principle. Virtue: our following of these rules must be through force of our own characters, as a result of having internalized the proper principles, and following them as a matter of what Aristotle calls "second nature" habit. In new or hard cases, we have to rely on our good judgment, but then we routinize the judgment and its attendant feedback so that it too becomes part of our second nature. Utilitarianism: we do all of this ultimately because it conduces to our eudaimonia, and increases the chances that we and others will achieve such a life.

Conclusion

There has been a substantial and unprecedented increase in human prosperity since around 1800, beginning in northwestern Europe and then spreading to other parts of the world. This Great Enrichment resulted from a change in attitude about what McCloskey calls the "bourgeois virtues," leading in turn to a change in both formal and informal institutions. The formal institutions allowing this enrichment included protections of "justice," that is, person, property, and promise, while the informal institutions included an internalization of a specific code of ethics to which people developed a principled adherence and for which their culture provided support. While money is of course not all that matters, what it can do is enable the things that truly do matter in life—including eudaimonia. A just and humane society, then, is one in which ever more people, including especially the least among us, are able to achieve eudaimonic lives. The achievement of such lives requires both freedom and responsibility, and it is by exercising these capacities, and recognizing and respecting them both in ourselves and in others, that we achieve dignity as full moral agents. The completed argument requires, then, both individual virtuous character and deontological adherence to proper rules and codes, all of which is defended on utilitarian grounds according to which "utility" is understood as conducing ultimately to eudaimonia.

6

Obstacles to Achieving
the Purpose of Business

Introduction

If the arguments of the previous chapters are sound, then the path to prosperity and, ultimately, eudaimonia seems relatively straightforward: get the moral codes and our attitudes about those codes right, get the institutions right, and voilà—honorable business, and thence prosperity, ensues. But can it really be that easy? Well, yes and no. It is easy insofar as listing the required formal and informal institutional elements may be relatively easy. It proved exceedingly difficult to discover what those institutions are, however, and it has taken the concentrated work of many of humanity's greatest minds to figure them out. Yet even that was relatively easy in comparison to the truly difficult part of our story: how do we implement those institutions where they do not already exist? And if we could somehow overcome that enormous problem, we would then face the further difficulty of maintaining them over time.

There are in fact numerous obstacles facing us in the implementation and maintenance of the right kinds of institutions—indeed, too many to address within the compass of a single book. In earlier chapters we have looked at several specific objections people have raised to the markets and business activity described herein, including worries about inequality, fairness, manipulation, lying, exploitation, and negative externalities. There is more to say about these worries and about several others. In this chapter, I propose to consider not just objections to specific aspects of my argument, but also some potentially major obstacles to achieving the prosperity and then eudaimonia that our recommendations propose.

"Capitalism"?

Until now, I have not used the term "capitalism." That was deliberate, and for several reasons. First and foremost, I want the argument of this book to stand or fall on its own terms, not on whether it comports with any particular ideology or with some prior conception of political economy. Though Adam Smith is often referred to as the "father of capitalism," he himself never used the term,[1] and applying it to him would distort the purpose and nature of his recommendations. He was not interested in making the world safe for capital or capitalists, any more than he wanted to construct an apology for businesspeople or for the rich—though that is often how his recommendations are mischaracterized. He was instead concerned about the nature and causes of genuine wealth, with the primary motivation being to improve the stations of the least among us. That is akin to one of the purposes of this book. The argument is not "pro-capitalism" (whatever that would mean, exactly) any more than it is "pro-business." To the contrary, it is pro-*prosperity*. I have been concerned to understand how we can have what Edmund Phelps (2013) calls "mass flourishing," and the role that markets and business—*honorable* business—can play in achieving it. The institutions enabling this mass flourishing often, in fact, come at the expense of particular firms: because they are entitled to, and would receive, no special protections or favors or subsidies, many of them will fail. That is part of the process of "creative destruction," in Joseph Schumpeter's memorable phrase. I will address an aspect of Schumpeter's argument later in this chapter, but for now what is important to see is that our political-economic goal is prosperity, so that our moral goal can be eudaimonia—and neither of these are what people typically mean by the term "capitalism."

A second reason I have avoided speaking of "capitalism" is that this term, like the terms "socialism" and "communism," comes fraught with connotations, usually negative, and that can prejudice one's evaluation of the argument. Karl Marx (1818–1883) popularized the term "capitalism," and he applied it to the systems of political economy advocated by people like Adam Smith and James Mill (1773–1836, father of John Stuart Mill). Marx did not intend it as a compliment. As we will discuss more fully below, Marx thought of free trade, free markets, and private property as elements of an exploitive system whose adherents were victims of an "ideology"—or comprehensive conceptual system that was impervious to argument or evidence—that poisoned both their minds and their virtue. He called it "capitalism" in part because he saw it as a kind of intellectual and moral disease, which the "-ism" helps convey. My argument, however, supports

---

[1] Smith used the words "capital" and "capitals," but never "capitalism."

institutions that enable honorable business as one element of the construction of eudaimonic lives. It is therefore predicated on no ideology, let alone on any particular political ideology.

A third and final reason I have not used the term "capitalism" is because people often mean by it something like the cronyism that we often see today in so-called capitalist countries. Cronyism is a system in which some industries, firms, families, or individuals get special government favors to protect their interests. Although such arrangements are often defended as being in the public interest, in practice they almost always benefit the favored party at the expense of the public. Barriers to entry into the market, subsidies, trade restrictions, limits on competition, legally granted monopolies, occupational licensure requirements, and so on are usually described by their beneficiaries and their government proponents as in some way portending benefit to the community: protecting consumers, protecting firms or industries vital to the national interest, generating future increased revenue, and so on. But when one looks at the actual cases in detail, they are instead typically characterized by the concentration of benefit on the protected industry or firm itself, and the spreading of the costs—including opportunity costs—on to others. The owner of a professional sports team, for example, certainly benefits from having the cost of his new stadium subsidized by taxpayers, and because the costs are spread among thousands, even millions, of taxpayers, they may hardly notice. Yet study after study has shown that the promised increased prosperity from professional sports stadiums not only does not materialize but often turns into net losses.[2] The same is true of cities that host the Olympics.[3] Some particular persons or businesses or organizations will benefit, but usually at the expense of everyone else—consumers, taxpayers, and competitors alike. "Concentrated benefits and dispersed costs" are the stock-in-trade of many such public-private partnerships. It is the core of cronyism, and, because it is extractive in nature, my argument opposes it.

For all these reasons, then, I decline to use the word "capitalism." *Prosperityism* might be closer, but it is rather infelicitous.[4] Smith referred to "the obvious and simple system of natural liberty," which also captures much of the sentiment, but it too is a bit cumbersome. Given my defense of the ultimate aim of the argument, perhaps "eudaimonism" is the most accurate term. That is a bit esoteric, and would require some explanation, but perhaps those are good things. In any case, "eudaimonism" captures my argument about the ultimate purpose of human life, and about how social and public institutions should be arranged to enable it—as well as the role that honorable business plays in its achievement.

---

[2] See, for example, Parker 2015.

[3] See, for example, Applebaum 2014.

[4] McCloskey 2016a suggests "trade-tested betterment" or "innovism."

The Inhuman Alienation of Markets

As we have seen, one central promise of Adam Smith's system of political economy was that it would, as it were, deliver the goods: It would lead to increasing supplies of goods and services, to increasing material prosperity. And, as we have also seen, at this it seems to have succeeded to unprecedented levels. And yet, many people remain suspicious of markets and business. More than just suspicious: many blame markets and business for a wide variety of the economic and social problems we face. Why?

I would like to propose a partial answer. In 1755, over two decades before the publication of his *Wealth of Nations,* Adam Smith wrote:

> Little else is requisite to carry a state to the highest degree of opulence from the lowest barbarism but peace, easy taxes, and a tolerable administration of justice: all the rest being brought about by the natural course of things. All governments which thwart this natural course, which force things into another channel, or which endeavour to arrest the progress of society at a particular point, are unnatural, and to support themselves are obliged to be oppressive and tyrannical.[5]

That statement contains several ideas, but let us focus on one in particular, namely, Smith's reliance on the "natural course of things," which he contrasts with governments that are "unnatural" when they try "thwart this natural course." What exactly is the "natural course of things"? Does being "natural" mean that it is good? Smith seems to believe it does, but I think in fact that markets and business are, in some important ways, quite *un*natural. They rely on an understanding of the world, and of our place in it, that may be contrary to some of our fundamentally natural ways of thinking, behaving, and relating to each other. They may be *so* unnatural, in fact, that even when they succeed—indeed, sometimes *because* they succeed—at increasing material prosperity for all, they often struggle to overcome our instinctive suspicion and distrust of them. The animus we seem to have toward markets and business is, I suggest, at least partly a result of their being contrary to some of our natural inclinations and of their requiring us to act in ways we would not naturally do. I believe that anyone proposing to defend markets and business—including not only Smith but the argument of this book—should face these facts squarely. Doing so will force us to come to terms with abiding difficulties inherent in business and markets, difficulties that

---

[5] Reprinted in Smith 1982, 322.

change, or should change, our understanding of the relation between markets and business, on the one hand, and human nature, on the other.

Here is my hypothesis.[6] Human beings are a small-group species. Those of our ancestors who survived the gauntlet of a nature red in tooth and claw did so because they were able to create small, close-knit bands of people who were willing to sacrifice for one another if, and when, it was required. Long-term survival of individuals was not at issue: By their early thirties people's teeth fell out anyway.[7] What mattered instead was the survival of the band, most of whom were one's blood relations and with whom one had lived since birth. For the band to survive, each member had to believe with certainty that he could rely on all of the others: everyone did his job, whatever it was, in the service of the band's survival, and when necessity required it, each was ready to sacrifice for others. Any hint that a member of the band was not up to the band's demands was taken as a threat to the entire band, and it was disapproved of as required. Moreover, any individual's success (or luck) and any individual's failure (or misfortune) were felt to be those of the entire band, not just of the individual. So if you were successful in, say, a hunt, you were expected to share. If you fell into misfortune, everyone was expected to do what they could to help. The band rose or fell as a united community; we were all in it together.

Now extend the story just a bit. As we now know from multiple sources,[8] the level of wealth human beings enjoyed throughout almost all of their history, and likely during their evolutionary periods, was both extremely low and extremely consistent: $1–$3 per day in constant purchasing power parity per person. Consider a few implications of that fact. First, most people spent most of their lives close to death. They were often undernourished or sick or both, and they often did not ingest enough calories to engage in very much activity.[9] Moreover, they did not have enough wealth to allow for saving, capital investment, or for substantial improvements of any kind. Even if someone invented some new technology, there was typically neither the wealth nor the peace nor the leisure to build on it. Second, their precarious position led them to be suspicious of people who were not in their own band, because one principal and regular way for rival bands to survive was stealing the possessions, and killing or enslaving the men, women, and children, of other bands. Given that, if you came across someone you did not know, often the prudent choice was rather to kill him than to spend time trying to find out whether he might be friendly.

---

[6] I here draw on Rose 2011, as well as Collier 2017; Scheidel 2017; and Sznycer et al. 2017. See also Otteson 2012.

[7] See Ridley 2011.

[8] See Jones 2000; Cameron and Neal 2003; and Maddison 2007.

[9] See Fogel 2004.

Third, this meant that markets were extremely limited. Trading did occur, but it was typically based on personal knowledge, personal bonds, and personal encouragements and threats of retribution for reneging. And because the fear of predation was ever present, there was a significant pressure against accumulating anything worth stealing.[10]

Consider one more aspect of this dynamic: If anyone in your small, close-knit community began to accumulate possessions or tokens of wealth that were greater than what everyone else had—or if any household or family had more than what the other households and families had—the obvious and likeliest explanation was that this person or family was cheating. Either they were stealing it from the other members of your community, or they were cavorting treasonously with members of another community. There were very few other ways to accumulate more than others within your own group. Because of how close the group always was to subsistence, anything that was killed, captured, or discovered was typically shared within very small margins. It might not have been exactly equal sharing—the best hunter might have gotten a tad more, or the first serving, for example—but the differences in absolute terms were small. And everyone knew why anyone who got more, got more. There were no secrets. So if you started accumulating a bit too much, it must have been because you had found a secret cache of something and were not sharing, or you were taking more than your proper share of the communal bounty, or you were getting subsidized by someone outside the community. Because markets, opportunities for investment, and capital itself were so limited, transactions tended to be zero-sum: I, or we, gain only by taking something either from you or from the commons (without sharing). Thus my increasing wealth would usually have been the result, in one way or another, of my impoverishing the others in my band. These constituted direct threats to the unity and hence the survival of the community. Thus everyone would have been on the alert for any signs of such treachery, and any discovery of it could not be tolerated. It was punished swiftly, and often mercilessly. Ultimately, those bands that survived were those that were marginally better at maintaining community unity and a sense of individual sacrifice for the community, and at detecting and punishing threats to that unity.

I suggest that we today are the inheritors of those psychological instincts, and that that fact helps explain why we often seem to be so quickly and so instinctively hostile to many of the institutions, and particularly to some of the results, of markets and business. Markets and business require, first of all, a willingness to deal with and even trust complete strangers. We trade and exchange with people who look, speak, and live entirely differently from us, people with whom we

---

[10] Scheidel 2017, chaps. 1 and 2, lays out this history in considerable, and fascinating, detail.

have no chance of developing any kind of personal knowledge, bond, or affection.[11] Moreover, business, or at any rate honorable business, allows inequalities. Business in markets allows people around us to have more, sometimes much more, than we do. Yet if business is conducted honorably, the transactions in which businesspeople engaged to generate and achieve their status would have been voluntary, based on negotiations that were beneficial to all the parties to them. Because people's talents, skills, and values vary, because people's desires and preferences and motivations vary, and, of course, because of sheer luck, some people will be able to generate more wealth through these voluntary transactions than others will—and inequality will result. Such transactions are not zero-sum, in which there is a loser for every gainer, but are instead positive-sum, in which everyone wins. We are thus all better off for the existence and repeated iterations of such transactions, even those transactions in which we ourselves played no direct role. This is Smith's "invisible hand" at work. Even given all this, however, observing inequality nevertheless often seems to elicit in us an instinctive disapproval.

I have argued that honorable business can succeed only when two separate kinds of things are in place: first, a set of political and economic institutions approximating what Smith articulated; and second, an internalized moral code that is open to and trusts strangers, that does not automatically suspect inequality, and that sees people's successes and failures—and their schedules of values and worldviews—as being their own and not others' business. This, I submit, is an unnatural way of viewing the world for human beings constructed as we are. It goes against central and enduring aspects of our psychological instincts, and, even if it has its advantages (even enormous advantages), it must continue to contend against the recurring suspicions triggered by the instincts our species developed through thousands of years of hard-won evolutionary selection.[12]

Thus when Karl Marx argued that capitalism was an "alienating" force wrenching people from their natural "species-being," he was on to an important insight.[13] Markets and business *are*, in an important sense, alienating: you trade, interact with, and come to rely on people outside your band, outside your community, even on the other side of the world. Moreover, markets and business contravene our "species-being" by allowing the development of *individual* goals, values, and ends, and by going so far as to recommend that we not enforce small-group or communal equality or conformity but instead respect individual pluralism and diversity.

[11] See Seabright 2010.

[12] Hayek 1978 makes a somewhat similar claim, though with important differences.

[13] Marx (1844) 1994, 58–68. See also Heath 2010, chap. 1.

Smith claimed, however, that the "division of labour, from which so many advantages are derived" is "the necessary, though very slow and gradual consequence of a certain propensity in human nature [... namely,] the propensity to truck, barter, and exchange one thing for another" (WN, 25). He wrote later of the natural "higgling and bargaining of the market" (WN, 49), and we might perhaps connect this principle with that articulated by Smith in his *Theory of Moral Sentiments* that the "desire for mutual sympathy of sentiments" is not only one of our most fundamental desires but also one that maintains our natural sociability.[14] Thus some aspects of markets and business—trading, negotiating, deal-making—seem to comport with and even reflect, rather than contradict, some aspects of our nature. Moreover, if Smith is right that human ingenuity is one of the hallmark characteristics of commercial society,[15] then perhaps the entrepreneurship that markets allow would also give license to a natural impulse in humankind. My argument would hold, then, that certain important features of markets and business conflict with some aspects of human psychology, while other features comport with and even summon other aspects. That might explain why our attitude toward markets and business is not entirely and always negative. Perhaps the best way to put it is that our attitude toward them is deeply ambivalent, and often, though not always, hostile.

If I am right, then one of the chief political difficulties in today's world of global communication and trade is trying to ensure that our small-group species will tolerate and even embrace large-group exchange. We naturally like the idea of small groups; we feel safer and more secure when we personally know everyone we deal with and when we have a single leader who determines the direction the entire community takes; and the simple, traditional lifestyle of yesteryear—or, at least, our romantic images of such a life—continues to call to us like a siren song. How we were able to break free from those deep-seated psychological strictures in northwestern Europe around 1800 is therefore a real puzzle, all the more puzzling if it constituted as stark a break as I have suggested. It would reveal just how fragile what we call "civilization" really is, just how anomalous it has been in human history—and just how easy it would be to return to the Hobbesian nasty, poor, brutish, and short status quo ante of human life. But the benefits that that break enabled were and are enormous and cannot be gainsaid. They have meant the difference between life and death for billions of people.

If we propose, then, to extend those benefits rather than curtail them, we face a considerable challenge. We must first of all internalize the requirements of honorable business into our own characters, which will include the willingness

---

[14] See TMS, 9–16.
[15] See, for example, WN, 10 and 19–21.

to see the world and wealth and other people differently from the way we seem naturally inclined to do. But we must also understand that markets and business are, and will likely continue to seem to us, exactly what Marx called them: inhuman and alienating.

Lying and Exploitation

Marx (1844) raised two other objections to Smithian political economy that deserve attention. The first is that negotiations in markets are essentially extended exercises in lying. Consider buying a car. You say to the car dealer, "I won't pay more than $20,000 for that car." (That is a lie.) The dealer responds, "I won't take less than $30,000 for it." (That too is a lie.) As the negotiation proceeds, at each stage each of you lies to the other. Even if you eventually agree on a price, and even if you both voluntarily agreed to the price and you both benefit from the transaction, nevertheless the transaction is based upon, and mediated through, lying. Marx argued that what he called "capitalism" involves, in fact, systematic lying on virtually everyone's part, and, more than this, that this is an immoral way for people to deal with one another. Lying is morally wrong, after all, and any system of political economy that not only allows it but, apparently, endorses it is morally wrong as well.

A related second objection Marx raises is that participants in a market come to view one another not, as I have suggested, as full moral agents with dignity, but, rather, as mere tools to be manipulated into giving us what we want. I want that car, so I say the words necessary to get the dealer to give it to me. Even more insidiously, when I work and earn a paycheck, Marx says I am not actually providing a service to my company or producing a good at the behest of my company. What I am actually producing instead is the means for me to manipulate you into giving me what I want:

> When I produce *more* of an object than I myself can directly use, my *surplus* production is cunningly *calculated* for your need. It is only in *appearance* that I produce a surplus of this object. In reality I produce a *different* object, the object of your production, which I intend to exchange against this surplus, an exchange which in my mind I have already completed. The *social* relation in which I stand to you, my labour for your need, is therefore also a mere *semblance*, and our complementing each other is likewise a mere *semblance*, the basis of which is mutual plundering. The intention of *plundering*, of *deception*, is necessarily present in the background, for since our exchange is a selfish one, on your side as on mine, and since the selfishness of each seeks to get the better

of that of the other, we necessarily seek to deceive each other. (Marx 1844, §3)

Thus I do not actually care about my company or about you; I care only about what it or you can give to me. And the same is true for you—and for everyone else engaged in business in markets. So life under "capitalism" becomes a duplicitous pretense whereby everyone tries to manipulate everyone else, a multiplayer strategic game in which each participant tries to dupe and manipulate the others so as to achieve her own goals, regardless of what this means for or does to others.

These are damning criticisms. How might we respond? For his part, Adam Smith would likely remind Marx of his claim that a central and enduring feature of human psychology is the desire for mutual sympathy of sentiments, a desire that makes us genuinely interested in others.[16] The first sentence of Smith's *Theory of Moral Sentiments* is, "How selfish soever man may be supposed, there are evidently some principles in his nature, which interest him in the fortune of others, and render their happiness necessary to him, though he derives nothing from it except the pleasure of seeing it" (TMS, 9). Smith later emphasizes the point: "Sympathy, however, cannot, in any sense, be regarded as a selfish principle" (TMS, 317). So Smith's response to Marx would be to deny his claim that human beings are fundamentally, or only, selfish, and claim instead that, as a matter of empirical fact, we do care about the "fortune of others."[17]

A second response would be to claim that the offers we make to other people to buy from them, sell to them, or cooperate or associate with them all come with the recognition of the other's right to say "No, thank you" and go elsewhere. When we recognize this right, we do show respect for the others, and treat them as our peers who have the same free moral agency we do. We do not presume to know what is best for others, and we do not presume that we are in a better position to know what others should do than do those others themselves. We might also point out what the alternatives are to encouraging people to pursue their ends by making offers to others that those others are free to decline: the alternatives are either to prohibit offer-making altogether, or to prohibit people from exercising their opt-out option. But both of these would restrict people's autonomy and moral agency and hence disrespect their dignity.

Third and finally, we might also argue that negotiation, which is indeed a central part of a market economy, can just as often be a genuine discovery process as an exercise in lying. Perhaps people do not actually know what something is

[16] See McCloskey 2016c.

[17] For recent evidence that Smith had a point, see Bowles and Gintis 2011 and Haidt 2013. See also Sober and Wilson 1998.

worth to them—in which case negotiating with others might help them clarify for themselves what their actual schedule of value, preferred tradeoffs, and
opportunity costs are. How much are you willing to spend on that new house?
How much are you willing to sell your house for? How much is a house actually
worth? Perhaps people are often genuinely unsure about such things, in which
case entering into a negotiation with others can help them figure it out. That is
not lying. It is instead a mutual exploration of new potential ways to generate
mutual benefit.

It is also important to point out that third parties are typically in no epistemic
position to know whether first and second parties are not in possession of the
relevant local knowledge, and the farther away third parties are from the first
and second parties, the less they know. Although we often have or form beliefs
about what others should do, and we often negatively judge others when they
do not behave or choose in ways we believe they should, our beliefs are usually
a reflection of what *we* would do or would have done in others' shoes. Because
others are not us, however, and hence have preferences, schedules of value and
purpose, resources, and opportunities that differ from ours, it is not clear that we
are in a position to criticize their choices when those choices are not what ours
would have been. For all we and other third parties typically know, others may
be making exactly the right decisions in their own situations. At any rate, the fact
that others choose differently from how we would does not by itself suffice to
show that they are making a mistake, and therefore it is not yet sufficient reason
to intervene.

Asymmetries of Knowledge

In a commercial society with extensive division of labor, people develop specialized knowledge and skills. The more division of labor there is, and the more
advanced the economy is, the more specialized will individuals' knowledge
and skills be. This is a good thing: it not only leads, as Adam Smith showed,
to increasing production, thus to decreasing prices, thus to increased standards
of living and increased prosperity; but it also, as Smith also argued, enables an
increasing scope for people to develop their unique talents and realize their
"dissimilar geniuses" (WN, 30), for both their own and for others' benefit.
Throughout most of their history, human beings lived in small groups that were
largely self-sufficient, though, as we have seen, at extremely low levels of prosperity. Intergroup trading occurred—indeed, wherever there have been humans
there has been trading, owing to what Smith called humans' natural "propensity to truck, barter, and exchange one thing for another" (WN, 25)—but it was
limited, typically able to extend only as far as our personal familiarity with our

trading partners extended, and it faced retarding pressures from the ever-present risk of predation.

As protections of person, property, and promise were introduced, however, and spread to encompass larger groups of people, the opportunities to trade with more people increased the incentives to create goods and services that others find valuable. Smith: "When the market is very small, no person can have any encouragement to dedicate himself entirely to one employment for want of the power to exchange all that surplus part of the produce of his own labour, which is over and above his own consumption, for such parts of the produce of other men's labour as he has occasion for" (WN, 31). Where, by contrast, a market grows larger—meaning including more people, and thus more "dissimilar geniuses"— more opportunities present themselves. In small communities, like the clans of "the Highlands of Scotland," Smith says, "every farmer must be a butcher, baker and brewer for his own family" (WN, 31). Smith continues: "In such situations we can scarce expect to find a smith, a carpenter, or a mason, within less than twenty miles of another of the same trade" (WN, 31). Remember that he wrote this in the eighteenth century, when a distance of twenty miles was a significant obstacle—a full day's journey or more. And these downward pressures limiting trade were exacerbated if the small communities in question—like the Highland clans of Scotland—were marked by mutual animosities, and even internecine conflict. Without extensive protections of the "three Ps," Smith argued, "There could be little or no commerce of any kind between the distant parts of the world" (WN, 33).

It turns out that Smith was right about that. Contemporary empirical studies examining the extent to which different peoples traded with others, and comparing this to their overall levels of prosperity, demonstrate a pattern exactly like what Smith would have predicted: the more intergroup trade—that is, the greater the "extent of the market"—the more prosperity; the less such trade— the smaller the "extent of the market"—the less prosperity.[18] The next step in the Smithian argument is that as the market gets bigger, with more people bringing their differing talents and the fruits of their labor "into a common stock" from which others too can benefit (WN, 30),[19] the opportunities to divide the labor also increase. A small community cannot afford to have its members be scientists or writers or artists, except perhaps as part-time hobbies; but a larger and more prosperous community can begin, as its wealth increases, to afford such luxuries. In time, such communities can begin to think about things like education

---

[18] See Ridley 2011 for evidence, including many specific examples, of this.

[19] Hume (1754) 1985a wrote that the increasing fruits of people's labor "serve to the ornament and pleasure of life" generally, and the increasing prosperity that they portend generate "a kind of *storehouse* of labour, which, in the exigencies of state, may be turned to the public service" (272).

and healthcare and pure research and concern for the environment—but only as their wealth enables it. Gradually what were once considered unaffordable luxuries can become real possibilities, even, eventually, expected necessities. In this way, as the standards of living rise, more and more former luxuries become standard parts of even the common person's life.[20] Think of contemporary commonplaces like anesthesia, telephones, automobiles, air conditioning, televisions, commercial air transportation, personal computers, cell phones, and internet access. Although it may be hard to imagine now, when each of these products entered the market, it was considered a fabulous, even obscene, luxury, only for the superrich; many indeed speculated aloud that each of these were in fact needless, even potentially dangerous, luxuries.[21] Paul Krugman, for example, who went on to win the Nobel Prize in 2008, wrote this in 1998: "The growth of the Internet will slow drastically, as the flaw in 'Metcalfe's law'—which states that the number of potential connections in a network is proportional to the square of the number of participants—becomes apparent: most people have nothing to say to each other! By 2005 or so, it will become clear that the Internet's impact on the economy has been no greater than the fax machine's."[22] As silly as such a prediction seems to us now, the point is that these now commonplaces were enabled only because of the vast interconnected markets in which people traded goods, services, and ideas—and such vast markets are themselves possible only because of relatively widespread protection of Smith's three Ps.

Today people can be specialized to extents that could not have been dreamed of in previous generations. This is a great achievement for human expression and individuality, but it can also run a risk. Because people are so specialized, their knowledge of their own fields may vastly exceed the knowledge of their field that people not in their fields have. Think of medicine: this has become so multifaceted, with specialties and subspecialties, that even doctors are hard pressed to know much about fields of medicine outside their own specialties. A friend of

---

[20] As Smith acknowledged: "Under necessaries therefore, I comprehend, not only those things which nature, but those things which the established rules of decency have rendered necessary to the lowest rank of people" (WN, 870).

[21] Some examples: in 1839, surgeon Alfred Velpeau argued against anesthesia on the grounds that pain was necessary and anesthesia a "chimera" (see Gumpert and Shuman 1936, 232); in 1881, the *New York Times* reported a ban on bicycles in Central Park because people claimed that they were a threat to horses, who were made "crazy" by them; in 1907, the *Pittsburgh Gazette Times* discussed "the automobile terror" and the "terrorism" of "the automobile craze" and argued in favor of arresting anyone who drives an automobile; in 1914, the *Gettysburg Gazette* claimed that "wireless telephones" were "for wealthy only" and unsuitable as "a public service"; and in 1936, the *Spokane Spokesman-Review* argued in favor of banning radios on the grounds that they were antidemocratic and corrupted "the purity of elections." Similar arguments have been raised against everything from elevators to video games to hover boards; see Follett 2016.

[22] Krugman 1998.

mine is an orthopedic surgeon, but he concentrates only, as he says, on the shoulder to the hand; as he will be the first to tell you, you should go to someone else if you have a problem with your hip or knee or ankle. Another friend is a neurosurgeon; his niche is to have mastered a specific technique to address aneurysms in the brain. He is excellent at it, has saved hundreds of lives, and is very well remunerated for what he does—justifiably so. But if you have other kinds of problems with your nervous system, he will send you elsewhere. Or consider finance: it too has become so complex, with specialized terms, concepts, and techniques, that unless one is oneself a specialist, it can be overwhelming and bewildering.

This is not a criticism of specialized knowledge, which may be deep but not broad. On the contrary. Economists have developed a concept called "rational ignorance": as counterintuitive as it may sound, it is actually rational for us *not* to know many things.[23] Consider again my neurosurgeon friend. I know very little of his field or his technical training; similarly, he probably knows little about eighteenth-century British moral theory. And probably neither of us knows much about engineering or pipefitting. This is not a criticism of either of us or of the electrical engineer or pipefitter. Given our respective specialties, and the value each of us can contribute to the world on the basis of those specialties, the opportunity cost for any of us to learn the others' specialties would be high, probably too high. It could take months or years for any of us to learn the other specialties—but that would be time lost to doing what we are already good at. If there are other people who specialize in neurosurgery, electrical engineering, and pipefitting, then that frees me to become a specialist in eighteenth-century British moral philosophy. And vice versa. The beauty of this is that, since not everyone *wants* to be a specialist in neurosurgery, engineering, pipefitting, or eighteenth-century British moral philosophy, markets and business have allowed our society to achieve sufficient division of labor and wealth to provide each of us ever more opportunities to find a unique path. In the process, we are able to discover ways not only to express and develop our own individuality but also ways to be, as Smith puts it, "of use to one another" (WN, 30).

The good news, then, is that markets and business have enabled these specialties, which create enormous generalized benefit. There is a worry, however, which comes under the heading of asymmetrical knowledge: it can be difficult for nonspecialists to judge whether what a specialist is telling them is true or not. If your neurosurgeon tells you that this is what you need to do, are you really in a position to disagree? If your financial adviser tells you that this is what you need to do, to what extent can you be expected to evaluate the proposal if you are not yourself also a specialist? If your car mechanic tells you this is what you

[23] See Caplan 2008.

need to do, how are you to know? Even a casual consumer of news will see an almost endless barrage of reports about the healthful or baleful effects of this or that food, drink, supplement, drug, or medical treatment; about the good or bad effects of this or that economic policy, regulation, or law; about this or that way to finance one's house or car or education; and on and on. As markets continue to spread around the globe, and as millions, even billions, of people enter them, the opportunities for specialization continue apace, which means that the potential opportunities for those in the know to exploit those not in the know will increase as well.

Some suggest that this implies a role for government regulation to help constrain sellers and producers of goods and services so that they cannot talk unwitting people into things that the latter would not want if they knew what the former do. Proposals for regulatory protections, safety standards, building codes, occupational licensing, and many other kinds of governmental action are often made on the basis of the claim that many people, perhaps most people, cannot be expected to know what is safe, or what are best practices, or what will actually accomplish what is advertised. The conclusion is that if most of us cannot in fact know these things, this will provide opportunities for the unscrupulous among us to take advantage of these asymmetries of knowledge. A car mechanic, financial adviser, politician, lawyer, doctor, dentist, or any other person with specialized knowledge is thus in a position to exploit people not similarly specialized. One might think that this worry is particularly acute in business, however, because, as some claim, businesspeople's drive to turn a profit makes them especially inclined to exploit others when they can. Thus, the argument might run, the government needs to be especially vigilant in regulating, overseeing, and monitoring business, increasingly so as specialized knowledge becomes even more difficult for nonspecialists to assess.

Our increasingly globalized market indeed creates widespread knowledge asymmetries. As we saw a moment ago, not attempting to learn everything about everything can actually be an example of "rational ignorance" allowing us to focus on a narrower range of activities that conduce more directly to our eudaimonia. But what should we do about the opportunisms enabled by these asymmetries? Proposals for governmental regulation of business activity are what we might call "front-end discipline": it requires or prohibits various kinds of activity before it happens. The effectiveness of front-end discipline is, however, mixed. Sometimes the regulators and regulatory agencies get coopted by the very firms or industries they are to regulate: lobbying, consulting, and selective campaign donation enable entrenched firms and industries to get regulations to favor themselves, often at the expense of smaller firms, of new potential entrants into the markets, or of taxpayers or consumers. As is now well documented, this regulatory capture is disappointingly widespread and commonplace.[24] Another obstacle to effective front-end discipline is connected with the local knowledge argument we have discussed: legislators and regulators, however expert in their fields and even assuming virtuous motives, do not know the varying values, purposes, and opportunities of their individual citizens. Because of that, they are typically not in a position to know what decisions citizens should make in their individualized local situations. Suppose that experts have decided that there is reason to worry about people's salt intake, because they believe it is connected with heart disease, and so they move to restrict the salt that restaurants can supply in your city. But suppose it turns out that my particular heart condition actually requires elevated amounts of salt.[25] Your policy might then affect me negatively rather than positively, even if it is true, or at least might be true, that statistically such a policy should have positive effects on more people than those on whom it has negative effects. But expert knowledge is general and aggregated, not particular and individualized, which means that their policy recommendations will address averages—which may or may not benefit any particular individuals.[26]

We also need to beware of what we might call the "averaging fallacy." Suppose it is the case that the people in your community are on average twenty pounds overweight. Suppose on that basis we impose a new policy restricting everyone's caloric intake to 2,000 calories per day for women and 2,520 for men, which are based on recommendations for average women and men who are "moderately active," but with a 10 percent reduction because we average twenty pounds too heavy.[27] Will this policy be right for all of the members of our community? Highly unlikely. We said that our community members are "on average" twenty pounds overweight: Does it follow from that that *everyone* is twenty pounds overweight? No. Does it follow from that that even a *single* person is twenty pounds overweight? No. We cannot determine how much over- or underweight any single individual is from knowing the (correct) mean average. Perhaps some of us are athletes, and need many more calories; perhaps some of us are facing medical issues that require more or fewer calories; perhaps we have a few morbidly obese members, which skews our average upward. Distant regulators cannot know these particularities, and

---

[24] For classic accounts, see Stigler 1971 and McChesney 1987. For a more recent, and comprehensive, account, see Lindsey and Telles 2017.

[25] Neither of these is hypothetical. In 2009, then–New York mayor Michael Bloomberg launched what he called the "National Salt Reduction Initiative"; see New York Global City Partners 2014. Moreover, I do have a heart condition that means I need to ingest more salt daily than most people require.

[26] See Tetlock 2006 and Easterly 2013.

[27] See WebMD, n.d.

hence any policies they enact are highly unlikely to turn out to be those that best serve individuals.

There is another concern. If I am the one making the decisions about how much salt, for example, I ingest, I will probably respond relatively quickly to the effects of those decisions. I am not infallible, of course, so my responses will not be perfect. But regulators are not infallible either, and I, unlike them, have the benefit of receiving the feedback from my actions. Hence I am better positioned to make decisions about my situation than they are, even given my fallibility. Because I experience the consequences, I have strong incentives to get decisions right; the more important the decision—meaning the more consequential the potential effects on my life or on the lives of those I care about—the stronger the incentive I face to get things right. Regulators, by contrast, face no such incentives because the consequences of their policies in my life will likely be completely unknown to, and hence will have little or no effect on, them. Hence they are in a worse position from which to hope to make good decisions for me or for you. This is not an indictment of their character, just as it is no encomium to mine or yours: It is merely a consequence of the knowledge they do not have—namely, knowledge about you and me—and the feedback they neither receive nor feel.

There is another way of disciplining businesses against exploiting opportunisms, however, and even incentivizing them so that not exploiting opportunisms actually serves their interests (while thus serving ours). It is what we might call "back-end" discipline: the choices of consumers, which are more powerful than we might initially suspect. As we have seen, the majority of businesses fail. This is not because they are run by bad or unintelligent people; it is rather a necessary part of the process of discovery leading to betterment. An example will illustrate. My field is higher education, which means that I, like my colleagues, deal principally in ideas. Yet most of the ideas we have are, unfortunately, bad ones. Success is dependent on getting rid of the bad ideas as quickly as possible, and then capitalizing on those few ideas that are good. Often, however, we will not be able to know which of our ideas are good until we test them out: we tell others about our ideas, submit them to others' scrutiny and criticisms, and see how things shake out. Those few that survive this gauntlet will turn out to be the good ones—at least until they are refuted or superseded by yet other ideas, as most of them eventually will be. But we would not have known which were the good ones unless they had entered and survived this gauntlet, this, as we call it, "marketplace of ideas."

There is a clear analogy here to business activity in markets. We do not know in advance which business ideas are good ones either, until they survive the gauntlet of selective, picky, and critical consumers. Thus markets are not only competitive crucibles within which to test business ideas, but they also constitute a vehicle through which consumers choosing decentrally and independently can bring enormous pressure to bear on businesses.[28] In a Smithian "well-governed society," a business can succeed only if it pleases its customers. They all enjoy their opt-out option, and they exercise it liberally, so businesses have to pay constant attention to figuring out ways to satisfy their changing, even fickle, preferences, goals, resources, and so on. This is a perhaps surprisingly powerful disciplinary force. If a company produces a good or service that is subpar, defective, or that otherwise does not satisfy customers, word spreads. If a firm does not treat its employees well or engages in trades, associations, partnerships, or exchanges that are morally dubious, again word spreads. They may lose their best employees, they may see fewer other potential partners willing to work with them, and they may lose customers; if they do not right their ship, they may well go under. Now, assuming that businesspeople and firms do not want to lose their money or waste their time—not a controversial assumption—they thus have a natural, and indeed very strong, incentive to produce goods and services that will please their customers (whom they hope will become *repeat* customers) and to do so in a way that meets the moral and other value expectations consumers have. Because the market is a competitive arena—because businesses must respect our opt-out options and because our resources are scarce—bad business offerings and practices will, like bad ideas in the marketplace of ideas, eventually be uncovered, exposed, and rooted out.

This is a very real threat, and thus a very real disciplining factor. Joseph Schumpeter (1883–1950) argued, however, that these competitive pressures are yet even more effective. Schumpeter wrote: "Competition of the kind we now have in mind acts not only when in being but also when it is merely an ever-present threat. It disciplines before it attacks" (1942, 85). In other words, the mere knowledge that one *might* lose customers or business, or that others *might* compete with one, is often by itself enough to make businesspeople anxious to do the right things the right way. The connection to the worries about asymmetrical knowledge is that although opportunities to exploit them exist and may multiply as markets expand, so too does the ability for individual consumers to protect themselves because they have more options. They can say, "No, thank you" and go elsewhere. If you have one bad experience at a restaurant, you do not return. You check the ratings sellers receive from buyers before you buy on eBay or book with Airbnb or ride with an Uber or Lyft driver. You check Yelp or TripAdvisor. You might also give your own ratings—good and bad—based on your experiences. Millions of people today do, and millions of people consult, and then act on, that feedback.

---

[28] See Heath 2007.

This is not a perfect system, of course. Some of the information available from these sources is not reliable, and some of it is fake. The more sources of information there are, and the more people contributing to and relying on them there are, the more reliable they get. But of course mistakes will still happen. And there will always be some proportion of people who will try to exploit others nonetheless. Similarly, in the marketplace of ideas, there will still be bad ideas that have not yet been refuted, and there will remain some proportion of people who will try to pull the wool over others' eyes by plagiarizing, faking their data, exaggerating their findings, and so on. But if the markets in both cases—business and academia—are open and free, if anyone can enter, anyone can criticize, anyone can "opt out" or disregard, then the logic of the competitive system will bend, relentlessly and remorselessly, toward creation of genuine value.

Conclusion

One significant obstacle to business in markets providing the benefits it proposes arises from our natural suspicion of both its activities and effects. As the inheritors of psychological instincts that were selected for in our small-group history, we have an abiding suspicion of large, complex networks of trade, exchange, and association that involve people different from and even unknown to us. We also find it difficult to trust people we do not know, especially if they speak different languages, have different cultures, worship different gods, and so on. Moreover, our small-group instincts give us a strong and natural suspicion of inequality. Because business in markets involves intergroup exchange, and because it can lead to inequality, for many of us our first reaction will be to be skeptical, even condemnatory, of inequality, even before we know any details. This explains the sense in which Marx was right to say that what he called "capitalism" is inhuman and alienating. It goes against many of our natural human instincts, and it weakens the bonds to our local communities by expanding our horizons of association beyond those local ties and constraints.

Marx also argued that "capitalism" involves systematic lying and exploitation, though our conception of honorable business rules out and opposes lying and unjust exploitation. Moreover, much of the process of negotiation and bargaining that goes on in markets can be seen as a mutual discovery process in which participants clarify their own values and uncover possible points of contact with others' values. The vast majority of successful mutually voluntary transactions remain, then, mutually beneficial, and there is typically little reason to suppose that a third party could have known antecedently that there were any better choices, all things considered, for first and second parties to make. Though worries about potential exploitation of asymmetries of knowledge are real, the structure of properly functioning markets, and the honorable business that operates within their constraints—subject to the disciplining "back-end" forces of consumer choice aided by ease of communication—provides mechanisms that tend to discover and punish people who extractively exploit such asymmetries and then to incentivize people to look for ways to cooperatively create and provide genuine value.

7

Honorable Business and Treating People the Right Way

Introduction

In chapter 6, I offered reasons to avoid terms like "capitalism" to describe the system of political economy offered and defended in this book. Political institutions that enable honorable business and reward it for contributing to the creation of genuine value in a just and humane society in which ever more people have a chance of leading eudaimonic lives are not properly captured by the narrow and loaded term "capitalism." I suggested instead "eudaimonism," which, though it would require explanation, nevertheless gives a better indication of the nature and purpose of the system of political economy defended here and the role that honorable business plays in it.

As I have developed my account of this system, I have had occasion to raise and address several worries and objections. In this chapter, we turn our attention to three large worries people have raised about systems of political economy like what I have described, each dealing with concerns about how we should treat other people—and whether business encourages proper relations among people. The first objection relates to equality. We raised this worry in chapter 4, but because it is such an important concern and has so many facets, it warrants further discussion. The second worry, or cluster of worries, concerns the fairness (or unfairness) of the outcomes of our recommended political economy. This worry, too, we raised in chapter 4, but it too has many facets and thus warrants further discussion. The third and final worry we will address is connected with the "destructive" part of the "creative destruction" that seems to be an essential feature of markets and business. Increasing prosperity seems dependent on progress and innovation, but if this also leads to the destruction of industries, firms, and jobs, is it worth it?

The worries I discuss in this chapter, as well as in the next, are perhaps more general and philosophical than one might expect to see in a book about business ethics. Thus a prefatory word is required about why I discuss them. Before we are in a position to make well-informed decisions regarding our day-to-day business activities, we need to have an understanding of what the proper criteria are for making good decisions. This requires having an understanding not only of the purpose of business but also of the proper context of business—including, as I have argued, how it integrates into the institutions that contribute to a just and humane society. But that means, in turn, that we should have some reasonable conception of the extent to which those institutions themselves are morally justifiable. In this and the next chapter, we look at a handful of worries that have been raised about the kinds of large-scale political-economic institutions that comprehend the conception of honorable business I have defended. If those institutions are themselves problematic, then that would call into question this conception of honorable business as well. So if, for example, the institutions lead to an immoral inequality, to fundamentally unfair outcomes, to the distortion or even destruction of important values, or to the production of immoral goods or the sale of immoral services, then that would constitute serious problems for those institutions. In that case they might, in fact, question the entire hierarchy of moral value of which, I have argued, honorable business forms an integral part—perhaps entailing that this conception of business is not so honorable after all.

I propose, therefore, to address these more philosophical worries squarely, in the hope of clarifying the extent to which the business activity that is part of these institutions can itself be justified.

Equality

In a short book entitled *Why Not Socialism?* (2009), the late distinguished Oxford philosopher G. A. Cohen defended socialism on the basis of two central moral principles: equality and community. Cohen begins his book by describing an imaginary camping trip attended by several different families, and he argues that the trip realizes two principles—"an egalitarian principle" and "a principle of community" (2009, 12)—that together capture his vision of a just socialist society. Because Cohen thinks any reasonable person would have endorsed his two socialist principles in the camping trip, he argues that we should therefore endorse them in society generally.

A lot hangs, therefore, on Cohen's description of the camping trip. Here is the opening description:

You and I and a whole bunch of other people go on a camping trip. There is no hierarchy among us; our common aim is that each of us should have a good time, doing, so far as possible, the things that he or she likes best (some of those things we do together; others we do separately). We have facilities with which to carry out our enterprise: we have, for example, pots and pans, oil, coffee, fishing rods, canoes, a soccer ball, decks of cards, and so forth. And, as is usual on camping trips, we avail ourselves of those facilities collectively: even if they are privately owned things, they are under collective control for the duration of the trip, and we have shared understandings about who is going to use them when, and under what circumstances, and why. (2009, 3–4)

Cohen argues that the first moral principle that would organize a camping trip like this is equality. This principle is suggested in his language of having "no hierarchy among us," having a "common aim," using our "facilities collectively," and having everything be "under collective control."[1] As Cohen goes on to argue, the "egalitarian principle realized on the trip" is one "that is a radical principle of equality of opportunity, which I shall call 'socialist equality of opportunity'" (2009, 13). Cohen also describes an alternative version of a camping trip, one based not on his preferred "socialist" principles but rather "on the principles of market exchange and strictly private ownership of the required facilities" (2009, 6). In this latter version, Cohen argues, "Everybody asserts her rights over the pieces of equipment, and the talents, that she brings, and where bargaining proceeds with respect to who is going to pay what to whom to be allowed, for example, to use a knife to peel the potatoes, and how much he is going to charge others for those now-peeled potatoes that he bought in an unpeeled condition from another camper, and so on" (2009, 5–6). Cohen argues that such a "market" version of the camping trip, however, is quite unattractive: "Most people would hate that" (2009, 6).

Cohen's preferred "socialist" version of the camping trip raises some questions, however. One might wonder, for example, why there is no hierarchy among us. Is there no one who knows the area better than others or has more camping experience than others, and thus has opinions that should be granted more weight? Are there no heads of the respective households, or no natural leader or two to whom people would defer when conflicts arise or when decisions must

---

[1] Perhaps not coincidentally, the description Cohen gives of his camping trip recalls a description from the Bible of life among Jesus's apostles: "The community of believers was of one heart and mind, and no one claimed that any of his possessions was his own, but they had everything in common. With great power the apostles bore witness to the resurrection of the Lord Jesus, and great favor was accorded them all. There was no needy person among them, for those who owned property or houses would sell them, bring the proceeds of the sale, and put them at the feet of the apostles, and they were distributed to each according to need" (Acts of the Apostles 4:32–35).

be made? A second question is why we would assume that our "common aim" is that "each of us should have a good time." Perhaps we all care about that to some extent, but presumably each of us would have other aims as well, including aims that might be more important to us individually or within our own families than the "common aim" Cohen identifies. Perhaps I want to teach my children to fish. Perhaps you want some time away from it all and hence want to be left alone. Perhaps another wants to hike and explore, and another wants to read a book. Any of these aims, none of which are jointly shared, might be more important to us than making sure others are having a good time.

One also wonders where the camping "facilities" came from. Where did we get the pots and pans, canoes, soccer balls, and so on? Cohen does not discuss the question of production, but goods do not appear out of nowhere—an important point to keep in mind if one wants, as Cohen does, to adapt principles from his imaginary camping trip and apply them to actual human society. The answer, of course, is that they came from the productive labor of others—from businesses operating within markets. If we were to simply assume the existence of all the necessary facilities for society, if we assumed that we would not ever need anything more—and that nothing breaks or gets used up—and if we further assumed no special attachment to the facilities by members of our camping trip (because, for example, they themselves made or bought them, and hence believe them to be their own property), then, perhaps, the question of how to distribute these found goods and services might be the only, or the main, concern. But goods and services must be created by human beings. People must use their time, talent, and treasure to create them, in cooperation with others. And it would not suffice to have people create just anything: we need and want particular things, given our circumstances. How could we be sure not only that goods and services get created but that the goods and services created are what we in fact need and want? It seems the only way we have discovered to both incentivize production *and* coordinate it with people's actual and changing needs and desires is by having in place systems of production that require people to seek to create value for others, which requires institutions that protect person, property, and promise, that allow prices to emerge to coordinate differing wants in a world of scarce resources, and that are disciplined by people's choices and their opt-out options. But these are not the features of socialism; they are, instead, the features of the system advocated by Adam Smith. It would appear, then, that the only way to have a socialist camping trip is if it takes place within the larger context of markets and honorable business.[2]

---

[2] As indeed Cohen perhaps inadvertently implies when he reveals that he himself does not like camping trips and prefers instead his comfortable accommodations at Oxford: "I'd rather have my

Cohen's description of the camping trip includes discussions of four objections one might raise. The first comes from "Harry," who "is very good at fishing" and thus "catches, and provides, more fish than others do" (2009, 7). Because of this, Harry thinks it is "unfair" that he is allowed to eat no better than everyone else; should he not get something extra in return for his greater contribution to the community's bounty? Cohen's answer: "Harry, don't be such a schmuck. You sweat and strain no more than the rest of us do. So, you're very good at fishing. We don't begrudge you that special endowment, which is, quite properly, a source of satisfaction to you, but why should we *reward* your good fortune?" (2009, 7–8). Note two things in particular about Cohen's response to Harry. First, Harry "sweat[s] and strain[s] no more than the rest." Why is that relevant? Because Cohen is claiming that people should be rewarded based on their *effort*, not their *production*; on their inputs, not their outputs. If you and I gave equal effort, Cohen argues, then you and I should be rewarded equally. Second, Cohen speaks of Harry's "good fortune." Why is that relevant? Because Cohen is claiming that people's differing abilities are often more a matter of luck than of deliberate effort. If you are able to produce more than I can, but that is because you just happen, through luck, to have certain skills or abilities that I lack, then, Cohen argues, you can claim no special reward because you cannot claim credit for luck.

The second objection Cohen entertains comes from "Sylvia," who, while hiking around the campsite, "stumbled upon a huge apple tree, full of perfect apples" (2009, 8). In exchange for telling the group where the apple tree is, however, Cohen tells us that Sylvia asks for special considerations: she asks them to "reduce my labor burden, and/or furnish me with more room in the tent, and/or with more bacon at breakfast" (8). Cohen writes that Sylvia's "claim to (a kind of) ownership of the tree revolts the others" (8) because Sylvia is improperly claiming that she should be rewarded for something that was again a matter of luck: she "stumbled upon" the apple tree. The moral Cohen draws: you are not entitled to what you have only because of luck. The third objection comes from "Leslie," "who has been endowed from birth with many knacks and talents" (9), including being the only one who knows how to crack nuts the group discovered. The fourth and final objection is raised by "Morgan," who realizes that the group's campsite is located next to a pond that her father dug and stocked with fish with the specific intention of Morgan's one day coming upon it and thus being able to enjoy its bounty. Cohen rejects both Leslie's and Morgan's requests for greater reward, however, by claiming that their ability to provide more than others is also the result of luck and hence undeserved.

socialism in the warmth of All Souls College than in the wet of the Catskills, and I love modern plumbing" (2009, 10).

Each of these four scenarios is intended to forestall a claim that an opponent of socialism might make: the first suggests that your ability to produce more than another is due to an undeserved natural talent and that you thus have no claim to its produce; the second, that your good fortune results from sheer luck and thus again you have no claim to exclusive enjoyment of it; and the third, that your skill is undeserved and that you thus have no right to hold out a higher price for its use. The lesson from the fourth case is less clear; it might mean to suggest that what your father intended thirty years ago is irrelevant to today, or perhaps that because you did nothing to deserve the pond and its fish you can claim no special title to it. The key moral concept linking each of these scenarios and Cohen's responses to them is luck. The egalitarianism he defends is based in large part on this set of claims: (1) we do not morally deserve that which we have as a matter of (good or bad) luck; (2) a moral system of political economy is one in which the results of luck are equalized; (3) markets and business routinely reward people for good luck and punish people for bad luck and are therefore immoral; and (4) socialism is a system that equalizes the results of luck and is therefore moral.

One might raise rejoinders to each of the lessons Cohen draws from his four scenarios, but let us mention just one general concern about Cohen's overall position. Human beings respond to incentives, so it might be appropriate to ask what kinds of behaviors we are encouraging, and what kinds of behaviors we are discouraging, by transforming central social institutions like property, ownership, and reward, from "individual" to "collective." On what seem to be plausible assumptions of human motivations, people under Cohen's "socialist" collectivism might be discouraged from developing or using their "undeserved" skills that enable higher production, from seeking out "lucky" discoveries from which we could all benefit, and from saving and investing rather than simply consuming wealth from which others, including future generations, could benefit. If so, one might predict that the incentive structure created by socialist collectivism would lead to declining wealth and prosperity. Several political experiments of the twentieth and twenty-first centuries would seem to confirm this prediction.[3]

Let us look a bit more closely, however, at the particular version of equality for which Cohen argues. He calls it "socialist equality of opportunity," and he

---

[3] The high correlation between socialist-inclined governments and their citizens' low scores on standard criteria of human well-being discussed in chapter 2 provides some evidence. The human tragedy currently unfolding in Venezuela may provide another current example; see Worstall 2017. Perhaps it should also be noted that twentieth-century experiments in collectivism resulted in some 100 million innocent deaths; see Rummel 1997; Courtois et al. 1999; White 2011; and Pinker 2011.

argues that it "seeks to correct for *all* unchosen disadvantages" (2009, 17–18).[4] Cohen argues that this form of equality goes beyond merely "bourgeois equality of opportunity," according to which legal barriers to success based on race, sex, class, and so on are removed; and beyond the next level of equality of opportunity, which Cohen calls "left-liberal equality of opportunity," according to which not only "bourgeois equality of opportunity" is accomplished but in addition the "circumstances of birth and upbringing" are also corrected (14–17). Cohen's preferred "socialist equality of opportunity" not only corrects for artificial legal barriers and for the accidents of birth and upbringing that might restrict opportunity, but goes beyond them to seek correction for "native differences" among people (17)—which would presumably include differences in personality and temperament, differences in cognitive ability and IQ, and differences in physical abilities.

Before evaluating these conceptions of equality, I would note that Cohen's first, "bourgeois equality of opportunity," is similar to what my argument would incorporate into the institutions of government as part of its duty to protect justice. As I have argued, justice includes protecting the person, property, and promises of everyone—regardless of race, sex, class, and so on. I have defended this not only because such institutions enable generally increasing prosperity, but because they are reflective of the dignity of each individual as a full and equal moral agent. Cohen's second, "left-liberal equality of opportunity," would seem to fall under what Adam Smith called the obligations of "beneficence." If we learn of people in difficult situations—not because of another injuring them, which would be injustice and a duty of the government to remedy, but, rather, because their (undeserved) circumstances have unduly limited their options—then we may have a personal obligation to help them if we can. We would of course have to balance this against our other values, purposes, and obligations, and against our available resources and their opportunity costs; but there will be many situations in which we indeed ought, morally, to help. That these cases are instances of generosity or charity would not make them any less obligatory. It means only that they are our own responsibility, not those of the government—a proper function of Smithian beneficence.

Let us also pause a moment to make a high-level observation about Cohen's argument. The fact that almost all human societies throughout most of human history have failed to achieve even Cohen's "bourgeois equality of opportunity"—let alone his two more extensive levels of equality—is an indication of the difficulty of instituting it. The fact that in today's (Western) world Cohen

---

[4] Rawls similarly argued that "undeserved inequalities call for redress; and since inequalities of birth and natural endowment are undeserved, these inequalities are to be somehow compensated" (1971, 100).

could simply, and almost casually assert it—and that most of his readers, myself included, view it as all but self-evident—is an indication of just how far the prosperity we enjoy has enabled us to extend our care and concern. It was not that long ago in human history when even protections like this would have been impossible to entertain because people were too concerned about the bare survival of themselves, their families, and their small communities. The idea of a universal principle of respect for the persons, property, and promises of all people would have seemed a fantastic dream. So we have come a long way, despite the difficulty.

Returning to Cohen's argument, the next point to make is that achieving his second-level "left-liberal equality of opportunity" would be difficult, for two principal reasons. First, it depends on the prior production of substantial wealth. Charitable activities and welfare policies redistribute wealth people have already created; they do not by themselves generate new or their own wealth. Substantial, large-scale charitable or other redistributive projects can be contemplated, then, only within already wealthy societies, and they can flourish and are sustainable only when they do not endanger the prosperity that their societies generate. Second, it is often difficult to know when a particular charitable allocation of resources is worth it. Some acts of charity do not accomplish their intended effects; some, alas, are actually counterproductive.[5] Yet others that might help unfortunately cannot be justified given their cost, including the opportunity cost. Perhaps I have the resources to build a public library in my town, but it would mean that I would not be able to send my children to college. Or perhaps our town has the resources to cover your expensive medical treatment, but the higher taxes that we would have to impose mean that some planned business openings—which would have employed and provided resources and benefit for other people—never happen. Deciding which is the more valuable use of resources in cases like these, and any number of other similar cases, is very difficult to do. Consider also that there are currently approximately 1.5 million charities in the United States.[6] To which of them should we give that would be the best use of your and my available resources? Every dollar that federal, state, and local governments spend on charitable or welfare projects—which currently amounts to several trillion dollars per year in the United States—comes from taxation on private businesses and individuals. What would they have done with that money if the government did not take and spend it? In order to know whether government or any other spending is worth it, we would have to answer that question,

---

[5] See Easterly 2007 and 2013; Lupton 2011; and Coyne 2013.
[6] See National Center for Charitable Statistics 2013.

and then compare the two to see which provides greater benefit. Again, this is extremely difficult to do.

As difficult as it would be to achieve the best charitable uses of our limited resources even if we relied on people's local knowledge, Cohen's preferred "socialist equality of opportunity" would involve difficulties so great as to make it implausible even to attempt. I think it would also run dangerous risks. Imagine the possible consequences of empowering a government to attempt to compensate people for differences in personality, IQ, and physical ability. What would be involved? Would recombination of people's DNA be required? Or, as Plato suggested, selective sterilization?[7] Imagining things like this conjures up dystopian science-fiction stories like Kurt Vonnegut's "Harrison Bergeron" and Aldous Huxley's *Brave New World*.[8] Both history and common sense, therefore, would seem to provide strong caution against empowering some group of centralized authorities with the responsibility of "correcting" our "native, or *inborn*" differences (Cohen 2009, 17). As Adam Smith wisely warned over two centuries ago, a power like this might be such that it "could be safely trusted, not only to no single person, but to no council or senate whatever, and which would nowhere be so dangerous as in the hands of a man who had folly and presumption enough to fancy himself fit to exercise it" (WN, 456).

Inequality and Enforceable Rights

In chapter 4, I argued that much of the material inequality that arises from business activity in markets is morally unobjectionable—the result of people making free choices that they are entitled to make as full moral agents. If Jill one day meets and decides to marry Joe rather than her longtime boyfriend Jack, Jack may be justifiably disappointed at this turn of events, which would certainly count as unlucky for him. But he has no claim to press against Jill. Jill is a full moral agent and thus entitled to make decisions like this, even if they lead to the unequal distribution of her affections to Joe rather than to Jack. Similarly, the owner of a coffee shop has no claim to press against customers who choose to go to the new coffee shop that opened across the street. The owner of the former might be justifiably disappointed at her bad luck of having a new coffee shop open across the street, but customers are full moral agents and thus within

---

[7] Plato argued that selective human "breeding," including selective sterilization, abortion, and infant exposure, would be necessary to achieve the ideally good city-state; see his *Republic* (1992), book. 5.

[8] Of course, we do not only have science fiction to which to turn when contemplating such nightmarish scenarios. There were numerous grisly and horrific actual experiments conducted in the twentieth century. If you have the stomach for it, you might see Baumslag 2005 or Spitz 2005.

their rights to say, "No, thank you" to her and go elsewhere. Even if that means that the customers' resources are unequally distributed from her to the owner of the competing shop, and even if she should go out of business, customers are entitled to patronize whatever shop they wish—just as Jill is entitled to marry whomever she wishes. Jack and the owner of the failing coffee shop suffer real losses, and their situations might now be unequal to that of Joe and the owner of the successful coffee shop, respectively, but these eventualities resulted from people's voluntary and unobjectionable choices that should be respected.

I suggest that these examples warrant a general conclusion: inequalities resulting from voluntary choices people make are not, by themselves, cases of actionable injury. We may not like some of them, and we may decide—and even, in some particular situations, be morally obliged—to engage in beneficent action to help those who do not succeed as a result of others' choices. But if we call for government interference, forcible redistribution of wealth, or coercive charity, we are calling for violations of justice—the one thing we may not do. We may give charitably out of our own resources; we may try to persuade others to give, or to choose differently; we may engage in honorable business to increase the total sum of prosperity and opportunity available in society; or we may do some combination, or all, of these. But we may not interpose ourselves uninvited into others' choices, or into others' business or affairs, without privileging our own agency over theirs and thus disrespecting their dignity and moral agency.

Some inequality arises, however, not, or not only, from unobjectionable individual choice, but from systematic interference in people's choices. Elizabeth Anderson (2017) has recently argued, for example, that many firms have codes of conduct or behavior, or place expectations on their workers, that amount to compulsion and even coercion. Unrealistic expectations, onerous work rules, or imperious bosses or managers can create environments that are toxic, stifling, and even psychologically damaging. Anderson is clearly right about this. Yet there are at least two reasons to resist her conclusion that therefore businesses coerce in the way governments can and do—that private firms are in fact "dictatorships," as she puts it, governed by "unaccountable" bosses (2017, xxii).[9] First, workers always at the limit have a right both of voice and exit. Except in the rare case of monopoly or monopsony, the threat of exit is real and thus provides workers more leverage than Anderson allows. Workers in America today in fact change their jobs and even occupations repeatedly throughout their careers, and with over 30 million businesses in America, there are typically many potential

---

[9] For what it is worth, here is Adam Smith's answer to Anderson: "The real and effectual discipline which is exercised over a workman, is not that of his corporation, but that of his customers" (WN, 146).

options available.[10] Second, it does not follow from the fact that one can imagine, for a given worker or group of workers, better situations for them either that we should intervene on their behalf or even that, all things considered, this is not the best overall option for them given the relevant circumstances. We cannot know from afar whether another person's choices are the right ones for her, and it seems condescending to merely assume that people who make choices that we would not have made must therefore be making mistakes. On the contrary, the way to respect them as equal moral agents to us is precisely to assume that they do have their own reasons for their choices, and hence to respect those choices. Unless there is actual coercion or fraud involved—if, for example, they in fact had no exit option—our default position should be to trust that they are making the best of the opportunities available to them that can be done.

In contrast to private business, federal, state, and local governments produce laws and regulations from which one may not exit or opt out. They often do so on a massive scale, and in many countries they can amount to substantial restrictions on what people may freely do as peaceful individuals or in mutually voluntary exchanges with others. The restrictions governments create can sometimes reach absurd levels—in some countries it can take years to get the legal permissions required to start a business, for example.[11] In other cases, the rules are so numerous, and sometimes contradictory and arbitrarily enforced, that they can effectively become prohibitions on people seeking good-faith ways to engage in honorable business.[12] Often these rules and restrictions hurt the poor or new entrants in the market most, as they do not have the resources to navigate them that richer people or larger or more entrenched firms do.

Though these restrictions are sometimes implemented out of corrupt motivations—to benefit one favored person, family, firm, or industry over others—other times they arise from the good intention of wishing to protect citizens or consumers from dangerous or destructive goods, services, or business practices. Drawing on my argument here, I can perhaps offer a general principle, namely, that the first rule of government regulation should be similar to the first rule of medicine's Hippocratic Oath: First, do no harm. Applying that to the regulations government place on business, the principle should be not to interfere in people's peaceful and voluntary activities in ways that would make things worse than they already are or otherwise would be. Unless people's actions are extractive, the default position should be to allow them wide latitude to find ways to improve their lives through voluntary cooperation with others without

---

[10] It is also the case that in the United States approximately three million workers *voluntarily* quit their jobs each month. See Bureau of Labor Statistics 2018.

[11] See de Soto 2000.

[12] See Silverglate 2011 and Murray 2015.

third-party interference. As Adam Smith wrote regarding his "obvious and simple system of natural liberty": "Every man, as long as he does not violate the laws of justice, is left perfectly free to pursue his own interest his own way, and to bring both his industry and capital into competition with those of any other man, or order of men" (WN, 687). Permissionless innovation is one of the keys to increasing prosperity, and should be given the widest scope possible.[13]

Shipwrecked on an Island

Let me close this discussion of equality by offering a thought experiment that proposes a contrasting moral to that of Cohen's camping trip scenario.

Suppose that you and I and hundreds of other people are sailing on a cruise ship across the Pacific Ocean. A storm assails us, however, and shipwrecks us on an uninhabited island. To our dismay, we discover that the island has little by way of flora or fauna capable of sustaining us for long. Our situation rapidly begins to deteriorate as a result. Suppose we can see another island in the distance, however, and so you and I and a handful of others decide to hazard a swim to it—against the advice of the other shipwrecked islanders. Suppose that, against all odds, we make it, and we few are delighted to discover that it has abundant flora and fauna. We manage to get a message to the inhabitants of the first island to that effect, but none of them decide to risk the uncertain and dangerous swim. In the meantime, we start a relatively flourishing life for ourselves: we eat well, and we are able to create adequate shelter and clothing. We send yet another message to the inhabitants of the first island informing them of our good fortune and imploring them to join us; this time, a few decide to join us, though most do not. Despite their straightened circumstances, most of them decide the risk is too high. Perhaps some of them are weak swimmers or have physical conditions that make them believe they are unlikely to make it. Perhaps some of them do not believe our tales of relative prosperity. In any case, months go by. During that time, a small stream of brave inhabitants decide to hazard the trip to our island, some of them surviving the journey, others, tragically, not. Over time, the disparity between our circumstances and theirs grows, not just because of the better resources, but because we are able to put them to use to multiply their benefit to us.

Now, a question: Have those of us who left the first island for the better-supplied island acted unjustly? Have we wronged the people who chose to stay behind? Does the fact that our situations—partly through luck, partly through deliberate choice and effort—are better, and getting increasingly better, than the

---

[13] See Erixon and Weigel 2016.

situation of the others create an enforceable moral duty on us toward those others? I suggest the answer to these questions is no. We have not made their situation worse; we have not wronged them in their persons, property, or promises. If we do not help them, we do not worsen their situation: we leave them as they otherwise are. Perhaps it would be generous or charitable or humane for us to try harder to help them. Perhaps, but perhaps not: it would be hard to know in the abstract because it might be that doing so could pose a significant risk to our own well-being; if so, then that would seem to lessen any obligation on our part to help. But would it be *unjust* for us not to do so? If we are not preventing them from joining us, or from attempting to better their own conditions in some other way, and if the prosperity we are enjoying on our island does not come at the expense of the others, then I do not believe our actions are unjust. Because they, like us, are full moral agents, they deserve to have their choices respected—and to accept responsibility for them. If they had forcibly prevented us from trying to swim to the new island, they would have been disrespecting our choices and thus acting unjustly. In the same way, if we tried to force them to join us, or forcibly prevented them from joining us, that would be to disrespect them and act unjustly. Once they learn of our greater prosperity, they are in full possession of the relevant knowledge; indeed, they know more than we did when we first ventured the swim. Respecting their agency requires respecting their decision to stay. Precisely the same requirement of respect is what debars them from making a claim on us after we arrive.

So although our situations are now unequal, no injustice has been done, and the inhabitants of the poorer island have no reasonable grounds of complaint. They might wish we would help them or hope that we do, or they may envy our situation, but those do not create grounds for enforced compensation.

What *would* create an obligation on us to help? The inhabitants of the poorer island would have a justifiable complaint if we had entered into some kind of agreement with them. Suppose we all decided together to build a makeshift raft, and selected by lot some people to hazard the journey to the other island. Suppose also that we agreed that should those who were selected arrive and find supplies, they would then help those on the initial island. In that case, the new islanders would indeed have morally enforceable obligations to help the others. If they did not, they would have violated the promise they made, which is an injustice. Or suppose that those who struck out for the new island built their raft with the only available trees on the initial island without getting the consent of the others—in other words, they impoverished the other inhabitants to facilitate their attempt to leave. In that case, the prosperity they enjoyed on the new island resulted in part at the expense of the other inhabitants. That, too, could generate an obligation on their part to help. Or, finally, if we lied to the others about the circumstances on our island, or if we prevented others from coming to our island, or drowned or killed them upon their arrival, then these would be obvious injustices, licensing punishment. But in the original scenario envisioned, no such agreement, no benefit at others' expense, and no force or fraud are in place. In such a case, there would be no nonoptional obligation on the part of the newly prospering adventurers to help the others. Again, they may choose to do so out of generosity or charity, and we might applaud and approve of their efforts; but we would have no grounds to justify forcing them to do so or punishing them for not doing so.

I offer this scenario as an alternative to Cohen's camping trip scenario. Cohen argues that equal sharing of all things is morally required, that departures from equality are prima facie morally suspect, and that this holds as a requirement of justice. Because business activity in markets would lead to departures from Cohen's recommended conception of equality, his argument constitutes a criticism not only of market economies generally but also of the conception of honorable business I have defended. On the basis of the shipwrecked-on-an-island scenario and the preceding discussion, I suggest instead that material inequality by itself is not necessarily morally blameworthy, and that many aspects of inequality are morally unproblematic and do not require correction, compensation, or redistribution of resources. The kind of inequality that I argue would require rectification is inequality in moral agency. If some are granted rights or freedoms that others are not, if some are able to exert their wills over others, if some have opt-out options but others do not: cases like these imply and issue from a moral inequality—some people's agency can trump that of others—that is disallowed by a proper conception of justice.

A justifiable set of political and economic institutions, then, is one that first and foremost enforces equal moral agency, not material equality. Such institutions allow people the opportunity to improve their situations in cooperation with willing others all of whom enjoy an opt-out option. If those institutions also allow material inequality, the increasing overall prosperity and the equality of moral agency they portend are, I suggest, more than sufficient compensating differentials.

Fairness

Any parent can attest to the fact that one of the first, and evidently favorite, expressions children learn is "That's not fair!" This phrase is used so often, and in so many different circumstances, that it is difficult to find a common thread connecting them. Sometimes it means a departure from exact equality: if your brother got a slice of cake, then you should get a slice of cake (of exactly the same size and quality) too. Sometimes it means not properly recognizing one's status: if a younger brother gets to sit in the front seat of the car instead of his older sister, a violation of fairness has occurred. Sometimes it means an unreasonable expectation: too much homework on a given night is unfair. Sometimes it means a failure in proper proportionality: the bigger brother should get two bags of chips, not just one like his younger brother, because he is bigger. Yet other times it means dashed hopes: each child got to pick one piece of candy out of the bag, but one child got a piece that it turns out she does not like, while the others all like theirs—which is unfair. Or it means dashed expectations: my sister got three gifts on her birthday, so I should get three as well; but I only got two, which, even if the cost of my two equals the cost of her three, is unfair. And so on.

Though parents often struggle mightily to be "fair" in their dealings with their children, if they are honest they will tell you that that frequently entails treating different children differently, and even at times unequally. One child has a harder time with math, and so he gets more help than the other children; one needs more frequent positive reinforcement, and so she gets more compliments; one has a harder time filtering his thoughts before they come out of his mouth, and so he gets more correction and rebuke; and so on. Some children get more of their parents' time than others, some get more of their parents' physical affection than others, some get more money spent on them than others, and so on. Sometimes we comply with the wishes of one child when we do not comply with the similar wishes of another child; sometimes we let one child drive the car and another not; sometimes we let one child stay out a bit later than another child; one child we send to a private school, another we send to the public school, another we homeschool. All of this might, it should be emphasized, issue from equal love for the children. The disparities in treatment result, instead, from the children's different situations, different personalities and temperaments, different needs, different abilities and skills, and different interests and goals, as well as the different resources or capacities or judgment of the parents at different times in their lives.

This discussion is not meant to disparage or belittle concerns about fairness. On the contrary, the fact that such concerns are so ubiquitous indicates how important they are to us. But this discussion does suggest that we may have differing and even competing conceptions of fairness, and that we may well not be able to settle on a single proper definition. Many philosophers have discussed fairness with considerable sophistication and subtlety. John Rawls, for example, perhaps the preeminent political philosopher of the twentieth century, argued that the first principle of any defensible liberal society was justice, and his conception of justice he called "justice as fairness."[14] According to Rawls, if

[14] See Rawls 1971.

the institutions that constitute the "basic structure" of one's society are just, that means they are fair, and each person then receives his "fair share" from the "cooperative labors of others"—as long as we also *do* our "fair share" in maintaining the institutions and engaging in cooperative labor (1971, 111–12).

In the eighteenth century, when Adam Smith was writing, the opposite of "fair" would not have been "unfair" but, rather, "foul"—in other words, in violation of the rules of the game or of good sportsmanship. The opposite of "fair" could also have meant ugly or unbecoming, with a long tradition of use of "fair" to mean, as the first definition in Samuel Johnson's *Dictionary* (1755) has it, "beautiful." But perhaps a relatively uncontroversial contemporary definition of fairness is getting what one deserves, whatever that is. A trade, exchange, or association, or a rule or set of institutions, is fair insofar as it results in the relevant parties getting what they deserve. It seems different from saying that one is "entitled" to something; if you were entitled to something but did not get it, that would seem an infraction of justice, not merely fairness. But if an exchange was unfair, that seems to suggest that there was perhaps something more or better that you should have gotten, without, however, rising to the level of injustice. It may not be fair of me to keep my whole piece of cake to myself, but not giving some of it to you would not seem to count as an injustice—unless, of course, I had made you some promise or we had a contract or some other agreement.

So in what way might honorable business in markets be unfair? Perhaps I am just as smart or talented as you, but I went into academic philosophy and you became a businessperson, so you make much more money than I do. Perhaps I think that philosophy is intrinsically more valuable than what you do in business, so I think that I should, in all fairness, be paid as much, if not more, than you get paid. Or perhaps I think that I contribute more value to the company than is reflected by what it is paying me, so I think it is unfair for it not to pay me more. Or, again, perhaps I think that you and I are intrinsically equally valuable, but I grew up in a poor household with a single working mother, while you grew up in a wealthy household with an intact family; the opportunities you had that I did not, through no fault of mine and through no desert of yours, seem unfair. Or perhaps we look on the sometimes dissolute and vacuous lives of the rich and think how unfair it is that people like them should have so much while we have so comparatively little.

We could multiply these examples, but to bring the discussion to a more focused point, let us ask what role honorable business and markets play in the creation or extension of such unfairnesses, and thus what actions should be taken, perhaps by government, to remedy them. Because, as I have argued, a government that restricts its activities primarily to enforcing negative justice—that is, protection of person, property, and promise—seems to be an indispensable key for allowing increasing overall prosperity, we should be cautious about asking the government to do more than that. Remedying individual cases of unfairness in personal relations or in individual persons' lives requires, as the above discussion of parenting suggests, intimate and detailed knowledge of the local situations of the persons involved—including their histories, their relations to others, their opportunities, their values and goals and capacities, and so on. This is knowledge not likely to be had by distant third parties, like legislators and regulators, so the chances that any intervention they contemplated would make things better are slim. How could your senator, for example, know what you deserve? Does your senator even know who you are?[15] So if the question is what political or economic policies are implied by many of these kinds of cases of unfairness, the answer might appear to be none. There is too much variation in cases, too much disagreement—even good-faith disagreement—about what fairness would require in any particular cases, and too much difference in individuals to license any general policy.

But not all hope is lost. Let me make two positive recommendations that follow from the argument about honorable business offered in this book. The first concerns one part of the discussion of fairness that I believe is often wrongly omitted from consideration. The second concerns what we have in our power to do to remedy unfairness. I will then close this discussion of fairness by discussing a perhaps unexpected worry arising from what Joseph Schumpeter identified as the central defining characteristic of competitive market economies, namely, "creative destruction."

The "Forgotten Man"

An influential school of thought in political philosophy called "luck egalitarianism" holds that because luck plays a substantial role in everyone's relative success in life, and because one cannot be credited or blamed for the presence or effects of luck in one's life, then those who are benefited by good luck should have some of the fruits of their success redistributed to those who are hindered by bad luck.[16] The goal of luck egalitarianism is to equalize the effects of luck in people's lives—hence the name—and thus let everyone's relative level of success be the result, to the extent possible, of only their deliberate choice. This position is difficult to implement in practice, however, since the mechanisms available for such redistributive ends in practice often benefit or impose costs on the wrong people. They often end up not only benefiting the unlucky and

---

[15] Most Americans do not know who their own senators are, and each American has only two senators to remember; senators, by contrast, typically have millions of constituents. See Caplan 2008 and Somin 2016.

[16] See Anderson 1999 for a review of luck egalitarian positions.

burdening the lucky, who are the respective intended targets, but, because they focus on proxies for luck like wealth, they often end up also benefiting the lucky and (further) burdening the unlucky, which is the opposite of what is intended.[17]

Discussions of luck egalitarianism, and justifications for various types of redistribution more generally, rightly focus their concern on the least well-off in society.[18] John Rawls, for example, argued that the public institutions of a well-ordered society would satisfy two main principles of justice: "The first requires equality in the assignment of basic rights and duties, while the second holds that social and economic inequalities, for example inequalities of wealth and authority, are just only if they result in compensating benefits for everyone, and in particular for the least advantaged members of society" (1971, 14–15). Rawls's second principle, called the "difference principle," requires that whatever inequalities might exist in society should benefit, perhaps first and foremost, the least well-off in society. They may also benefit those who are better-off in society, but if they do not benefit the least among us, then, Rawls argues, they are not worthy of our support. As positions like Rawls's get translated into political-economic considerations, and then into discussions of business and markets, the concerns for the least well-off become worries about those who do not fare as well as others in market exchanges and business transactions.

In markets and business, some people do not make as much money as others. Indeed, some people make much more than others. Perhaps it is the case that substantially everyone in market economies is better off than they would be in nonmarket economies; regardless, some do not fare as well as others, as well as they would like or believe they deserve, or as well as others believe they should or deserve. Think of the person who cannot get a job, or who cannot get a good job; think of the person who starts a new business, into which she put all her savings, but that nevertheless fails, and she loses everything; think of people who cannot afford a reliable car to get them to work, or who cannot afford to send their children to the school of their choice, or who cannot afford the medical care they need.

As difficult as their situations are, evidence suggests that all of these kinds of people are better off overall if they live in a country that has markets and honorable business.[19] In such a country, the overall levels of prosperity increase, raising the standard of living for everyone, including in particular that of the poorest in the country. The best antipoverty program we have been able to discover is a system of political economy that enables growing prosperity: it creates more options, more affordable goods and services, and thus more means for achieving

---

[17] See Otteson 2017 for this and other criticisms of luck egalitarianism.
[18] See Tomasi 2012 and Piketty 2014.
[19] See chap. 2.

one's ends. Indeed, policies and programs of government-supervised wealth redistribution surprisingly, and perhaps disappointingly, tend to have little positive effect on the poor (there is even evidence that they tend to have a *negative* effect on the poor);[20] but protections of the "three Ps" in markets that incentivize honorable business have a significant, and positive, effect on the standard of living of the poor.[21] Still, it is undeniable that some people continue to face significant hardship because of their relative poverty that others who are relatively wealthier do not. Should they not remain a cause for concern?

In 1883, Yale political scientist William Graham Sumner published an essay called "The Forgotten Man."[22] In this essay, Sumner claimed that in discussions about poverty relief, the two main figures in the discussions are (1) the person, or persons, who need help and (2) those publicly advocating on their behalf. Sumner notes, however, that that leaves one important person out of the discussion—namely, the person asked to pay for whatever policy those in the second group devise. This is his "forgotten man." Sumner writes:

> As soon as A observes something which seems to him to be wrong, from which X is suffering, A talks it over with B, and A and B then propose to get a law passed to remedy the evil and help X. Their law always proposes to determine what C shall do for X or, in the better case, what A, B and C shall do for X. As for A and B, who get a law to make themselves do for X what they are willing to do for him, we have nothing to say except that they might better have done it without any law, but what I want to do is to look up C. I want to show you what manner of man he is. I call him the Forgotten Man. (Sumner 1992, 202)

Sumner argues that this Forgotten Man is the unduly neglected taxpayer. In Sumner's telling, this is a person who does his job and provides for his family and manages to be upright enough in his life that he can do both. In other words, he has done nothing wrong—indeed, he is doing right—and yet he is the one who is, in effect, punished for doing so. He is made to pay not only for his own obligations but also for the programs that A and B devise; whereas if he decided not to work or provide for his family, he would then become the beneficiary of A and B's programs, and in effect rewarded. Sumner's argument is that this person deserves our praise, not blame, and should be rewarded, not punished. We want more people to be like him, Sumner argues, not fewer. Similarly, Sumner argues that the programs A and B propose create what we today would

---

[20] See Dollar and Kraay 2016.

[21] See Hall and Lawson 2014.

[22] Sumner 1992.

call "moral hazard": at the margins, some might decide that working and providing for one's own obligations is not worth the effort, which risks creating more people for the Forgotten Man to support.

There is some evidence suggesting Sumner may have been on to something. Expanding welfare benefits correlates with increasing, not decreasing, numbers of people signing up for their benefits; and as welfare benefits become less generous, we see fewer people signing up for them.[23] Adam Smith's economizer argument might help explain this. People respond to incentives, and if they get rewarded for something, we will tend to see more of them doing it. A recent study suggested that upwards of 90 percent of people receiving welfare benefits in the United States do not, by objective standards, actually need them.[24] Why, then, do they take them? Because they can. Why do politicians, regulators, and government program administrators tolerate that? Because it is in their interest to do so. The budgets of government agencies do not increase if fewer people need their help; so it is in their interest to maintain, and indeed expand, the numbers of people to whom they are administering. In the fifty years since Lyndon B. Johnson launched the War on Poverty, the United States has spent over $22 trillion on its increasing array of poverty and welfare programs.[25] And yet the proportion of people at or below the official poverty line has remained relatively constant, with little or no positive change. Indeed, there is now a higher proportion of people receiving government-supervised supplemental food subsidies and Social Security disability than at any time in American history. Despite our unprecedented levels of overall wealth, over 20 percent of all Americans today receive some form of direct federal government welfare, some 70 million people.[26]

If Harvey and Conyers (2016) are right, or even close to being right, then the majority of this spending is unnecessary, and may indeed even be counterproductive. But put that aside for the moment and consider instead: Who pays for it? The answer is taxpayers—those who create, have, and keep jobs, those who engage in productive, cooperative, and thus honorable business. But they are not the only ones paying for it. Our children and future generations will pay for it as well. As of this writing, the current national debt of the US federal government has surpassed $21 trillion, higher than its current annual gross domestic product

[23] See Brooks 2006.

[24] Harvey and Conyers 2016.

[25] See Sheffield and Rector 2014.

[26] If we add in the number of people receiving Medicare, Medicaid, Supplemental Security Income, housing subsidies, and other benefits, the number of US citizens receiving governmental aid increases to some 166 million, or approximately 51 percent of the population. See US Census Bureau 2015.

(approximately $19 trillion), and is climbing rapidly. As large, and unsustainable, as that is, that number does not include so-called off-budget items like Social Security, Medicare, and Medicaid. If we add to our national debt the estimated obligations we and our future generations have committed ourselves to and thus face from those programs, our total indebtedness rises considerably. Estimates vary—necessarily so, because they depend on projections regarding how long people will live, how many of them will avail themselves of these programs, and so on—but educated guesses range from $70 trillion on the low end to as high as $222 trillion, or between 3.5 and 11.5 times the current total domestic product of the entire United States.[27] For comparison, the total gross product *for the entire world* in 2017 was $127 trillion.[28] Now, of course not all of America's debt comes from welfare and aid programs. But $2.5 trillion, some 62 percent of the federal government's current (2017) $4 trillion budget, is dedicated to "entitlements," which includes Social Security, Medicare, and Medicaid.[29] Another $315 billion, or 8 percent of the budget, is spent in paying interest on our debt, which is now the fastest-growing part of our budget expenditures. Spending on the military, for comparison, is approximately $825 billion, about 20 percent of the overall budget. Thus the lion's share of our total current and future indebtedness is accounted for by our "entitlement" expenditures.

Again, who pays, or will pay, for this? For the most part, it is future generations. But that means that we today who are benefiting from these expenditures are in fact benefiting at the expense of those future generations. The value of what they will have to pay should, however, be discounted, since we can plausibly assume that future generations will be richer than we are today; yet even granting that discount, this nevertheless constitutes a large wealth transfer from those too young to vote or not yet even alive to beneficiaries today. That would therefore seem a clear example of a zero-sum extraction. Not only have those future generations not voluntarily consented, they have not even been asked— and yet every child today faces an individual personal share of $213,496 of America's current national debt, and it is climbing.[30] We can certainly see who benefits from these programs: the current beneficiaries, as well as the politicians and government officials who administer the bureaus, agencies, and offices. But those who will be required to pay these unsustainable levels of spending and promising are the future generations—unseen, and so unheeded. They are Forgotten Girls and Boys.

---

[27] See Kotlikoff 2010 and Lawler 2012.

[28] See Central Intelligence Agency, n.d.

[29] See Amadeo 2018.

[30] If we add to our national debt the United States' current unfunded liabilities, then each individual's share, as of this writing, rises to $930,121.

In his Farewell Address in 1796,[31] President George Washington warned members of Congress to avoid the accumulation of public debt. We should, he said, "cherish public credit." He continued:

> One method of preserving it is to use it as sparingly as possible, avoiding occasions of expense by cultivating peace, but remembering also that timely disbursements to prepare for danger frequently prevent much greater disbursements to repel it, avoiding likewise the accumulation of debt, not only by shunning occasions of expense, but by vigorous exertion in time of peace to discharge the debts which unavoidable wars may have occasioned, not ungenerously throwing upon posterity the burden which we ourselves ought to bear.

For Washington, this was much a moral mandate as an economic one. A large debt would make it more difficult for the country, just as it does for a household, to call upon the reserves necessary in times of emergency. More worrying than that, however, was what Washington saw as the immorality of "throwing upon posterity the burden which we ourselves ought to bear." Why was that immoral? Because it constituted a form of, to coin a phrase, *taxation without representation*—and a particularly egregious form at that, because our posterity does not even have the opportunity to voice an opinion.

But let us bring this reasoning to a more local and specific level. Recall our examples of Jack, Jill, and Joe, and of Coffee Shops A and B. I argued that Jack and the owner of Coffee Shop A had no grounds for seeking compensation from, respectively, Jill or Joe, and the owner of Coffee Shop B. I argued that this followed from the fact that Jack had no right to Jill, and the owner of Coffee Shop A had no right to her (former) patrons. But we can understand these examples using Sumner's argument as well. For those who would feel and express (justifiable) sympathy for the plights of Jack and the owner of Coffee Shop A, the parties who figure most centrally in the conversations are Sumner's A, B, and X. A and B are the people who feel the justified sympathy and discuss ways to help X; X is Jack or the owner of Coffee Shop A. The persons left out of the conversations are not just those who might be called on to compensate the Xs, but also those whose free and voluntary choices led to the situation in which those Xs find themselves. Disappointments we experience in life are often the result of others having made choices that did not lead to benefit we expected or hoped for, but those are choices that those others were, as full moral agents, nevertheless entitled to make.

---

[31] See Washington 1796.

If I do not get into the college I wanted to, if I do not get the job I wanted, if I do not get paid what I would like (or even believe I deserve), or if I cannot afford many of the things I would like: whatever hardships or disappointments these cause for me, though real, they frequently result from choices that others made to which we have no grounds to object. I have no more claim to having been injured and no more cause to call for compensation than I would if I do not get love or companionship from the person I wanted. Just as others are entitled to choose whether to give their love or companionship to me, others are also entitled to choose whether to admit me, hire me, pay me more, and so on. I may not like their choices, I may wish, even desperately wish, they would choose otherwise, and I may even believe that they are wrong to choose the way they do; but if I interfere with their free choices, or visit cost or harm or injury on them, then it is I, not they, who have committed injustice. It is I, not they, who have disrespected another's autonomy and dignity, and thus it is I, not they, who have acted unacceptably.

Among those who are often forgotten, then, are those on the other sides of potential exchanges, trades, partnerships, and associations. They are moral agents, just like us; they deserve respect for their autonomy and dignity, just like us; and they deserve to have their choices, and the exercise of their opt-out options respected, just like us.[32] When thinking about our own situations or those we know whose plights we lament, we must not forget that morally proper, as well as mutually beneficial, associations with others must be *mutually* voluntary—and that means that others get to have a say as well.

Social Power

As we have seen, in his *Theory of Moral Sentiments*, Adam Smith distinguished between "justice," which he argued required protection of person, property, and promise; and "beneficence," which required taking steps to improve the situation of others. To be fulfilled, the former required merely restraint—refraining from injuring or interfering with others' three Ps. By contrast, to be fulfilled, beneficence required the expenditure of resources—time, money, and so on—to generate actual benefit in others' lives. Smith considered the protection of justice necessary for the survival of any society, and so he assigned it as the prime duty of government. Beneficence, however, he considered to be the "ornament which embellishes, not the foundation which supports" society (TMS, 86). Moreover, because he thought that providing actual and real help to others required detailed knowledge of their local situations, he argued that distant legislators

---

[32] See Shapiro 2007.

would be unable to engage in beneficence effectively. Smith also thought that "beneficence is always free, it cannot be extorted by force" (TMS, 78). If we are forced to help another, Smith argues, we would get no moral credit for it. For these reasons, he assigned the duties of beneficence to those who (a) had the relevant local knowledge to know which ostensible help would in fact be helpful and (b) could exercise their free moral agency to help those who needed it and whom they could actually help.

Smith's answer to critics who suggest that the free and voluntary charitable action he envisions and extolls would be insufficient to meet all of the needs of the poor was, *Look in the mirror*. If there is someone you know who needs your help, then give it. If there are people in need whom you can help, do so. Each of us should do the same. These are, in other words, personal obligations on Smith's account. If no one of us can meet all the needs of others, then we should voluntarily band together and pool our resources to do what we can and believe we ought. Smith would counsel us not to underestimate the good that can be done by even the single committed individual—not only directly, by helping specific others with one's time, talent, and treasure, but also indirectly, by serving as an example and model to others. He would similarly counsel us not to underestimate the power of such moral example and witness. People often do not respond well to being lectured about what they should do; but they often do respond to the power of personal example.

In a similar vein, John Stuart Mill argued in his influential *On Liberty* ([1859] 1978) that there are strict limits on the power society may justifiably exercise over any of its citizens.[33] Indeed, he argued that the central purpose of his essay was to assert "one very simple principle": "That principle is, that the sole end for which mankind are warranted, individually or collectively, in interfering with the liberty of action of any of their number, is self-protection" ([1859] 1978, 9). He elaborated: "That the only purpose for which power can be rightfully exercised over any member of a civilized community, against his will, is to prevent harm to others. His own good, either physical or moral, is not a sufficient warrant. He cannot rightfully be compelled to do or forbear because it will be better for him to do so, because it will make him happier, because, in the opinions of others, to do so would be wise, or even right" (9). But what if we believe that others are making choices or engaging in conduct that is in fact detrimental to their "physical or moral" good? Are we left no recourse? Mill answers: "These are good reasons for remonstrating with him, or reasoning with him, or persuading him or entreating him but not for compelling him, or visiting him with any evil,

---

[33] See Mill 1978.

in case he do other wise. To justify that, the conduct from which it is desired to deter him must be calculated to produce evil to some one else" (9).

Mill's full justification for this clear demarcation between what is acceptable and what is unacceptable in our treatment of others is too elaborate for us to do it justice here. But we can note two important points. First, Mill's distinction between what is unacceptable—"visiting him with any evil"—and what is acceptable—"remonstrating with him, or reasoning with him, or persuading him or entreating him"—maps directly on the distinction Smith draws between justice and beneficence. To visit a person with evil would be to cause her harm or injury, which Smith identifies as injustice and Mill says we "cannot" do. On the other hand, part of what Smith envisioned under the heading of "beneficence" would include teaching, mentoring, and advising others—as long as those others were willing to listen—which is what Mill here identifies as remonstrating, reasoning, persuading, and entreating. Both Smith's and Mill's arguments suggest an important vehicle for the alleviation of poverty that is today often underappreciated. Not only institutions protecting every person's, including every poor person's, person, property, and promises, and not only the increasing prosperity and "mass flourishing" that this enables, which raises the standard of living of the poor especially. Beyond that, and on a much more personal level, Smith's and Mill's arguments constitute reminders of our *personal* obligations. They ask us to call upon what Nock (1994) called our "social power," as opposed to "political" or "state power."

Political power has two characteristic features that distinguish it from social power. First, it operates on the basis of coercion. Every dollar that the government spends, whether for good or bad ends, has been taken from its current or future citizens, whether they agreed or not.[34] The second feature of political power, however, is that it reduces the opportunity of fulfilling our personal moral obligations, and thus it diminishes our opportunities to develop our own moral character. If the state takes on the duty of caring for the poor, the unemployed, the indigent, the injured, the sick, the retired, the undereducated, and so on, then that is proportionately less opportunity for you and me, and all other private citizens, to exercise the self-command required both to help others and to develop our own, as Nock (1991) puts it, "moral fibre." Perhaps, then, beneficence might instead be properly a role for our social power.

The control any of us individually has over what our government does is in any case negligible. Almost no election turns on any one vote, and the vast majority—over 99 percent—of the 23.7 million officials who administer America's federal, state, and local governments are unelected. Thus the government will end up

---

[34] See Brennan 2016, chaps. 6 and 9. See also Scheidel 2017, chaps. 1 and 2, esp. pp. 43–61.

doing whatever it will do, almost regardless of what any of us individually wants. Perhaps, then, you and I should turn our attention to something over which we actually have some control: what we personally do. Thus we should look for ways to use whatever resources we have available to us to help us achieve not only our own ends but to help others achieve theirs, ways to benefit not only ourselves but others as well. Sometimes our judgment will determine that this requires charitable activity on our part—directed, focused, and specific acts of charity that our local knowledge suggests has a chance at actually helping. In order to enable charity like this, however, we have to have sufficient resources available to us that are beyond what we, and those who depend on us, need. The more resources we have, the more of such effective charitable activity in which we can engage. So, taking the argument one step further, what should we do to enable ourselves, and as many others as possible, to be in possession of enough resources to engage in the charity our judgment obliges us to? If we cannot steal those resources from others, that would seem to leave us with only one option: *generate* them—through honorable business.

Creation and Destruction

In his influential book *Capitalism, Socialism, and Democracy* (1942), Joseph Schumpeter offered one of the now most-cited descriptions of what he called "capitalism." He was using the then-standard definition of "capitalism," by which was meant an economic system that allowed the private ownership of the means of production and that allowed competition for scarce resources. Given this definition of capitalism, Schumpeter wrote: "The essential point to grasp is that in dealing with capitalism we are dealing with an evolutionary process" (1942, 82). He claimed that capitalism "is by nature a form or method of economic change and not only never is but never can be stationary." Why? "The fundamental impulse that sets and keeps the capitalist engine in motion comes from the new consumers' goods, the new methods of production or transportation, the new markets, the new forms of industrial organization that capitalist enterprise creates" (1942, 83). He might have added all the new ideas given life, and the new desires created by business in markets. But he went on to elaborate on the biological metaphors he was borrowing from evolutionary theory: in markets there is "industrial mutation," which, he says, "incessantly revolutionizes the economic structure *from within*, incessantly destroying the old one, incessantly creating a new one" (1942, 83). And then comes his now famous phrase: "This process of Creative Destruction is the essential fact about capitalism. It is what capitalism consists in and what every capitalist concern has got to live in" (83).

The creative destruction that takes place in markets and business occurs at many levels.[35] Individual businesspeople find their jobs eliminated or obviated by other workers or new technologies; firms go out of business and are replaced by new ventures, which themselves usually go out of business eventually and get replaced by yet others, and so on; and entire fields and industries find their usefulness surpassed and disappear into the mists of history. This process has been going on at least since Adam Smith's time, and it shows no sign of slowing now. If anything, the rates of failure and replacement have been accelerating. This is a great benefit to all of us who increasingly enjoy the products, goods, and services that this progress brings to us. And the regular trajectory of prices for any good or service is to go steadily downward, often beginning at a point where only the rich can afford it and then eventually decreasing until the former luxuries become commonplaces. By the time they become commonplace, they are typically much better than they were when the rich first bought them. Think of cell phones: the first cell phones, which cost thousands of dollars and only the rich owned, were nowhere near as powerful and capable as the phones that today almost all adults in America (and many children) have in their pockets or purses. A similar pattern holds for virtually every good introduced and sold in markets—everything from refrigerators to televisions to personal computers to building materials to automobiles: the real prices go down and the quality goes up.[36]

In all this talk of abundance, however, the focus is typically on innovation and progress—in other words, the *creative* aspect of capitalism. But that is only one half of Schumpeter's description. The other half is *destruction*. It can be easy, perhaps all too easy, to forget that as new products emerge that satisfy our needs and wants, old ones go away. When a business goes under, people lose money, jobs, and perhaps their livelihoods. The competition in the market might produce benefit to the world, but it often comes at the price of those people who lose their jobs and who are displaced. In a growing and vibrant economy, perhaps we can be fairly confident that there will be other opportunities for these people, and even that the new opportunities might be better than what they had before. In some cases, however, the immediate loses can be substantial. Consider a whole town built up around coal mining. If the coal-mining industry wanes, businesses might go under or pack up and move away—leaving effectively the entire town in the lurch. There are many cases like this in the history of American markets,

---

[35] See Munger 2018.

[36] The main exceptions to this general rule are things like education and healthcare, which, perhaps not coincidentally, tend to be dominated by governments instead of markets. See Cox and Alm 1999; Goodman 2012; and Laffer 2014.

many businesses and people left languishing in the detritus of the destructive part of creative destruction.[37]

Consider the fracking revolution, for example, which has produced thousands of new jobs and has led to significant decreases in the prices of energy production—but has also displaced other, older means of producing energy, which means the displacement of workers, families, and even whole communities.[38] Perhaps the workers who lose their jobs in coal mining can take jobs in the fracking industry. But if my family has been in coal mining in West Virginia for generations, and it is all I have ever known, it is a tall order to expect me to just pick up and move to North Dakota and take a job there in fracking—and what guarantee do I have that the new job in North Dakota will last? It is also true that displacement involves not just economic hardship but psychological hardship. Most people do not like change, let alone complete upheaval. The uncertainties and insecurities involved with the process of creative destruction can lead to significant anxiety, which is a real, if nonmonetary, cost in people's lives.[39]

These are indeed part of the "perennial gale of creative destruction" (1942, 84), in Schumpeter's words, that takes place in markets and business. New opportunities arise, but others go away. Unfortunately, the institutions that lead to increasing overall prosperity require this. Even the poor, indeed especially the poor,[40] are benefited by living under such institutions. That is what can give us a confidence that those who are displaced are still, despite the real hardship, overall better off than they likely otherwise would have been for being part of country with such institutions. The "incessant revolution" and "incessant destruction" can create real pain and cost that should not be discounted, but in the long run everyone is better off for it. One might think of an analogy to surgery. It involves the infliction of significant pain, but it is temporary, and in the long run one is (one hopes, at least) better off for it. No one wants to face the prospect of potentially losing a job or having to close a business, but, like surgery, one can perhaps find some comfort in the probability that one will ultimately be better for it.[41]

But there will be some who are not better off for it. Some people lose their jobs or lose their business—and never recover. In a growing and prospering economy, such cases will mercifully be relatively infrequent, and such people will be relatively few. But they will still exist. And in such cases, have we no

---

[37] For two vivid accounts of the destructive part of "creative destruction," see Smith 2013 and Reeves 2017.

[38] See Sernovitz 2016.

[39] See Schabas 2005.

[40] See Deaton 2013; Wilkinson 2016; and McCloskey 2016b.

[41] Taleb 2012 argues that experiencing setbacks and even failure in fact strengthens systems, institutions, and individuals, making them more resilient and better able to work productively in the future. See also Ubel 2006.

obligation to help them? The answer is yes, we do have an obligation to help. This is precisely a role for our social power in the service of the virtue of beneficence. If there are people who need our help, we should roll up our sleeves and help them. We may not be able to help everyone we believe needs help, but we will be able to help some. If we can help just one person, or just one family, then that is a great good in itself. And the more of us who undertake this obligation to help where we can, the more people and families we can help. If we live in a country with the right institutions, we may thankfully find ourselves in a situation where we have the resources to give considerable help. And if we are engaged in honorable business, we will be creating both opportunities and value that can improve the lives of others. This may not solve all problems, but, of course, nothing will solve all problems. The human condition is frustratingly hard, and there is no way to eliminate all setbacks, disappointments, failures, and displacements. If we take it upon ourselves to alleviate some of that, including perhaps working to ensure that we ourselves do not become among those needing others' help, then we will be fulfilling our obligations of both justice and beneficence.

Creative Destruction of Community

The two principles G. A. Cohen (2009) argued that his "socialist" camping trip scenario implied were an egalitarian principle and a principle of community. We discussed earlier in this chapter Cohen's egalitarian principle, but his worry about the deleterious effects of markets and business on community are also shared by many critics. The worry has two main aspects. First, if there is great disparity of wealth in one's community, then people will have widely divergent lives and experiences, making it difficult for them to enter into engaged community with one another. Cohen asks us to imagine a wealthy person and a poor person on a bus.[42] The wealthy person typically does not take the bus, but on this day his luxury automobile is in the repair shop, and so he finds himself sitting next to a person of far humbler means who does regularly take the bus. What, Cohen asks, would they have to speak about? Their lives are so different, and their experiences are so different, there would be few if any points of contact. Cohen fears they would have little occasion to interact with one another and would thus probably just sit in silence, forgoing an opportunity for human contact and community. A second worry about the effects on community of markets and business is that the "creative destruction" of the latter leads people to be mobile and itinerant, taking jobs and pursuing opportunities in many different places, possibly far away from one's friends, family, and community. This can

---

[42] Cohen 2009, 35–36.

give those who move frequently a rootlessness, disconnecting them from the grounded ties and bonds that enable full community, perhaps therefore robbing them of one central element of eudaimonia.[43]

Both of these are very real possibilities, and so both of these are real worries. The "incessant revolutions" of markets and business mean that opportunities for work and creating value will arise and fall away, and will move from place to place. This means that there will be a natural and dynamic cycle of birth, life, and death to communities, towns, and cities,[44] just as there are to ecosystems, languages, cultures, and even civilizations. In all of these transitions, there will be both cost, loss, and displacement, as well as gains from creation and innovation. To a large extent, this is merely a reflection of the at-times tragic nature of the human condition. Heraclitus (535–475 BC) said that one cannot step into the same river twice: continuous change is the nature of both nature and human life, and there is little anyone can do to stop it. That does not mean we have to like it, or at least not all of it, but it does mean we have to resign ourselves to it and do the best we can in the face of it.

The same will be true of community. Cohen is correct to claim that a sense of community seems necessary for human fulfillment and ultimately happiness. He is also correct that the wealthier people become, the more opportunities they will have to move, dissociate themselves from one community or set of communities, and associate themselves with or create new communities. The problem, however, is that neither he nor anyone else knows which communities others should associate themselves with. Would it be better for the rich person and the poor person to talk on the bus, or is it, all things considered, better for them to remain in silence? Is it a net loss if they do not speak or do not try to become acquaintances or even friends, or would attempting to do so be a waste of time? Not everyone, after all, should be friends with everyone. Personalities, goals, values, and preferences differ, which means that people will naturally sort themselves into groups if granted the freedom to do so. But how could we know from afar whether any two people should be friends or should associate—or, if they should associate, in what ways? The answer is that we cannot know this from afar. The local knowledge argument applies here as well. We no more know with whom people unknown to us should become friends than we know what lines of work they should go into or what church (if any) they should go to.

Markets and business generate new options for people, as well as the wealth to pursue them if they choose. That will indeed mean that people will leave some communities, and over time it may mean that some communities die

---

[43] See Deneen 2018.
[44] See Jacobs 1961.

altogether. Is that always bad? Markets and business also create entirely new communities—fresh, vibrant, and unpredicted communities. Think of the new communities created by Facebook, for example, or by the myriad other digital forums, platforms, and spaces that people now frequent but before they existed did not. Are all of them on balance good? Probably not, but some of them might be—and for some people, these new opportunities are godsends. The stifling nature of a local parochial community is the stuff of legend. For someone who wishes to explore a new (or no) religion, or a new way of relating to others, or hobbies, interests, or passions that are not on offer in one's hometown community, the opportunities, and the wealth, generated by markets and business can give the dissenter, the maverick, the rogue, the outcast, the misfit, the eccentric, the risk-taker, the adventurer, the iconoclast, and the entrepreneur a new lease on life, and open up vistas of possibility that could enable a eudaimonic life that might otherwise have been impossible. So, yes, community is important. But so is the ability to choose which community is right for one. And no society creates more opportunities to construct the kind of life that is uniquely right for an individual, according to each individual's own lights, than the free and prospering society of markets and honorable business.

Conclusion

An abiding concern that many of us share is equality. But there are different kinds of equality. One kind of equality we might call "formal," which pertains to the way our institutions treat us. Honorable business requires public institutions that do not distinguish citizens according to things like race, sex, or class but instead grant all of us equal protections in our persons, property, and promises as required by justice. A different kind of equality, however, which we might call "material," addresses the degree to which all of us have the same material wealth. This kind of equality is advocated by socialists like G. A. Cohen and is defended by "luck egalitarians" who argue that much of the wealth disparity we see is the result of undeserved luck and is hence unjust. The system of political economy defended here requires formal equality, but allows material inequality—as long as it results only from exchanges, transactions, and associations that abide by our code of business ethics, or, in other words, from honorable business. Empirical evidence suggests that societies approximating the institutions and moral attitudes embodied in our code enjoy increasing prosperity for all, including especially the poor.

There are also many conceptions of fairness, but one perhaps uncontroversial conception is that a fair transaction is one in which each person gets whatever she deserves. The system of political economy we defended stands the best chance of achieving this aim of fairness, as long as we also consider those "forgotten" men, women, and children who are affected by departures from this system. For those who remain in need, we should summon our social, not political, power to help them. This is the argument of both Adam Smith and John Stuart Mill, and it has the virtue of not only enabling increasing prosperity but also maintaining proper moral relations among people—respecting the autonomy and dignity of every person.

The creative destruction that Schumpeter argued was the "essential" characteristic of what he called "capitalism" involves, as the phrase implies, both creation and destruction. We should not ignore, discount, or disparage the costs in human lives of the destructive part of this process. Nevertheless, there are reasons to be hopeful that even for people adversely affected by this process, their setbacks will be only temporary and they will in the long run be benefited overall for living in a country with the institutions we defended. For those, however, whose situations are not improved, or who remain in need of help, we should give it—voluntarily and personally.

Schumpeterian creative destruction applies also to communities: some wither, some flourish; some die, new ones are born. The "perennial gales of creative destruction" are the spontaneous evolution of communities, driven by the needs and desires of human beings making choices. Although sometimes their choices will lead to the death of communities, conventions, and traditions we may hold dear, they also give rise to new ways of conceiving of human possibility and human association, and new ways and fresh opportunities to achieve eudaimonia.

8

Honorable Business and Valuing
What We Ought

Introduction

Should everything be for sale? Is there anything that should not be for sale? What about prison cell upgrades, access to the car pool lane while driving solo, the services of an Indian surrogate mother to carry a pregnancy for a Western couple, the right to immigrate into the United States, the right to shoot an endangered black rhinoceros, the personal cell phone number of your doctor, the right to emit a metric ton of carbon into the atmosphere, or the admission of your child into a prestigious university? Each of these, as well as many other cases, is raised by Michael Sandel in his book *What Money Can't Buy* (2012), and he argues that each of them is morally problematic.[1] Debra Satz, for her part, in her book *Why Some Things Should Not Be for Sale* (2010), focuses on women's reproductive and sexual labor, arguing that such things arise from what she calls "noxious markets."[2] Others describe and enumerate yet other potential members of the class of "what should not be sold"—though commentators disagree about what, if anything, should in fact belong to this class.[3]

The problem, according to these critics of markets, is summed up by Sandel: "Markets don't wag fingers. They don't discriminate between admirable preferences and base ones" (2012, 14). He has a point: markets do not wag fingers or discriminate among preferences. But *people* do. Markets are not, in fact, agents that act at all: they are merely the arenas in which people

---

[1] These examples come from Sandel 2012, 3–4. But see also pp. 4–5 and *passim*.

[2] See Satz 2010, chaps. 4, 5, and 6.

[3] See Skidelsky and Skidelsky 2012 and Brennan and Jaworski 2016. Brennan and Jaworski note wryly that there seems to be "a limitless market for books about the moral limits of markets" (2016, 7).

transact voluntarily.[4] Like many other critics of markets, Sandel wants to argue that markets are "amoral." That is, they take no position on the morality of what is bought and sold—hence anything goes. This can give rise to the idea that markets are a kind of moral anarchy, not only indifferent to morality but perhaps actually undermining it by their very indifference. It is, after all, but a short conceptual leap from "x is for sale" to "It's all right to buy x." Even if the latter does not follow logically from the former (which it does not), nonetheless many people may be inclined to believe that it does; hence if it is legal to buy or sell x, more people may buy (or sell) x than otherwise would, even if morally they should not. That is why Sandel argues that there should be extramarket limitations placed on what may be bought or sold, limitations drawn from our considered moral judgments and not produced by markets themselves.

Another worry that Sandel raises is about precious natural resources. He is concerned about endangered species, like black rhinos, and about beautiful vistas and landscapes, like Yosemite National Park. He fears that if we allow "the logic of buying and selling"—to which we might add competition and ownership as private property—to extend to things like this, it will degrade and corrupt them.[5] But we might extend and generalize this worry: perhaps markets and business endanger not only specific animals or species or parks, but ecosystems or even the entire environment. Do the presence and activity of markets and business lead to the destruction of our natural resources? Do they lead to the exploitation of the commons? Do they lead to higher levels, or worse kinds, of pollution?

Let us take these two sets of questions up in this chapter. We will first examine the arguments supporting the idea that some things should not be for sale and that markets are amoral (if not immoral). Then we will examine the worries raised about nature, the commons, and the environment more generally when they become part of the "logic of buying and selling." The connection to the conception of honorable business we have articulated lies precisely in the question of whether what we have described as "honorable business" always issues in the production of morally defensible goods, in the sale of morally defensible services, or in the (morally) sustainable use of resources. If "honorable business" allows—or, worse, even encourages—transactions in immoral goods or services, or in the destructive use of resources, then perhaps it is not so honorable after all. So, does it?

---

[4] Imagine a person arguing that there should be limits on boxing rings because boxing rings hurt people. Boxing rings do not hurt people—though the people in them sometimes do.

[5] See Sandel 2012, 79–82 (on black rhinos), 35–36 (on Yosemite), and 6 for the "logic" quotation.

Commodification

The first person to make an extended case about the "commodification" to which markets lead was Karl Marx. In 1867, Marx published the first (and sole during his lifetime) volume of his projected four-volume work, *Capital*. In it he devotes many pages to discussing the origin, nature, use, and effects of commodities. Economists today tend not to give Marx much attention because subsequent developments in the discipline of economics have superseded or disproved most of Marx's economic claims. But some aspects of Marx's thought continue to inspire the thinking of some philosophers, as well as some anthropologists, literature scholars, historians, political scientists, theologians, and sociologists.[6] If economics has largely moved beyond Marx, why do these other scholars continue to find value in returning to him? One answer might be found in his chapter in *Capital* called "The Fetishism of the Commodity and Its Secret."

In this chapter, Marx says that although a "commodity appears at first sight an extremely obvious, trivial thing," in fact, he claims, "It is a very strange thing, abounding in metaphysical subtleties and theological niceties," and he goes on to speak of the "mystical character of the commodity" ([1867] 1994, 230–31). What is so strange or mystical about commodities? He argues that in markets commodities come to have the appearance of separate, independent entities with their own values, unconnected with the values and labor of the humans who created them or the purposes those humans had in creating them. Commodities are in fact, Marx argues, extensions of human labor, thus of humanity itself, and therefore are properly seen only in their relation to human beings. In markets, however, they take on a life of their own: they are bought and sold, move from place to place, and can become assets figuring in a much larger context of financial arrangements—without anyone caring or even knowing about the people and labor that brought them into being.[7] Marx's concern here is connected to a much earlier essay he wrote entitled "Alienated Labor," which is part of his *Economic and Philosophic Manuscripts* of 1844.[8] In this essay, Marx argues that capitalism is alienating in several ways: workers become alienated from the productions of their labor, the commodities; they become alienated from each other, because they now view their coworkers as competitors rather than comrades; they become alienated even from their own labor, which they now view as itself a commodity that is bought and sold; and they become alienated, as we

---

[6] Some recent examples include, from philosophy, Barker 2018; from anthropology, Harvey 2018; from literature, Eagleton 2018; from history, Claeys 2018; from political science, Blackledge 2013; from theology, Boer 2014; and from sociology, Crossman 2018.

[7] For a more recent explication of this Marxian claim, see de Soto 2000, chap. 3.

[8] Marx (1844) 1994, 58–68.

saw in chapter 6, from their "species-being," from the natural connection they should feel as members of a single species united in a common humane project. This alienation Marx believes is literally dehumanizing: because it strips from us essential parts of our identity—our labor, our connection to nature, our connection to other humans—it renders us something less than human. It reduces us to mere commodities.

Many contemporary anticommodification theorists[9] are moved by similar worries. Selling and buying the rights to kill an endangered black rhino, for example, fails, according to Sandel, to show proper respect for the rhino. It is "morally disagreeable," "morally objectionable," "caters to a perverse desire" that "is not worthy of being fulfilled," and "corrupts the meaning and purpose" that such creatures should hold for us.[10] Similarly with scalpers selling tickets to Yosemite National Park: Sandel claims "national parks are not merely objects of use or sources of social utility. They are places of natural wonder and beauty, worthy of appreciation, even awe. For scalpers to auction access to such places seems a kind of sacrilege" (2012, 37).[11] The language of corruption here is similar to that of Marx's language of "alienation":[12] it is a disrespecting of the value and dignity of the thing bought and sold, a rendering it less than what it is. This process of disrespect, or "commodification," inspires many of the criticisms of markets and business that we see today.

One difficulty facing the anticommodification argument, however, is that people disagree about what the value of things is. Marx argued that human labor gives things value, an idea he may have gotten from Adam Smith, who may have held a similar idea.[13] Marx's claim was that human labor is intrinsically valuable, and thus what human labor creates gets its value from this labor. To the extent that the market price for a good or service departs from this intrinsic value, the price is unjust. As we saw in chapter 4, however, the idea that things have intrinsic value is difficult to sustain. It creates many more philosophical problems than it solves, and it renders common, everyday experiences unintelligible, immoral, or both. Suppose the market price for a baseball signed by Babe Ruth is $5,000. Is that the correct price? Who knows—and how would we even answer that question? Looking to the labor involved in producing the baseball would not get us very far. Suppose you would pay $5,000 for it, but I would pay only $50. If

[9] I borrow this term from Brennan and Jaworski 2016.

[10] Sandel 2012, 79–84.

[11] Pope Francis uses similar terms to describe capitalism. See Francis 2015. For commentary, see Whaples 2017.

[12] Many others use similar language. See Brennan and Jaworski 2016, chap. 5, for a survey.

[13] But see Otteson 2013, chap. 8, which departs from the standard interpretation of a Smithian "labor theory of value."

there is an intrinsic value to the baseball, one or both of us must be wrong—but who is to say? A more straightforward and common-sense way to think of this is that the baseball is worth $5,000 *to you,* while it is worth $50 *to me.* Thus its worth depends on particular valuing agents, and is indexed to them. That means that a given commodity might have any number of values, based on the subjective preferences, which include the subjective values, of different people. The "right" price would be what is right for given individuals; but there would be no single "right" price for everyone.

Apply this reasoning to the kinds of cases that Sandel, Satz, Skidelsky and Skidelsky, and others entertain. The first conclusion would be that the goods and services—the commodities—have no value other than what valuing agents give them. Consider an analogous case. We often speak of "natural resources." Strictly speaking, however, there is no such thing as a "natural resource."[14] Things in nature are not resources until human beings turn them into something that can be put to their purposes. The black tar-like substance beneath the ground in many places on earth has been there far longer than humans have; it did not become the commodity "oil," however—that is, it did not become a *resource*— until human beings figured out what they could do with it. Similarly with other things in the natural world, and with the things we transform them into or the uses to which we put them: they do not become commodities or resources until human beings figure out something they can do with them that benefits them. The value, then, is not intrinsic in things. It is created by human beings.

If so, then there can be no such thing as disrespecting the inherent value of things. But that leaves us with the problem that people value things differently. Some, for example, will value a black rhino for the enjoyment they receive from hunting and killing it. Others, like Sandel, do not value the enjoyment that hunters receive but instead value the enjoyment they get from knowing that rhinos live in the world without being hunted. Whose value is more important? It is this question that brings us now into the realm of political economy. If we assume that different and competing estimations of value are an enduring part of the human condition, we have two ways we can reconcile the differences: we can let one person or group mandate to others how they should value things or forbid them from valuing them otherwise, or both; or we can let people make offers and bargain with one another based on their respective individual valuations. The former, which is what Sandel and other anticommodification theorists endorse, involves the privileging of one person or group's schedule of value over that of others; the latter, by contrast, assumes that no one's schedule of value should be granted special privilege over that of others.

[14] See Simon 1998.

I argue for the latter. But how would that work in practice? If Sandel believes that black rhinos should be protected from hunting, one thing he could do is buy them. If they become his property, he can forbid people from hunting them, in the same way that he can forbid people from entering his house or using his car without his permission. If others agree with Sandel—and presumably many would—then they could pool their resources, giving them yet more ability to protect yet more endangered species. I would make a similar argument with many of the other kinds of mutually voluntary and mutually beneficial transactions Sandel and others want to forbid: if it is land or something else that is being consumed or used in ways they do not like, they could buy it and use it for whatever purpose to which they think it should be put.[15] If Sandel instead wants to use law and government action to enforce his preferences, however, then he is disrespecting, not the rhino, but rather the other human beings whose agency is now curtailed. He may not like their choices, but "I don't like your preferences" is not sufficient ground for forcible restriction of others' liberty—at least not when we assume an equality of moral agency, as I have defended.

But what about when the allegedly unacceptable commodification is in things like people's own bodies? Sandel asks: "Should we regard our bodies as possessions that we own and can use and dispose of as we please, or do some uses of our bodies amount to self-degradation?" (2012, 47).[16] Sandel poses this question rhetorically and so does not answer it; but it has an answer: These are not mutually exclusive. It can be true *both* that we own our bodies and may do with them what we please *and* that some uses to which we might put our bodies are degrading. Sandel goes on to argue that our goal should be "developing the right attitude to our physical well-being and treating our bodies with care and respect" (2012, 59). I agree; but this has little to do with markets and business, let alone constituting any criticism of it. In fact, it trains its fire at entirely the wrong target. Let me explain.

Recall that a central distinction we have been at pains to make in developing our case for markets and honorable business is that between what Smith called "justice" and "beneficence." Both are virtues, and both create moral obligations. But only the former is the proper duty of government; the latter is the proper duty of individuals and private groups, based on their local knowledge and using their personal moral judgment. That distinction articulates a much clearer way

[15] This is the strategy of, for example, the Nature Conservancy, which solicits charitable donations in order to buy, and then leave undisturbed, tracts of land around the world. According to the organization's website, it currently owns approximately 119 million acres worldwide. See https://www.nature.org/.

[16] Satz 2010 makes similar arguments, though with far greater sophistication, regarding prostitution, surrogacy, selling of eggs and sperm, and so on.

of handling cases like those Sandel raises than what Sandel offers. If what you are proposing to do, or what you are proposing to create, build, buy, own, sell, trade, exchange, or gift does not, at any point, violate the person or property of unwilling others, and does not violate any promise or contract (express or even implicit) you or others have made, then we have no justification for intervening to stop you. You will have made no one's situation worse than it was before you engaged in your action, and in the absence of injury there is no justifiable cause for punishing you. That does not mean, however, that I have to *approve* of your action. On the contrary. I retain every right to judge your decisions or actions negatively and, adapting Mill's language, to remonstrate with you, reason with you, persuade you, or entreat you. I can also publicly execrate or attempt to shame you. I can also refuse to be your friend, associate, or partner, and I can encourage others to do the same. But if you disagree with me and recalcitrantly decide to go against my argument or advice, these are reasons to lament your decision, "but not for compelling [you] or visiting [you] with any evil in case [you] do otherwise."[17]

To put my argument somewhat differently, it is entirely possible to advocate *both* individual liberty *and* virtue. That is, I can respect your moral right to engage in behavior that I at the same time believe would be vicious. As the nineteenth-century constitutional scholar and abolitionist Lysander Spooner put it, "Vices are not crimes."[18] Respecting both liberty and virtue is the moral foundation of the system of political economy I have defended here.[19] I can respect the moral right of businesses or industries to exist that engage in practices or produce goods or services that I find repugnant or disagreeable, while at the same time refraining from attempting to interfere with the mutually voluntary actions of those full moral agents choosing otherwise than I would. As long as the businesses in question are not violating the code of business ethics—as long as they respect all persons, property, and promises, and proceed without threats, fraud, or coercion—they may exist. Indeed, justice requires that we let them exist.

Wage Slavery

But justice does not require that we have anything to do with them. In their *Communist Manifesto* (1848), Marx and Engels write the following of workers under what they call "capitalism": "Not only are they slaves of the bourgeois class, and of the bourgeois State; they are daily and hourly enslaved by the machine, by

---

[17] Mill (1859) 1978, 9.

[18] Spooner (1875) 2013.

[19] I defend this system of political economy much more extensively in Otteson 2006.

the overlooker, and, above all, by the individual bourgeois manufacturer himself. The more openly this despotism proclaims gain to be its end and aim, the more hateful and the more embittering it is" ([1848] 1994, 165). Can you relate to this sentiment? Perhaps you do not like your job, or at least certain aspects of it; perhaps you hate your boss, and perhaps too often you feel as though you are required to engage in needless, pointless, or mindless drudgery on behalf of your boss or your company. I suspect that substantially all of us have felt sentiments like this at various points, and so when we read these words of Marx and Engels, we might think: *Exactly! My job treats me inhumanely, as if I were a slave.*[20]

If experiences you have had in your life or career incline you to support the quoted passage from Marx and Engels, however, I respectfully ask you to reconsider using the language of "slavery" to describe your situation. Unless you are an *actual* slave, it is a gross exaggeration, and an offense to actual slavery. Human slavery has gone on throughout substantially all of human history, and it goes on in some places in the world yet today. It is a horrific, total elimination of a human being as a thinking, free moral agent and reduces the enslaved to a condition that is literally—not metaphorically or figuratively—subhuman. The term "chattel slavery" captures this: it treats humans as if they were mere movable property like any other kind of property, like a car, a hammer, a dog, or an ox. The key defining feature of slavery, however, is the abolition of autonomy. Nothing the slave does is at his own discretion; everything is at the behest of his enslaver. There is no opt-out option; there was never any opt-in. It is not just hard or grueling or unpleasant; it is not just occasionally or even often dreary, boring, or unfulfilling; it is not just that slaves wish they were paid more or had more generous health or retirement benefits; it is not that they wish they had more paid time off or that they wish they could get their education expenses reimbursed.

Working for a company in a market economy is, then, nothing whatsoever like slavery. The language of being a "slave to one's job" or of one's boss exercising "despotism" is not merely literally not true, not merely even an exaggeration: it is an affront to everyone implicated. It is an affront to the tragic victims of actual slavery; it is an affront to the billions of people who voluntarily work for wages; it is an affront to the millions of people who pay their employees wages. No company or boss in a market economy can compel workers to do anything. They make offers to employees, and to prospective employees, which they are free to refuse if they so choose. For their part, employees retain an opt-out option, and it is disingenuous to pretend otherwise. If you do not like your job, quit. Say, "No, thank you" and go elsewhere. But do not disrespect the suffering of actual victims of slavery by pretending that an unpleasant or uninspiring job is even in

---

[20] See Anderson 2017, who makes a similar case.

the same moral universe. You may feel unappreciated or overworked, you might think that your tasks are menial or beneath you, and your boss might be imperious, overbearing, demanding, or set unrealistic expectations. In honor of those people, past and present, who have suffered under the dehumanizing cruelty of actual slavery, however, I exhort you not ever to speak of your job in those terms. It was wrong even for Marx and Engels to use language like that 150 years ago. As unpleasant as the conditions in those nineteenth-century factories were, the workers nevertheless still chose to be there.[21] Still, their conditions were far more difficult, and often more dangerous, than those facing most workers in America today. So there is even less excuse for American workers today to use language like this. Unless what is being discussed is actual slavery, we should not use that language to describe anything else.

Exploitation

We have already discussed worries about various kinds of exploitation, including in particular exploitation of workers and exploitation of asymmetries of knowledge. Here let us discuss another kind of exploitation: of natural resources. In 1968, Garrett Hardin published a famous article in *Science* called "The Tragedy of the Commons." In it, he described why he believed we were heading to a population catastrophe: whereas the production of food increases, he argued, linearly, population increases exponentially. Drawing on Thomas Malthus (1766–1834), he predicted a time when the food and population curves would cross, leading to mass starvation and deprivation. Exactly when this would happen Hardin declined to speculate. Malthus had made a similar dire prediction in his *Essay on the Principle of Population* (1798), though it had failed to materialize in the 170 years between when he articulated the warning and the time Hardin was writing. In that same year, 1968, Paul Ehrlich wrote a book called *The Population Bomb*, in which he warned of impending mass starvation and death in the 1970s and 1980s. In the fifty years since Hardin and Ehrlich wrote, their predictions have still not materialized: though people have died, and continue to die, of starvation, it is now not because there is not enough food in the world. There is in fact more than enough food in the world to feed everyone on it, even given our highest-ever worldwide population levels.[22] The problem today is not food *production* but food *distribution*. Although many economists and demographers today no longer worry about the "Malthusian problem," some still do. Just

---

[21] See also Powell 2014 for a not unrelated discussion of sweatshops.
[22] See Oxfam, n.d.

because it has not happened in the last 220 years does not mean it still could not happen at some point in the future.

The more influential part of Hardin's article, however, is his discussion of "the commons," and his explanation for why human behavior in them is necessarily "tragic." Here is his argument. Consider a tract of land that is owned commonly and that many ranchers use for cattle grazing. Suppose they all want the land to sustain their use indefinitely into the future—in other words, they are genuine and good-faith conservationists at heart. But consider: if I add one more head of cattle to my herd, the benefit of that additional head is concentrated in me. I get the additional revenue from that additional head of cattle. But who pays the marginal cost of the extra bit of grazing? All of the ranchers do. In other words, we have concentrated benefits and dispersed cost. I get 100 percent of the benefit, but pay only $1/n$th of the cost (n = the number of ranchers, including myself). Inevitably, the benefit to me will outweigh the cost to me, which means it is in my interest to add that extra head. But all the other ranchers reason similarly. And the same reasoning holds for each additional head of cattle each of us might consider adding. What is the predictable result? We all add heads of cattle until the land is overgrazed and depleted. If I were to decide to unilaterally refrain from adding more cattle, that would just mean there is marginally more for everyone else. As long as I cannot stop others from adding more cattle—which, since the land is commonly owned, rather than being my own private property, I cannot do—I know that others will simply consume whatever benefit I leave behind. So all of us add ever more cattle, leading to a spiral downward that leads inexorably to depletion.

What is particularly "tragic" about this is that all the ranchers are acting rationally and reasonably, given their circumstances, and we have no reason to assume any of them are immoral. Their motivations may in fact be unimpeachable— they want to provide for themselves and their families. Given the logic of the commons, however, in order to provide for their families, they have to get everything they can *now*, because there might not be anything there in ten years, or in one year, or tomorrow. Their reasoning and their motivations are sound: and yet acting individually, they engage in behavior that leads to a result that none of them wanted—a destructive result for them and for the rest of us.

Hardin argues that because of this "tragic" logic of the commons, we must "exorcize the spirit of Adam Smith" (1968, 1244). Why? Smith had argued that when individuals act in their own interest they engage in transactions that lead to general benefit. This was Smith's invisible hand argument. Hardin's claim is that while Smith's argument might hold in some cases, the commons are places where we in fact get the opposite result—individual actions leading not to general benefit but to general loss. Hardin thought this was true of all commons, which would include land that is commonly owned, the oceans, the air, and, of most concern to him, population growth. With population growth, Hardin argued that a similar logic to that of the grazing commons applied. The marginal benefit of my having another child accrues to me, but the cost of feeding that child comes at the expense of the world's total food supply. Because others reason similarly, they realize that having more children will benefit them but the cost will be spread across the entire population. Thus they have more children, contributing to an inevitable crisis of overpopulation. Concentrated benefits and diffused costs again work their dark magic, leading, Hardin thought, to an unsustainable population growth that would eventually imperil us all.[23]

A potential solution to the tragedy of the commons was offered by Hardin himself: private property. If instead of leaving the grazing land in the commons—that is, under common ownership—we converted it to parcels that could be owned privately, the logic completely changes. If I can graze my cattle only on land I myself own, then it is now in my interest not to overgraze it—because if I did so, I would bear the full costs. Under conditions of private property rather than commons, I am incentivized to become a good steward of the land, using only so much as will ensure it will continue to provide value in the future. Similarly, if I have to pay you to use your land for my grazing cattle, I again bear the cost—which incentivizes me not to have more cattle than are sustainable. You, as the landowner, have a similar incentive not to let too many cattle graze your land so that you can sustain your land's value. In this way, private property internalizes the negative externalities. Instead of allowing me to impose the costs of my behavior on others, it now returns those costs so that they redound directly upon me. The lesson, then, would be to convert as much commons as possible into private holdings, to encourage sustainable use and long-term stewardship. This enables us, even when acting in our individual self-interest, to achieve the beneficial results that all of us prefer. Perhaps Adam Smith is alive after all.

But can this solution work in all cases? How could we convert the oceans, for example, or air to private property? Elinor Ostrom won the Nobel Prize in economics in 2009 largely for the fieldwork she conducted that discovered the surprising and innovative ways that actual communities facing problems with their common pool resources were able to overcome them. Economists at least since Hardin had held that natural resources that were collectively owned would be overused, exploited, and in the long run destroyed. Ostrom overturned this

---

[23] It is perhaps worth noting that the worries about an overpopulation crisis have largely dissipated as people around the world have voluntarily reduced the number of children they have. Every country in Europe today, for example, is reproducing at below replacement rates, as are the United States and many countries in Asia; and the consensus among demographers today is that global population will likely crest by approximately the year 2100. See Lal 2013; Rosling, Rosling, and Rönnlund 2018; and World Bank, n.d.

consensus by documenting how people in local communities discover ways to manage shared natural resources like pastures, fishing waters, and forests.[24] She showed that when natural resources are jointly used by members of their communities, they often develop rules for how these resources are to be cared for and used in a way that is both economically and ecologically sustainable. She also showed that these local communities devised mechanisms to monitor the use of the resources in question, to detect departures from the rules, and to punish people who violated the rules. She discovered that people used a variety of mechanisms that were tailored to their specific situations, that built on their local knowledge, and that served their particular purposes. Sometimes this included local government rules or regulations; sometimes this included self-enforcing community standards and conventions; sometimes there were hybrids. Her conclusion: "Policy analysts who would recommend a single prescription for commons problems have paid little attention to how diverse institutional arrangements operate in practice" (1990, 21). Perhaps most surprisingly, she found that "systematic empirical studies have shown that private organization of firms dealing in goods such as electricity, transport, and medical services tends to be more efficient than governmental organization of such firms" (1990, 21–22).[25]

The exploitation of commons is an example of what economists call "collective action problems," which are cases in which individuals would benefit from taking actions that they are not individually incentivized to take.[26] Consider hockey helmets. It used to be the case that professional hockey players did not wear helmets. Though they suffered sometimes horrific injuries and though hockey helmets existed, still they would not wear them. Ostensible reasons for why they did not wear them were that they were bulky and heavy and hence uncomfortable, and that they might limit peripheral vision. Neither of these seem like good reasons, however. Perhaps the real reason was the culture of hockey, which was one of machismo and affected indifference to pain. No player wanted to be the first to wear a helmet, because he knew that the others would mock him for it. So what happened? In 1979, John Ziegler, the president of the National Hockey League at the time, made the wearing of helmets mandatory for all incoming players in the league. And so they all, or almost all of them, began wearing helmets. Soon helmets became an accepted part of the game, and now no one plays without one. What is the lesson to take from this? The theory is that most hockey players secretly wanted to wear them but did not want to lose standing in their peers' eyes. When it was made mandatory by a third party,

---

[24] See also Ostrom 2005.

[25] See also Beito et al. 2002; Scott 2009; and Stringham 2015.

[26] See Olson 1965.

however, they could do what they had wanted to do anyway, but without losing face. The conclusion many draw: a third-party mandate is required to solve collective action problems.

Or take Christmas cards. Nobel laureate Thomas Schelling (1978) argued that most people in America do not actually want to write and mail Christmas cards every year, yet millions do. Why? Because although they would prefer not to, no one wants to be the first to stop: given the widespread convention, failing to comply with it would risk incurring the wrath or negative judgment of one's family and friends. So we all keep doing it, even though we mutually do not want to. What would be a solution to this collective action problem? Ban sending Christmas cards. If we imposed a fine of, say, $10,000 per card sent, almost everyone would stop sending them immediately. Schelling suggested that although people might complain about such a ban at first, they would come eventually to appreciate it, and then they would soon forget about the former practice altogether and wonder why they ever engaged in it. The lesson: a third-party mandate can solve collective action problems.

Consider one more example: the practice of shaking hands when you meet someone. We do not know exactly where this practice came from. Some hypothesize that it descended from an attempt to show that one was unarmed, but we do not really know. In any case, in previous eras people might not have known what we now know about shaking hands—namely, that it is one principal way we communicate microbes to one another. Shaking hands spreads disease and infection. We all know this now, yet we continue to shake hands. (People who "kiss hello" or "kiss goodbye" are running even greater risks.) Yet one could not unilaterally stop shaking hands even if one wanted to. Imagine you went for a job interview, your interviewer extends her hand, and you do not meet it with yours. Saying, "I don't want to spread bacteria" will not help and will almost guarantee that you do not get the job. Perhaps a preferable form of greeting would be, for example, the Far Eastern convention of bowing. That is the suggestion many have made, including President Donald Trump, a self-described "germaphobe."[27] How could we get Americans to change their convention of shaking hands? The hypothesis would be by legally banning it, on the theory that, once again, third-party mandates solve coordination problems.

Few disagree that third-party mandates can solve at least some collective action problems. The question, rather, is whether this is the best way to do so, or whether, perhaps, there might be at least some situations in which other mechanisms are better. Social convention, as one example, is surprisingly powerful. Many aspects of behavior and etiquette change not because

---

[27] See Guarino 2017.

of third-party mandate but, rather, from changing social consensus. Indeed, most changes in manners and etiquette change in this way—as Adam Smith's theory about the development of moral standards explains and would predict. Conventions about appropriate attire, appropriate joke-telling, appropriate language, appropriate behavior at the office and at church and at school, and on and on: rules exist, though they change over time; and they are created and enforced typically not by the government but by the participants in or users of them. Everything from how long one should hold a door open for another to how loudly to speak or laugh in public to how to speak in a locker room versus how to speak in front of one's parents and their friends: in all of these cases, and numberless others, there are conventions that we know and understand and follow, even though no single person created or enforces them. A concrete example is the relatively recent change in what to do when one sneezes. The growing consensus of covering one's mouth and nose with one's elbow, as opposed to one's hand, is a change that has resulted from social pressures connected with concerns about spreading disease. Changes like these arise not from law or regulation but instead from the experiences we have with others in these situations, and from the feedback we both give and receive about our own and others' behavior. This is the spontaneous order of human life—a kind of marketplace of life.[28]

But are there cases when the government, or other third parties, should step in with mandates, enforcing them coercively if necessary? Local conventions often work well locally, but they work less well when dealing with large-scale, especially cross-national or cross-cultural issues—like pollution, for example.[29] If I create pollution in my company or on my land, its effects may produce consequences hundreds, even thousands, of miles away. Suppose you and I are owners of competing companies that produce electricity from burning coal. Suppose a new technology arises that would reduce our emissions, and suppose that because both of us care about the environment we both would like to adopt the new technology. But suppose adopting the new technology is costly, as it no doubt would be. We both want to do it, but if I adopted it and you did not, you would have a competitive advantage over me in the market—my prices would rise, yours would not. You reason similarly about me. So although individually we might both prefer to adopt the new technology, neither of us is incentivized to do so without assurance that the other would as well. By standard prisoner's dilemma reasoning, mutual defection is the dominant strategy. And although others who breathe our air might also like for us to adopt the new technology,

[28] See Otteson 2002.
[29] See Schmidtz 2011b.

without mutual assurance between you and me, we would likely not do so—and we would all, you, I, and others, be worse off for it.

One way to address this problem would be to ask the Environmental Protection Agency (or some other government agency) simply to mandate that we adopt the new technology. If we both have to, then we both bear the costs equally—so neither of us would be at a competitive advantage or disadvantage with respect to the other. Is this a good solution? Perhaps, but in fact it is hard to say. Equalizing the costs does not make them go away; it just redistributes them. You and I would both raise our prices, which means consumers would pay more for their electricity. Is the tradeoff of higher prices for the reduced emissions worth it? Again, perhaps, but to know for sure, we would have to reckon all the costs against the benefits. There is the cost of higher prices, but there is also the cost of the Environmental Protection Agency (EPA) itself (its 2017 budget was $8.2 billion).[30] We must also remember Bastiat's lesson about opportunity cost: what would those resources have done if they had not gone to pay higher prices for electricity and the EPA's budget (or the increase this new policy would require in monitoring, testing, reporting, and so on)? Moreover, what would the EPA's scientists do, and what other benefits might they generate, if they were not working for the EPA? Without knowing that, we cannot know for sure whether this is in fact a good use of our scarce resources. Again, it might be—we just do not yet know. Telling us only the proposed benefits is telling us only one side of the balance sheet.

Two final thoughts. First, we should remember Ostrom's caution that the mistake policymakers often make is to believe that only one kind of solution—typically a third-party, governmental, mandate—must fit all situations. There are other possible solutions we might consider. Given the beneficial results arising from systems of private property in so many other areas of social life, perhaps we should see if we can figure out a private-property solution. Perhaps ownable and tradeable pollution permits, for example? There have been many experiments with such things, with perhaps surprising success.[31] If we understand pollution as a private property trespass, or as another kind of damage to private property, then it would come under the heading of justice and license government action—or at least give reasonable grounds for negatively affected parties to demand compensation. This would avoid a "tragedy of the commons" scenario by eliminating the commons, and it would internalize the externalities in the same way that privatizing grazing lands would and does.

---

[30] See United States Environmental Protection Agency, n.d.
[31] See, for example, Global Water Partnership, n.d.

Second, there was an element in our example of the coal-burning electricity plants that might have gone unnoticed. We said that both you and I, the owners of the rival plants, wanted to reduce emissions out of our genuine concern for the environment. But we also said that others in the affected communities wanted this too. This latter point is crucially important. Why does almost every company in America—and, indeed, in most of the developed world—talk at length about and advertise their "green" credentials? Their sustainable uses of resources, their stewardship of the environment, their recycling, their "wise use," their Leadership in Energy and Environmental Design-, or LEED-, certified buildings, and so on? Many of these practices go well above and beyond what is mandated by law or regulation. Since they also are costly, why, then, do businesses not only adopt such practices but trumpet them to the world? The answer is *that is what we want*. In the last forty years or so, environmental consciousness has gone from a fringe interest to a mainstream one to a cultural consensus. Remember that honorable business seeks ways to create value—that is, it seeks to benefit itself only by benefiting others. In order to be successful, an honorable business must figure out what customers and consumers want and prefer. So the real power in this relationship belongs to the customers and consumers. If a business does not give us what we want—what we value in a way that we value it—we will go elsewhere. And if we are in a Smithian "well-governed society," we retain the opt-out option, the right to say, "No, thank you" and go elsewhere. So if businesses want to succeed, they must please us. What that means in the context of environmentalism and sustainability is that if we want sustainable business practices—and if we are willing to put our money where our mouths are—businesses will give them to us. This does not require front-end legislation or regulation; the back-end discipline that consumers provide in the market by their choices provides instantaneous feedback that businesses that want to succeed, as they all do, must heed.

Here, then, seems to be another responsibility that might be apportioned to our social power. If we care about the environment, about sustainable business practices, or about any other matter of large or small scale, then we as consumers should vote with our dollars. Michael Sandel (2012) repeatedly presses the need for what he calls a "national debate" and "conversation" about the moral values expressed in the market. Since the market itself is not a moral agent, this amounts to a call for us to take our moral values seriously when we make choices in the market—about what to buy and not to buy, with whom to work and with whom not to work, and so on. In a profound way, however, the market is itself an arena in which we have this debate and conversation on a daily basis. The choices we make determine who wins and who loses, what products and what practices get rewarded and what do not. Each of us can decide whether to eat at McDonald's or Chick-fil-A, buy from Nike, or shop at Walmart. Since we do not all value the same things the same way, there will be many choices catering to our disparate preferences. But if there is something that matters to enough of us, business will adapt to please us. And even if any one of them does not change the way we would prefer, there will be others who will.

By contrast, the government and its regulators and bureaucrats will do what they will do, and we, both individually and even collectively, will have, alas, little effect on it. Remember that the vast majority of government officials are unelected and so virtually immune from public scrutiny or accountability. And they are just as self-interested, biased, shortsighted, and susceptible to corruption as people in any other walk of life. Businesses, by contrast, are exquisitely sensitive to what we want—not because businesspeople are more virtuous than people in government, or even necessarily because they want to care about us, but rather because they have to do so if they want to survive. In business and in markets, then, we can have an effect, indeed a decisive one. We are full moral agents who can choose. We should use that agency.

Conclusion

In this chapter, we have discussed two broad categories of worries about markets and business: commodification and exploitation. Marx argued that under what he called "capitalism" workers suffer from a dehumanizing "alienation" as they see their work and indeed some of their identities turned into cold commodities that are indifferently bought and sold. Extensive commodification severs the connection between what is truly valuable—human beings and their labor—and the products sold in markets. Contemporary critics like Sandel and Satz worry similarly about the corrupting influences markets can create, claiming that in markets many goods or services may be bought or sold that are not properly respecting of their intrinsic value. But things have only the value that valuing agents—that is, actual human beings—give them. Because different people value things differently, however, we must look for peaceful and mutually respectful ways to reconcile these differences. Allowing people to make their own choices to exchange, transact, or partner with willing others, responding to the prices that naturally emerge from their choices, provides a way to allow competing conceptions of value and the good life to coexist peacefully. They also allow people to consider a broader range of potential courses of life that can help them achieve eudaimonia.

But legally allowing something to exist does not mean we must support it. It is possible to support both individual liberty and virtue and to respect others' decisions as licit even while disapproving of them. We can exercise, then, instead of political power, social power—by expressing our approvals and disapprovals, and by voting with our dollars—even while respecting the rights of others to choose differently from the way we would.

Nothing in markets or business resembles slavery. Marx and Engels's talk of "wage slavery," like similar sentiments one sometimes hears from people today who issue complaints about their careers, their companies, or their bosses, is not just an exaggeration but an affront to the actual victims of the brutal practice of slavery. If you and I do not like our jobs, we can quit. Slaves cannot quit. We should therefore cease talking about workers' lives in market economies as being even in the same moral universe as the lives of slaves.

The potential exploitation we discussed was that of the environment and natural resources. We considered Malthus's and Hardin's worries about an allegedly impending population bomb, and more generally about the "tragic" logic that leads, or can lead, to the depletion of commons. It turns out that private property rules can internalize the externalities of many problems of the commons. We also discussed other kinds of "collective action problems," including small and large scales, from hockey helmets to pollution. Although third-party mandates can solve many such problems, often their relative costs are unknown or unaccounted, which makes it difficult to know whether such coercive mechanisms are better than alternative methods—particularly private-property-based mechanisms—at solving the problems. As Ostrom argued, we must resist the temptation to assume that only one kind of mechanism must be used for all problems. Finally, we emphasized the influential role that individual consumers can play in affecting both the products and practices of businesses. While individuals have comparatively little control over governmental laws and regulations, they nevertheless do control the choices they make in markets, and thus they can exert considerable influence over the goods and services, and the business practices, of firms.

All things considered, then, is business a force for good? Is there a way to engage in business that is not only allowable but even admirable? To those questions we turn in our next and final chapter.

9

Why Business?

Introduction

As we noted at the outset of this book, business has a bad reputation. Indeed, the words "markets," "business," "profit," and "capitalism" all have negative connotations, as if people think there is something inherently suspicious about buying and selling, trading and exchanging, partnering and associating, negotiating and bargaining, and seeking a profit. I have argued for a different view. There are in fact two kinds of business, honorable and dishonorable. Dishonorable business proceeds through extraction. It enriches itself at the expense of others, through force, fraud, deception, and outright theft, and it denies to others an opt-out option. Such activity is rightly condemned, for two main reasons. First, it does not in fact lead to generalized benefit, to "mass flourishing." It engages in zero-sum transactions that take wealth from one place and reallocate it to another. Although some can grow quite wealthy through dishonorable business, this does not enrich others in the process. Second, it disrespects the humanity and dignity of those from whom it extracts. It treats them as if they were not full moral agents and presumes a moral superiority that arrogates to itself rights and privileges that it denies to others. It is thus deeply self-centered. It sees others as mere means or tools to its own ends, paying little regard to their interests or their personhood.

What I have defended, by contrast, is honorable business, which seeks to benefit itself only by simultaneously benefiting others. It engages in voluntary and cooperative exchange, which respects others' opt-out option. It leads to real, positive-sum gains for all parties, increasing the sum total of benefit, and thus prosperity, in society. It is thus deeply other-regarding. It does not deny itself or its own interests in prosperity, but it takes it as an absolute constraint that it may succeed only if it helps others to succeed as well. And it respects others' conceptions of success and benefit: others must succeed according to their own conceptions of success and benefit, on their own individual paths ultimately to eudaimonia. This kind of activity is not only not blameworthy, it is in fact praiseworthy, also for two main reasons. First, it is the path to mass flourishing. History and empirical evidence suggest that it enables everyone, even and perhaps especially the least among us, to improve their situations, satisfying ever more of their needs, opening up ever more options and opportunities, and providing ever greater horizons of possibility. Second, it respects the inherent dignity of every individual. By respecting their choices and their opt-out option, it makes offers of exchange and partnership that they are free to decline if they so choose. It thus meets them as peers, with the same full moral agency as everyone else. It respects their capacities of autonomy and rationality, and gives them the liberty to choose and respects them as accountable agents by letting them take responsibility for their choices.

In this final chapter I would like to summarize the moral argument for honorable business, and to make a case for why it is a worthy pursuit. Students who decide to study business are often asked why they are doing so, and the people asking them this question often seem to believe that there are only two possible answers: (1) to make money and (2) to get a job. While it is no doubt true that people studying business want to make money and to get a job—as, I suspect, most other students do as well—still, that is not a particularly inspiring vision, especially as it does not seem to connect to any higher or moral purposes or to anything beyond oneself. I have argued for a conception of honorable business that does connect to higher, moral purposes, and that does serve ends beyond oneself. In this concluding chapter, then, I would like to propose an answer the question of "Why business?" that speaks to higher aims. I begin with the conception of human moral agency that has been largely implicit, though at times explicit, in my argument, and then explain how honorable business not only reflects this conception but can also give it an appropriate and powerful avenue for expression.

Freedom and Responsibility

The person primarily responsible for the well-being of each individual is the individual himself. I am in charge of my life; I am its captain. I am responsible for taking my time, talent, and treasure and converting it into value for others that will enable me to create value in my own life. I am not entitled to the fruits of others' labor any more than I am entitled to others' lives. This means that although I have a right to seek to better my condition in cooperation with willing others, I have no right to a job, still less to any particular job. It means I have no right to any particular good or service, no right to any particular price, and no right to any particular wage.[1] The reason for this is that jobs, goods, services, and the resources to pay wages are produced by other human beings who take the resources available to them and labor to create value with them. They do not appear magically in the world but are instead the result of the applied and concerted effort of human beings. To claim a right to them implies an enforceable obligation on others, which is in other words to claim a right to extraction. But others are full moral agents, just like me, and are equally entitled to their opt-out option, even when I disagree with their choices or really, really want whatever good or service they might be able provide for me. I must respect them just as I wish to be respected, and I must remember that my needs and wants and preferences, however pressingly I feel them, are no more important than theirs—because I am no more important than they are. As Adam Smith wrote, "One individual must never prefer himself so much even to any other individual, as to hurt or injure that other, in order to benefit himself, though the benefit to the one should be much greater than the hurt or injury to the other" (TMS, 138). We are each precious, each valuable and unique centers of agency and creation. A peaceful and prospering society is one in which no one is accorded authority to direct the lives or mandate the activity of others without their willing consent. We must respect their agency, which can be demonstrated only by their retention of an opt-out option. They must be able to say, "No, thank you" to us.

The code of business ethics I have defended applies this moral framework to our professional lives and our business associations. It is an extension, and reflection, of the proper moral way to treat others. It thus begins, as does any proper moral code, with the "don'ts," that is, the things we may not do to others, before proceeding to the "dos," the things we should or must do for others. Actually, it begins even earlier than that. Before we get to the things we may not do, we must have the proper understanding of our moral agency that will provide conceptual and psychological space for us to control and direct our behavior. We are autonomous and rational: capable of freely making choices, and capable of constructing plans for our lives that can enable us to achieve our ends, including our highest ends. Because of this, we can and thus should be responsible for our choices, our activities, and our plans. Even more, because of this, we disrespect ourselves and dehumanize our own agency if we do not consider ourselves or hold ourselves to be responsible for what we do. That is why principle 1 in our code of business ethics is, "You are always morally responsible for your actions." It is important to see this as a personal commitment, the first step, or even pre-step, in moral agency: "*I* am always morally responsible for my actions." Accepting this not only

---

[1] This means that, as the *New York Times* editorial board argued years ago, the correct legal minimum wage is zero. See *New York Times* 1987.

affirms our identities as full moral agents but is also what grounds Adam Smith's claim that "self-command" is "not only itself a great virtue, but from it all the other virtues seem to derive their principal lustre" (TMS, 241). And letting others be responsible for their decisions is the primary way we respect them as full moral agents. They, too, are capable of self-command, which means that they too are and ought to be held accountable for their choices, actions, and behavior.[2] As difficult or unpleasant as it sometimes might be, *not* to let people be responsible for their choices, actions, and behavior is a principal way to *disrespect* their moral agency—and to disrespect them as persons. But the argument here makes an even stronger claim: not just that there are benefits to allowing people to choose their individual courses of life, but that we should, morally, do so. This is not an unalloyed good, however. As Schwartz 2016 argues, for example, choices can produce anxiety and even momentary paralysis; and the Schumpeterian "creative destruction" can produce displacement and loss even as it also produces other gains. Despite these worries, our argument is that respecting human moral agency is important enough to outweigh the justified concern over most of the negative consequences from individual choices.

The rest of the code of business ethics constitutes "don'ts": do not coerce or threaten; do not defraud, deceive, or unjustly exploit; do not disrespect others' autonomy and dignity; do not dishonor or renege on one's promises, contracts, and fiduciary responsibilities. These are not by themselves exhaustive of our moral obligations—we have positive obligations as well—but they are the necessary first steps. The "don'ts" come first, the "dos" second. This is precisely the same in other walks of human life. We do not say to the thief that it is all right to steal as long as she is polite or gives some of it to charity. We say, "Stop stealing." Once the thief stops stealing, then she can turn her attention to the positive aspects that round out a virtuous character. We do not say to the adulterer that it is all right as long as he buys his betrayed spouse something nice afterward. We say, "Keep your promise." Once the adulterer honors the promise he made, then he can turn his attention to providing the positive benefits to his spouse that makes him a good spouse and virtuous person. And so on. Similarly, the first rules we teach our children are "Keep your hands to yourself," "Respect other people's things," and "If you give your word, keep it." Whatever else our children do, or do not do, they must first follow these rules. Perhaps the central obligation parents have to society is instilling in their children an unwavering commitment to those principles, so crucial are they to ensuring that our children do not

---

[2] Some people cannot, in fact, exercise self-command, thus are not (yet) full moral agents, and thus cannot (yet) be held responsible for their decisions, actions, and behavior. This includes children who have not yet reached the age of majority and infirm adults. But these are exceptions that prove the rule. The account of moral agency described here applies to all normally functioning adults.

become undue burdens on others and thus can become full contributing and participating members of a civilized society.[3]

The Positive Obligations of Business

The code of business ethics comprises, then, a series of "don'ts." By itself, this may not be a particularly inspiring moral vision. Telling people that they should not injure others in their persons, property, or promises may be necessary, but surely that cannot be all we have to do to be fully virtuous. Indeed, that is not all. But it is already extremely hard to do, and because nothing else we do will have real value until we first master and internalize the principles in the code, we already have a lot of work to do to integrate the code into our habits, our judgment, and our character. So before asking what else we must do, let us take due time to contemplate all the aspects and elements required just by the "don'ts" of the code.

So the principles in the code are the first step in fulfilling our moral obligations, but they do not exhaust those obligations. What other obligations, then, do we have? The answer to this question comes from the hierarchy of moral value of which honorable business forms an integral part. We live in a world of scarcity. We have limited time, limited capacities, limited wealth. If our ultimate end in our all too short time on earth is to use all our skills and abilities, all our available resources, and all of our opportunities to achieve a eudaimonic life, then we must choose our actions, behaviors, and goals with deliberation and purpose. Every minute we spend doing something that does not contribute to our ends is a minute lost forever. Every minute, and every dollar, we dedicate to a purpose that is either not consistent with our considered hierarchy of value and purpose or, even worse, interferes with that hierarchy, is lost forever. A rationally ordered moral life, like a rationally ordered economy, is one that dedicates its resources first to our most important ends, second to our second-most important ends, third to our third-most important ends, and so on. Hence if we pay primary, or even too much, attention to our lower-ranked ends at the expense of our higher-ranked ends, we are choosing irrationally—according to our own hierarchy of value and purpose.

But we cannot rest content with a rationally ordered life: we must have a rationally ordered *moral* life. That means that the ends we pursue must not only be consistent and form a coherent whole, but they must also be *good* ends. They must be ends that are worthy to be pursued, ends that we believe, in our calm,

---

[3] See Rose 2019.

cool, and considered judgment, are virtuous. Now, putting it that way allows for some variation: not everyone will agree on what actions are virtuous. There is nothing wrong with that. In a free society, there will be reasonable pluralism among conceptions of the good life,[4] and even among the specific application and instantiation of the virtues in individual lives and situations. It is sufficient for the success of society, however, to rely on individuals' good judgment, honed by their experience, within the constraints of abiding by the code. If all you do is abide by the negative prescriptions of the code, and do nothing more, that will be enough, and society may demand no more of you. If, in addition, you then also take positive steps to improve others' situations—still within the constraints of the code—your contribution will be even greater.

This brings us to the positive obligations not just of the individual generally but of the individual's professional business activities in particular. If you consistently abide by the code, you will, as we have said, have fulfilled your minimum obligations to society. But you have much more to give. You have skills, abilities, and energies that can actually improve others' situations. One way you can do this is by charitably giving and sharing of your resources—including your time, talent, and treasure—with others. Assuming such sharing and giving is voluntary, these are positive-sum transactions: your beneficiary gets whatever you share or give, while you get the joy, happiness, and satisfaction of helping another. Both of your lives are improved. Yet sharing and giving do not generate new resources that can enable more enjoyment, consumption, or sharing and giving in the future. Charitable action reduces material resources: you give yours away so that another can use or consume them. You gain nonmaterial benefit, but a plan only to give, however much benefit it provides to others, is unfortunately not sustainable as a general or long-term plan.[5] Resources must be created before they can generate benefit, and the more resources we have the more benefit we can generate. That means we need business. But not just any kind of business—honorable business.

Thus the obligation of the professional business person is to use every iota of skills and resources she has to generate as much positive benefit for herself and others, to create as much value in the world, as she can. She may not know exactly how others will benefit, or what possibilities of fulfillment and joy her

---

[4] See Berlin (1958) 2002; Rawls 1971; and Sen 1995.

[5] Thus the example of Zell Kravinsky, who gave to the point of ruin both for himself and his family, is not a sustainable or universalizable model. See Singer 2009, chap. 8. Bill Gates, to take another example, has reportedly committed over $30 billion of his fortune to charity through his foundation, which is an enormous amount of money. Gates once told a reporter, "I have no use for money. This is God's work" (Tweedie 2013). With a net worth as of this writing of approximately $90 billion, perhaps he can afford to say he has no use for money. In any case, to give money like that away, he first had to generate it.

efforts enable, but she will know that she is contributing to both. In considering what education and training to pursue, in considering what lines of work to go into, in considering what companies to work for, and in every minute of every one of her days in business, she must keep ever in mind that her obligation is to create value. She must deploy her judgment in a complex calculation that factors in her values and purposes, her skills and abilities, and the resources and opportunities available to her, as well as the needs, wants, preferences, and desires of others. She must look for intersections between others' interests and her own and choose from among those intersections specific courses of action that maximize both others' and her own interests. She must ask, then, not only what would be *good* for herself and others, but what would be the *best* utilization of all that she is and has and can do both for herself and others.

She of course cannot achieve all of the things in life she might like to achieve: she cannot be a medical doctor and an astronaut and a concert pianist and an engineer and an artist and a CEO—even if she might be capable of being, and succeeding at, any one of them. Similarly, she cannot satisfy all the interests that others have, even though she might be able to satisfy some of the interests of many of them. Hence she will have to make choices, sometimes difficult choices, and often under uncertainty. Is she choosing wisely? Are her efforts going to issue in the results she hopes or expects them to? She will have to rely on her judgment in making her decisions, even while she will never know the answers to these questions with complete certainty. But the more experience she has, the better her judgment will be—and the more confidence she can have in her deliberations, even if this confidence will never reach perfection. If she follows the code, however, and while doing so looks for goods and services she can make and buy, partnerships and collaborations she can form, and exchanges and transactions she can pursue that she believes will lead to the greatest contribution she can make both to her own prosperity and that of others given her limited resources, given her fallible but ever-expanding knowledge, and given her imperfect but ever-improving judgment: then she will be leading a life of full virtue. She will be acting both justly *and* beneficently, improving her own *and* others' lives in the process. She may even find she was happy, and she may even have constructed for herself a life of eudaimonia.

Why Business?

The reason to pursue business, then, is not only because it can provide one a living. Neither is it because business is a necessary evil enabling one to do other things that are not evil. Still less is it to provide one a way to while away one's time on earth, because otherwise one's life would be too boring. These are not reasons to do anything. Why not? Because we are purposive creatures: rational and autonomous, constructed for action and capable of moral purpose. Thus the first step in thinking about how we should lead our lives is to realize and embrace the kind of creature we are, and to respect ourselves as what we are and not something else. If we lead a listless life of momentary pleasure, we are leading what Aristotle called a "bovine" life—a life fit for cows. Eating, sleeping, defecating, and reproducing are the sum total of the bovine life and are perfectly appropriate to the cow. We are not cows. The appropriate life for us includes those things, of course, but it goes well beyond them. So if we live our lives as if we were simply complicated cows, two things will result: we will ultimately be unhappy, and we will have forgone an indefinite amount of benefit we could otherwise have contributed to the world.

We are capable of far more, and our moral agency requires far more of us. The first step, then, is to respect ourselves as the active moral beings we are. Then we must examine ourselves and our lives to determine what kinds of life we could pursue that would enable us to achieve the highest ends of which we are capable. That will include a life that provides us a chance of reaching our highest sense of justified purpose and earned achievement. At the same time it will include a life that enables others with whom we interact to do the same.

Honorable business provides an opportunity and vehicle for both. It satisfies our need to act and do, not just be. And because honorable business requires benefiting ourselves only by benefiting others, it squarely addresses the require-ment of our moral agency to pursue virtuous purposes. What more moral pur-pose is there than using all one's talents, all one's abilities, and all one's efforts to achieve improvements in our own lives and in those of others? Our contribu-tions might be marginal—we might play just one small part in a company that provides only one product of seemingly little importance in the grand scheme of things. But every particle of benefit we add to others' lives adds to the sum total of enjoyment they have in life. The biggest sand castle is built one grain at a time, the biggest castle one brick at a time, the biggest bridge one rivet at a time, the biggest city one person at a time. If others want what we can provide and are willing to part with their own scarce resources to get it, we can know—and thus feel justified pride—that we have, somehow and in some way, improved their lives.

We will also have contributed to their freedom. By satisfying this one particu-lar need or desire of theirs, by giving them this even small piece of joy or use or pleasure, we have now provided something for them that frees up other particles of their capital, other particles of their time or attention or concern, which they can now put to yet other uses. We have liberated them from this one concern, or liberated just this one piece of their resources, which now makes them freer to focus on other, even greater purposes or concerns. This is no small feat, and it is not to be disparaged. To achieve eudaimonia, we must have the liberty to make choices in our own lives about how to expend our energies, how to spend our time, where to put our resources so that we can make steady progress up our hierarchy of moral value. We cannot climb to the top of the ladder of our lives, however, without first proceeding up the bottom rungs. The ladder that culminates in eudaimonia might be a high one indeed, with a very large number of steps; but the steps are finite and can be traversed within the compass of a finite human life. Each contribution we make, however small, to others' achievement of eudaimonia is a step on this ladder we helped them climb.

The decision to commit oneself to honorable business is, then, a decision to commit oneself to doing everything one can to helping oneself and others achieve their highest moral ends, to contributing to those material, moral, and psychological needs each of us has on the journey to finding our true and noble purpose in life. Dishonorable business is a betrayal of this high purpose, but honorable business is an affirmation of it, and a contribution to it. Engaging in no business at all may not violate the rules of justice or our code, and so is an allowable option. But is that all that you are capable of? Will you have lived a life that you will one day look back on and believe was worth having been lived—if the best you can say is that you injured no one? That is indeed a first and necessary step, but will that give you a sense of justified pride, of earned success and achievement,[6] of virtuous and worthy utilization of all the gifts and blessings and opportunities you will have had in life? Some of us have more wealth than others, some of us are born with greater opportunities than others, and some of us have better luck than others. But each of us is a center of consciousness that possesses a unique, irreplaceable, and inimitable signature of skills and abilities that can complement whatever else already exists in society—if we focus our energies and dedicate ourselves to cultivating them. We must therefore commit ourselves first to never engaging in dishonorable business, but at the same time we are called to make a positive commitment to ourselves to discover and engage the ways that we can uniquely contribute to the sum total of prosperity, benefit, joy, satisfaction, and, ultimately, eudaimonia, in the world.

Microactions and Macroresults

A former student of mine decided after graduating from college to go to work at a small start-up company that would keep records and complete paperwork for medical offices. He was good at his job, and his small company was starting to get

---

[6] See Brooks 2008.

more medical offices as clients. So things looked promising. But some members of his family disapproved. If he wanted to work in the medical field, they said, then he should be a doctor. If he did not want to be a doctor, they told him he should be a rabbi. They apparently could not bring themselves to see how filling out paperwork could possibly constitute a worthy and valuable use of his very considerable talents. He reached out to me to ask my advice: Was he wasting his life? In a way, the entire argument of this book is an elaboration of the response I gave to him.

Those medical offices that became his clients would not have done so if they did not value his services. This is not a small thing. It enabled the medical offices not to have to worry about keeping their records and filling out the ever-increasing and seemingly endless forms—and getting all of them right. These records and forms in many cases determined how and whether the doctors got paid, as well as whether their nurses, technicians, staff, suppliers, and so on got paid, and they thus directly implicated their ability to give good care to their patients and provide for themselves and their families. Relieving them of this burden meant they could instead turn more of their attention to what they were both genuinely good at and where their own comparative advantage lay: treating patients. The best use of a medical doctor's time is rarely filling out paperwork. But it has to be done, and it has to be correct, despite its complexity. If my former student and his company can meet this crucial need, and do so competently and well—that is, honorably—then they have now freed some of the doctors' time and talent for other concerns that better draw on and utilize their training, their abilities, their goals, and their values.

The services my former student's company are providing are thus creating real value in the world. He may not know exactly how those freed resources of time, talent, and treasure will be used, or exactly what benefits they will mean in the lives of his client doctors, their patients, their families, and their lives. But he can be sure that it will make a difference. And along the way he is able to provide an honest, and indeed honorable, living both for himself and his family. The money he will make, then, should be not only a source of material benefit to him, but of justified pride. And the services he is providing similarly provide a genuine benefit to others. He follows our code, and he is creating value both for himself and for others. *That* is honorable business.

This may seem like a small example, but it is repeated across millions of businesses and businesspeople, and their joint efforts are what have generated the unprecedented prosperity we enjoy today. And despite the few bad actors in business who unfortunately get all the press attention, it is these millions of largely unknown, often unsung, and unforgivably underappreciated value creators to whom we owe our thanks and who deserve our praise. It is they who shoulder the burdens of a peaceful and prosperous civilization, who create the goods and provide the services that constitute genuine prosperity, without which and without whose efforts all of our lives would be far, far poorer. To disdain what they do is to exhibit an ingratitude issuing from either vanity or ignorance—or both.

There is more to be done, of course, but that is where you come in. What should be your answer, then, to the question, "Why business?" I propose that it should be this: because in that way I contribute to a just and humane society. I treat people honorably and with respect, and I use what abilities and resources I have to make my own life—and that of my family and community—better but only by improving the lives of others. In that way I contribute my own particular part not only to a society of increasing prosperity, which generates ever more resources that can meet ever more people's needs, but also to a society of mutual respect for the autonomy, value, and dignity of all human beings. I use my limited and precious time, talent, and treasure to construct for myself a life that has a chance at achieving the highest human end of eudaimonia, but only in mutually beneficial cooperation with others, who themselves thereby have a greater chance of achieving eudaimonia. Not just business, then, but *honorable* business, which contributes both to prosperity and morality.

I propose that honorable business is not just *one* way to contribute benefit to the world, but may in fact ultimately be the *only* long-term, sustainable, and moral way to enable widespread eudaimonia. In that way, honorable business can indeed be a moral calling.

BIBLIOGRAPHY

Acemoglu, Daron, and James A. Robinson. 2012. *Why Nations Fail: The Origins of Power, Prosperity, and Poverty*. New York: Crown Business.

Allison, John A. 2012. *The Financial Crisis and the Free Market Cure: How Destructive Banking Reform Is Killing the Economy*. New York: McGraw-Hill.

Amadeo, Kimberly. 2018. "U.S. Federal Budget Breakdown: The Budget Components and Impact on the US Economy." *The Balance*. July 19. Available here: https://www.thebalance.com/u-s-federal-budget-breakdown-3305789.

Anderson, Elizabeth. 1999. "What Is the Point of Equality?" *Ethics* 109, 2: 287–337.

———. 2017. *Private Government: How Employers Rule Our Lives (and Why We Don't Talk about It)*. Princeton, NJ: Princeton University Press.

Applebaum, Binyamin. 2014. "Does Hosting the Olympics Actually Pay Off?" *New York Times Magazine*. August 5. Available here: https://www.nytimes.com/2014/08/10/magazine/does-hosting-the-olympics-actually-pay-off.html.

Aquinas, Thomas. 2002. *Aquinas on Law, Morality, and Politics*. 2nd ed. Trans. Richard J. Regan. Ed. William P. Baumgarth. Indianapolis: Hackett.

Aristotle. 2000. *Nicomachean Ethics*. 2nd ed. Trans. Terrence Irwin. Indianapolis: Hackett.

———. 2013. *Politics*. 2nd ed. Trans. and ed. Carnes Lord. Chicago: University of Chicago Press.

Arneson, Richard. 2004. "Luck Egalitarianism: An Interpretation and Defense." *Philosophical Topics* 32, 1–2: 1–20.

Badhwar, Neera K. 2014. *Well-Being: Happiness in a Worthwhile Life*. New York: Oxford University Press.

Balkin, Jeremy K. 2015. *Investing with Impact: Why Finance Is a Force for Good*. Brookline, MA: Bibliomotion.

Barker, Jason. 2018. "Happy Birthday, Karl Marx. You Were Right!" *New York Times*. April 30. Available here: https://www.nytimes.com/2018/04/30/opinion/karl-marx-at-200-influence.html.

Bastiat, Frédéric. (1850) 2017. *Economic Sophisms and "What Is Seen and What Is Not Seen."* Trans. Dennis O'Keeffe. Ed. Jacques de Guenin and David M. Hart. Indianapolis: Liberty Fund.

Baumslag, Naomi. 2005. *Murderous Medicine: Nazi Doctors, Human Experimentation and Typhus*. Westport, CT: Praeger.

Beinhocker, Eric D. 2007. *The Origin of Wealth: The Radical Remaking of Economics and What It Means for Business and Society*. Cambridge, MA: Harvard Business Review.

Beito, David T., Peter Gordon, and Alexander Tabarrok. 2002. *The Voluntary City: Choice, Community, and Civil Society*. Ann Arbor: University of Michigan Press.

Berlin, Isaiah. (1958) 2002. "Two Concepts of Liberty." In *Isaiah Berlin: Liberty*, ed. Henry Hardy, 166–217. New York: Oxford University Press.

Bernstein, David, and Ilya Somin. 2004. "Judicial Power and Civil Rights Reconsidered." *Yale Law Journal* 114, 3: 591–657.

Blackledge, Paul. 2013. *Marxism and Ethics: Freedom, Desire, and Revolution.* Albany: State University of New York Press.

Bobadilla-Suarez, Sebastian, Cass R. Sunstein, and Tali Sharot. 2017. "The Intrinsic Value of Choice: The Propensity to Under-delegate in the Face of Potential Gains and Losses." *Journal of Risk and Uncertainty* 54, 3: 1–16. Available here: https://link.springer.com/article/10.1007/s11166-017-9259-x.

Boer, Roland. 2014. *In the Vale of Tears.* Vol. 5 of *On Marxism and Theology.* New York: Haymarket Books.

Bostaph, Samuel. 2017. *Andrew Carnegie: An Economic Biography.* Updated ed. Lanham, MD: Rowman & Littlefield.

Bowles, Samuel, and Herbert Gintis. 2006. "The Evolutionary Basis of Collective Action." In *The Oxford Handbook of Political Economy*, ed. Barry R. Weingast and Donald A. Wittman, 951–67. New York: Oxford University Press.

———. 2011. *A Cooperative Species: Human Reciprocity and Its Evolution.* Princeton, NJ: Princeton University Press.

Brennan, Jason. 2016. *Against Democracy.* Princeton, NJ: Princeton University Press.

Brennan, Jason, and Peter M. Jaworski. 2016. *Markets without Limits: Moral Virtues and Commercial Interests.* New York: Routledge.

Bridges, Sheri. 2017. *Marketing in a Nutshell 3.* N.p.: Phandango.

Brooks, Arthur C. 2006. *Who Really Cares? The Surprising Truth about Compassionate Conservatism.* New York: Basic Books.

———. 2008. *Gross National Happiness: Why Happiness Matters for America—and How We Can Get More of It.* New York: Basic Books.

Bureau of Labor Statistics, United States Department of Labor. 2018. "Job Openings and Labor Turnover Summary." Available here: https://www.bls.gov/news.release/jolts.nr0.htm.

Burns, Judith. 2009. "BB&T Chair Blasts TARP as 'Huge Rip-Off.'" *Wall Street Journal.* June 12. Available here: https://www.wsj.com/articles/SB124482152282410185.

Business in the Community. 2016. "2016 CR Index Insights Report." London: Prince's Responsible Business Network. Available here: https://www.bitc.org.uk/our-resources/report/2016-cr-index-insights-report.

Cameron, Rondo, and Larry Neal. 2003. *A Concise Economic History of the World: From Paleolithic Times to the Present.* 4th ed. New York: Oxford University Press.

Caplan, Bryan. 2008. *The Myth of the Rational Voter: Why Democracies Choose Bad Policies.* Princeton, NJ: Princeton University Press.

———. 2012. *Selfish Reasons to Have More Kids: Why Being a Great Parent Is Less Work and More Fun than You Think.* New York: Basic Books.

Central Intelligence Agency. n.d. *The World Factbook.* Available here: https://www.cia.gov/library/publications/the-world-factbook/.

Chandler, David. 2016. *Strategic Corporate Social Responsibility: Sustainable Value Creation.* 4th ed. New York: Sage Publications.

Chandy, Laurence, and Geoffrey Gertz. 2011. "Poverty in Numbers: The Changing State of Global Poverty from 2005 to 2015." New York: Brookings Institution. Available here: https://www.brookings.edu/research/poverty-in-numbers-the-changing-state-of-global-poverty-from-2005-to-2015/.

Claeys, Gregory. 2018. *Marx and Marxism.* New York: Nation Books.

Clark, Gregory. 2007. *A Farewell to Alms: A Brief Economic History of the World.* Princeton, NJ: Princeton University Press.

Coakley, Matthew, and Michael Kates. 2013. "The Ethical and Economic Case for Sweatshop Regulation." *Journal of Business Ethics* 117: 553–58.

Coase, Ronald H. 1937. "The Nature of the Firm." *Econometrica* 4, 16: 386–405.

———. 1960. "The Problem of Social Cost." *Journal of Law and Economics* 3: 1–44.

Coase, Ronald H., and Ning Wang. 2012. *How China Became Capitalist*. New York: Palgrave Macmillan.

Cohen, G. A. 2009. *Why Not Socialism?* Princeton, NJ: Princeton University Press.

Collier, Paul. 2017. "Culture, Politics, and Economic Development." *Annual Review of Political Science* 20, 1: 111–25.

Conly, Sarah. 2013. *Against Autonomy: Justifying Coercive Paternalism*. New York: Cambridge University Press.

———. 2015. *One Child: Do We Have a Right to Have More?* New York: Oxford University Press.

Conn, Steven. 2018. "Business Schools Have No Business in the University." *Chronicle of Higher Education*. February 20. Available here: https://www.chronicle.com/article/Business-Schools-Have-No/242563.

Coolidge, Calvin. 2001. *The Price of Freedom: Speeches and Addresses*. New York: Fredonia.

Courtois, Stéphane, Nicholas Werth, Jean-Louis Panné, Andrzej Paczkowski, Karel Bartošek, and Jean-Louis Margolin. 1999. *The Black Book of Communism: Crimes, Terror, Repression*. Cambridge, MA: Harvard University Press.

Cowen, Tyler. 2013. *Average Is Over: Powering America beyond the Age of the Great Stagnation*. New York: Dutton.

———. 2017. *The Complacent Class: The Self-Defeating Quest for the American Dream*. New York: St. Martin's.

Cox, W. Michael, and Richard Alm. 1999. *Myths of the Rich and Poor: Why We're Better Off than We Think*. New York: Basic Books.

Coyne, Christopher J. 2013. *Doing Bad by Doing Good: Why Humanitarian Action Fails*. Stanford, CA: Stanford University Press.

Crossman, Ashley. 2018. "All about Marxist Sociology." ThoughtCo. January 1. Available here: https://www.thoughtco.com/marxist-sociology-3026397.

Cullity, Garrett. 2004. *The Moral Demands of Affluence*. New York: Oxford University Press.

Darwin, Charles. (1871) 1981. *The Descent of Man, and Selection in Relation to Sex*. Princeton, NJ: Princeton University Press.

Davis, Michael, and Andrew Stark, eds. 2001. *Conflict of Interest in the Professions*. New York: Oxford University Press.

Dawson, John W., and John J. Seater. 2013. "Federal Regulation and Aggregate Economic Growth." *Journal of Economic Growth* 18, 2: 137–77.

Deaton, Angus. 2013. *The Great Escape: Health, Wealth, and the Origins of Inequality*. Princeton, NJ: Princeton University Press.

DeLong, J. Bradford. 1998. "Estimating World G.D.P., One Million B.C.–Present." Available here: http://holtz.org/Library/Social%20Science/Economics/Estimating%20World%20GDP%20by%20DeLong/Estimating%20World%20GDP.htm.

DeMartino, George F., and Deirdre N. McCloskey, eds. 2016. *The Oxford Handbook of Professional Economic Ethics*. New York: Oxford University Press.

Deneen, Patrick J. 2018. *Why Liberalism Failed*. New Haven: Yale University Press.

Den Uyl, Douglas J., and Douglas B. Rasmussen. 2017. *The Perfectionist Turn: From Metanorms to Metaethics*. Edinburgh: University of Edinburgh Press.

De Soto, Hernando. 2000. *The Mystery of Capital: Why Capitalism Triumphs in the West and Fails Everywhere Else*. New York: Basic Books.

De Waal, Frans. 2006. *Primates and Philosophers: How Morality Evolved*. Princeton, NJ: Princeton University Press.

Diamond, Jared. 1999. *Guns, Germs, and Steel: The Fates of Human Societies*. New York: Norton.

Dollar, David, and Aart Kraay. 2016. "Trade, Growth, and Poverty." World Bank Policy Research Working Paper No. 2615. Available here: https://papers.ssrn.com/sol3/papers.cfm?abstract_id=632684.

Donaldson, John. 2017. "Poverty Reduction in China: Stellar, but Misunderstood." *Brink Asia*. June 7. Available here: http://www.brinknews.com/asia/poverty-reduction-in-china-stellar-but-misunderstood/.

Dunbar, Robin. 1998. *Grooming, Gossip, and the Evolution of Language*. Cambridge, MA: Harvard University Press.

———. 2010. *How Many Friends Does One Person Need? Dunbar's Number and Other Evolutionary Quirks*. London: Faber and Faber.

Eagleton, Terry. 2018. *Why Marx Was Right*. New Haven: Yale University Press.

Easterly, William. 2007. *The White Man's Burden: Why the West's Efforts to Aid the Rest Have Done So Much Ill and So Little Good*. New York: Penguin.

———. 2013. *The Tyranny of Experts: Economists, Dictators, and the Forgotten Rights of the Poor*. New York: Basic Books.

Ehrlich, Paul. 1968. *The Population Bomb*. New York: Macmillan.

Epstein, Richard A. 1985. *Takings: Private Property and the Power of Eminent Domain*. Cambridge, MA: Harvard University Press.

———. 1992. *Forbidden Grounds: The Case against Employment Discrimination Laws*. Cambridge, MA: Harvard University Press.

———. 1993. *Bargaining with the State*. Princeton, NJ: Princeton University Press.

Erixon, Fredrik, and Björn Weigel. 2016. *The Innovation Illusion: How So Little Is Created by So Many Working So Hard*. New Haven: Yale University Press.

Fleischacker, Samuel. 2016. "Adam Smith and the Left." In *Adam Smith: His Life, Thought, and Legacy*, ed. Ryan Patrick Hanley, 478–93. Princeton, NJ: Princeton University Press.

Fogel, Robert William. 2004. *The Escape from Hunger and Premature Death, 1700–2100: Europe, America, and the Third World*. New York: Cambridge University Press.

Follett, Chelsea. 2016. "Pessimism Viewed in Historical Perspective." HumanProgress.org. February 5. Available here: https://humanprogress.org/article.php?p=167.

Francis (pope). 2015. *Laudato Si'*. Rome: Vatican.

Frank, Robert H. 1988. *Passions within Reason: The Strategic Role of the Emotions*. New York: Norton.

———. 2012. *The Darwin Economy: Liberty, Competition, and the Common Good*. Princeton, NJ: Princeton University Press.

———. 2016. *Success and Luck: Good Fortune and the Myth of Meritocracy*. Princeton, NJ: Princeton University Press.

Frankfurt, Harry G. 1998. "Equality as a Moral Ideal." In *The Importance of What We Care About*. New York: Cambridge University Press.

Friedman, Milton. 1970. "The Social Responsibility of Business Is to Increase Its Profits." *New York Times Magazine*. September 13. Available here: http://query.nytimes.com/mem/archive-free/pdf?res=9E05E0DA153CE531A15750C1A96F9C946190D6CF.

Friedman, Milton, and Anna Jacobson Schwartz. 1969. *A Monetary History of the United States, 1867–1960*. Princeton, NJ: Princeton University Press.

Fund for American Studies. n.d. "Would You Give Up the Internet for 1 Million Dollars?" Washington, DC. Available here: https://tfas.org/give-internet-1-million-dollars/.

Gaus, Gerald. 2012. *The Order of Public Reason: A Theory of Freedom and Morality in a Diverse and Bounded World*. New York: Cambridge University Press.

———. 2016. *The Tyranny of the Ideal: Justice in a Diverse Society*. Princeton, NJ: Princeton University Press.

Gavett, Gretchen. 2014. "CEOs Get Paid Too Much, According to Pretty Much Everyone in the World." *Harvard Business Review*. September 23. Available here: https://hbr.org/2014/09/ceos-get-paid-too-much-according-to-pretty-much-everyone-in-the-world.

German, Chelsea. 2015. "Extreme Poverty's End in Sight." September 24. Washington, DC: HumanProgress.org. Available here: http://humanprogress.org/blog/extreme-povertys-end-sight.

Gettysburg Gazette. 1914. "Wireless Telephone for Wealthy Only." July 10. Available here: https://news.google.com/newspapers?id=ZQxUAAAAIBAJ&sjid=cTkNAAAAIBAJ&pg=5650%2C5522354.

Gintis, Herbert. 2016. *Individuality and Entanglement: The Moral and Material Bases of Social Life*. Princeton, NJ: Princeton University Press.

Global Water Partnership. n.d. "Tradeable Pollution Permits." Available here: http://www. gwp.org/en/learn/iwrm-toolbox/Management-Instruments/Economic-Instruments/ Tradable_pollution_permits/.

Goodman, John C. 2012. *Priceless: Curing the Healthcare Crisis.* Oakland, CA: Independent Institute.

Gordon, Robert J. 2016. *The Rise and Fall of American Growth: The U.S. Standard of Living since the Civil War.* Princeton, NJ: Princeton University Press.

Graham, Carol. 2017. *Happiness for All? Unequal Hopes and Lives in Pursuit of the American Dream.* Princeton, NJ: Princeton University Press.

Greif, Avner. 2006. *Institutions and the Path to the Modern Economy: Lessons from Medieval Trade.* New York: Cambridge University Press.

Guarino, Ben. 2017. "Shaking Hands Is 'Barbaric': Donald Trump, the Germaphobe in Chief." *Washington Post.* January 12. Available here: https://www.washingtonpost.com/ news/morning-mix/wp/2017/01/12/shaking-hands-is-barbaric-donald-trump-the-germaphobe-in-chief/?utm_term=.0a39002b140d.

Gumpert, Martin, and Edwin L. Shuman. 1936. *Trail Blazers of Science.* New York: Funk and Wagnalls.

Gwartney, James, Robert A. Lawson, and Joshua C. Hall. 2017. *Economic Freedom of the World Index.* Vancouver, Canada: Fraser Institute.

Haidt, Jonathan. 2013. *The Righteous Mind: Why Good People Are Divided by Politics and Religion.* New York: Vintage.

Hall, Brian J., and Jeffrey B. Liebman. August 1998. "Are CEOs Really Paid Like Bureaucrats?" *Quarterly Journal of Economics* 113, 3: 653–91.

Hall, Joshua C., and Robert A. Lawson. 2014. "Economic Freedom of the World: An Accounting of the Literature." *Contemporary Economic Policy* 32, 1: 1–19.

Hanley, Ryan Patrick. 2016. "Adam Smith and Human Flourishing." In *Economic Freedom and Human Flourishing: Perspectives from Political Philosophy,* ed. Michael R. Strain and Stan A. Veuger, 46–57. Washington, DC: American Enterprise Institute.

Hanson, Rick. 2013. *Hardwiring Happiness: The New Brain Science of Contentment, Calm, and Confidence.* New York: Harmony.

Haque, Umair. 2011. *Betterness: Economics for Humans.* Cambridge, MA: Harvard Business Review Press.

Hardin, Garrett. 1968. "The Tragedy of the Commons." *Science* 162, 3859: 1243–48. Available here: http://science.sciencemag.org/content/162/3859/1243.full.

Harris, Judith Rich. 2006. *No Two Alike: Human Nature and Human Individuality.* New York: Norton.

Hartman, Edwin M. 2008. "Teaching Business Ethics with Aristotle." In *Rethinking Business Management: Examining the Foundations of Business Education,* ed. Samuel Gregg and James R. Stoner Jr., 172–88. Princeton, NJ: Witherspoon Institute.

Harvey, David. 2018. *Marx, Capital, and the Madness of Economic Reason.* New York: Oxford University Press.

Harvey, Phil, and Lisa Conyers. 2016. *The Human Cost of Welfare: How the System Hurts the People It's Supposed to Help.* Santa Barbara, CA: Praeger.

Hasnas, John. 2013. "Teaching Business Ethics: The Principles Approach." *Journal of Business Ethics Education* 10: 275–304.

Hayek, Friedrich A. 1945. "The Use of Knowledge in Society." *American Economic Review* 35, 4: 519–30.

———. (1960) 2011. *The Constitution of Liberty: The Definitive Edition.* Ed. Ronald Hamowy. Chicago: University of Chicago Press.

———. 1978. "The Atavism of Social Justice." In *New Studies in Philosophy, Politics, Economics, and the History of Ideas.* Chicago: University of Chicago Press.

Heath, Joseph. 2010. *Economics without Illusions: Debunking the Myths of Modern Capitalism.* New York: Crown Business.

————. 2014. *Morality, Competition, and the Firm: The Market Failures Approach to Business Ethics.* New York: Oxford University Press.

Heath, Will C. Summer. 2007. "Hayek Revisited: Planning, Diversity, and the Vox Populi." *Independent Review* 12, 1: 47–70.

Heritage Foundation. 2017. *Index of Economic Freedom.* Washington, DC. Available here: http://www.heritage.org/index/.

Higgs, Robert. 1980. *Competition and Coercion: Blacks in the American Economy, 1865–1914.* Chicago: University of Chicago Press.

————. 2013. *Crisis and Leviathan: Critical Episodes in the Growth of American Government.* 25th Anniversary ed. Oakland, CA: Independent Institute.

HumanProgress.org. n.d. Washington, DC: Cato Institute. Available here: http://humanprogress.org/.

Hume, David. (1741) 1985. "Of the Independency of Parliament." In *Essays Moral Political and Literary,* ed. Eugene F. Miller, 42–46. Indianapolis: Liberty Fund.

————. (1754) 1985a. "Of Refinement in the Arts." In *Essays Moral Political and Literary,* ed. Eugene F. Miller, 268–80. Indianapolis: Liberty Fund.

————. (1754) 1985b. "Of the Jealousy of Trade." In *Essays Moral Political and Literary,* ed. Eugene F. Miller, 327–31. Indianapolis: Liberty Fund.

Hussain, Waheed. 2012. "Corporations, Profit Maximization and the Personal Sphere." *Economics and Philosophy* 28: 311–31.

Huxley, Aldous. (1932) 2005. *Brave New World.* New York: Harper Perennial.

Institute for Justice. n.d. "Kelo Eminent Domain." Available here: http://ij.org/case/kelo/.

Isaacson, Walter. 2015. *The Innovators: How a Group of Hackers, Geniuses, and Geeks Created the Digital Revolution.* New York: Simon and Schuster.

Jacobs, Jane. 1961. *The Death and Life of Great American Cities.* New York: Vintage.

Jensen, Michael C. 2001. "Value Maximization, Stakeholder Theory, and the Corporate Objective Function." *Journal of Applied Corporate Finance* 14, 3: 8–21.

Jensen, Michael C., and William H. Meckling. 1976. "Theory of the Firm: Managerial Behavior, Agency Costs, and Ownership Structure." *Journal of Financial Economics* 3, 4: 305–60.

Johnson, Samuel. 1755. *A Dictionary of the English Language.* London: Strahan.

Jones, Eric L. 2000. *Growth Recurring: Economic Change in World History.* 2nd ed. Ann Arbor: University of Michigan Press.

Joyce, Richard. 2006. *The Evolution of Morality.* Cambridge, MA: MIT Press.

Kahneman, Daniel. 2013. *Thinking, Fast and Slow.* New York: Farrar, Straus and Giroux.

Kahneman, Daniel, and Angus Deaton. 2010. "High Income Improves Evaluation of Life but Not Emotional Well-Being." *Proceedings of the National Academy of Sciences* 107, 38: 16489–93.

Kant, Immanuel. (1785) 1981. *Grounding for the Metaphysics of Morals.* Trans. James W. Ellington. Indianapolis: Hackett.

Kotlikoff, Laurence J. 2010. *Jimmy Stewart Is Dead: Ending the World's Ongoing Financial Plague with Limited Purpose Banking.* New York: Wiley.

Krass, Peter. 2002. *Carnegie.* New York: Wiley.

Kraut, Richard. 2002. *Aristotle: Political Philosophy.* New York: Oxford University Press.

Krugman, Paul. 1998. "Why Most Economists' Predictions Are Wrong." *Red Herring.* Available here: http://web.archive.org/web/19980610100009/www.redherring.com/mag/issue55/economics.html.

————. 2001. "Reckonings; after the Horror." *New York Times.* September 14. Available here: https://www.nytimes.com/2001/09/14/opinion/reckonings-after-the-horror.html?pagewanted=2&src=pm.

Laffer, Arthur B. 2014. *An Inquiry into the Nature and Causes of the Wealth of States: How Taxes, Energy, and Worker Freedom Change Everything.* New York: Wiley.

Lal, Deepak. 2013. *Poverty and Progress: Realities and Myths about Global Poverty.* Washington, DC: Cato Institute.

Landes, David. 1999. *The Wealth and Poverty of Nations: Why Some Are So Rich and Some So Poor.* New York: Norton.

Lawler, Joseph. 2012. "Economist Laurence Kotlikoff: U.S. $222 Trillion in Debt." *Real Clear Policy.* Available here: http://www.realclearpolicy.com/blog/2012/12/01/economist_laurence_kotlikoff_us_222_trillion_in_debt_363.html.

Layard, Richard. 2011. *Happiness: Lessons from a New Science.* 2nd ed. New York: Penguin.

LeBar, Mark. 2013. *The Value of Living Well.* New York: Oxford University Press.

Lindsey, Brink, and Steven M. Telles. 2017. *The Captured Economy: How the Powerful Enrich Themselves, Slow Down Growth, and Increase Inequality.* New York: Oxford University Press.

Lomasky, Loren E. 1990. *Persons, Rights, and the Moral Community.* New York: Oxford University Press.

———. 2016. *Rights Angles.* New York: Oxford University Press.

Lupton, Robert D. 2011. *Toxic Charity: How Churches and Charities Hurt Those They Help (and How to Reverse It).* New York: HarperCollins.

Lyubomirsky, Sonja. 2014. "Does Money Really Buy Happiness?" *Psychology Today.* September 29. Available here: https://www.psychologytoday.com/blog/how-happiness/201409/does-money-really-buy-happiness.

Macfarlane, Alan. 2000. *The Riddle of the Modern World: Of Liberty, Wealth, and Equality.* New York: St. Martin's.

Mack, Joanna. 2016. "Absolute and Overall Poverty." Poverty and Social Exclusion. October 27. Available here: http://www.poverty.ac.uk/definitions-poverty/absolute-and-overall-poverty.

Maddison, Angus. 2007. *Contours of the World Economy, 1–2030 AD.* New York: Oxford University Press.

Maine, Henry Sumner. 1861. *Ancient Law: Its Connection with the Early History of Society and Its Relation to Modern Ideas.* London: John Murray.

Malecki, Catherine. 2018. *Corporate Social Responsibility: Perspectives for Sustainable Corporate Governance.* Cheltenham: Edward Elgar.

Malthus, Thomas. (1798) 2015. *An Essay on the Principle of Population.* New York: Penguin Classics.

Mandeville, Bernard. (1714) 1988. *The Fable of the Bees: Or, Private Vices, Public Benefits.* Indianapolis: Liberty Fund.

Mansfield, Harvey C. 2016. "Aristotle on Economics and the Flourishing Life." In *Economic Freedom and Human Flourishing: Perspectives from Political Philosophy,* ed. Michael R. Strain and Stan A. Veuger, 1–8. Washington, DC: American Enterprise Institute.

Martin, Parker. 2018. "Why We Should Bulldoze the Business School." *The Guardian.* April 27. Available here: https://www.theguardian.com/news/2018/apr/27/bulldoze-the-business-school?CMP=share_btn_fb.

Marx, Karl. 1844. "Comments on James Mill, *Éléments d'économie politique.*" Available here: https://www.marxists.org/archive/marx/works/1844/james-mill/.

———. (1844) 1994. "Alienated Labor." In *Karl Marx: Selected Writings,* ed. Lawrence H. Simon. Indianapolis: Hackett.

———. (1867) 1994. *Capital.* In *Karl Marx: Selected Writings,* ed. Lawrence H. Simon. Indianapolis: Hackett.

Marx, Karl, and Friedrich Engels. (1848) 1994. *The Communist Manifesto.* In *Karl Marx: Selected Writings,* ed. Lawrence H. Simon. Indianapolis: Hackett.

Massachusetts Institute of Technology. 2018. "MIT Technology Review." Available here: https://www.technologyreview.com/lists/technologies/2018/.

McChesney, Fred S. 1987. "Rent Extraction and Rent Creation in the Economic Theory of Regulation." *Journal of Legal Studies* 16, 1: 101–18.

McCloskey, Deirdre N. 2006. *The Bourgeois Virtues: Ethics for an Age of Commerce.* Chicago: University of Chicago Press.

———. 2010. *Bourgeois Dignity: Why Economics Can't Explain the Modern World.* Chicago: University of Chicago Press.

———. 2016a. *Bourgeois Equality: How Ideas, Not Capital or Institutions, Enriched the World.* Chicago: University of Chicago Press.

———. 2016b. "The Formula for a Richer World? Equality, Liberty, Justice." *New York Times.* September 2. Available here: https://www.nytimes.com/2016/09/04/upshot/the-formula-for-a-richer-world-equality-liberty-justice.html.

———. 2016c. "Economic Liberty as Anti-flourishing: Marx and Especially His Followers." In *Economic Freedom and Human Flourishing: Perspectives from Political Philosophy,* ed. Michael R. Strain and Stan A. Veuger, 129–49. Washington, DC: American Enterprise Institute.

McDonald, Patrick J. 2009. *The Invisible Hand of Peace: Capitalism, the War Machine, and International Relations Theory.* New York: Cambridge University Press.

Mill, John Stuart. (1859) 1978. *On Liberty.* Ed. Elizabeth Rapaport. Indianapolis: Hackett.

Miller, Christian B. 2014. *Character and Moral Psychology.* New York: Oxford University Press.

———. 2017. *The Character Gap: How Good Are We?* New York: Oxford University Press.

Miller, Fred D., Jr. 1997. *Nature, Justice, and Rights in Aristotle's "Politics."* New York: Oxford Clarendon Press.

Mokyr, Joel. 1992. *The Lever of Riches: Technological Creativity and Economic Progress.* New York: Oxford University Press.

———. 2016. *A Culture of Growth: The Origins of the Modern Economy.* Princeton, NJ: Princeton University Press.

Monnery, Neil. 2017. *Architect of Prosperity: Sir John Cowperthwaite and the Making of Hong Kong.* London: London Publishing Partnership.

Montesquieu, Charles de Secondat, baron de. (1748) 1989. *The Spirit of the Laws.* Trans. Anne M. Cohler, Basia C. Miller, and Harold S. Stone. New York: Cambridge University Press.

Morris, Ian. 2013. *The Measure of Civilization: How Social Development Decides the Fate of Nations.* Princeton, NJ: Princeton University Press.

Morse, Jennifer. 1984. "Southern Labor Law in the Jim Crow Era: Exploitative or Competitive?" *University of Chicago Law Review* 51, 4: 1161–92.

———. 1986. "The Political Economy of Segregation: The Case of Segregated Streetcars." *Journal of Economic History* 46, 4: 893–917.

Munger, Michael C. 2011. "Euvoluntary or Not, Exchange Is Just." *Social Philosophy and Policy* 28, 2: 192–211.

———. 2018. *Tomorrow 3.0: Transaction Costs and the Sharing Economy.* New York: Cambridge University Press.

Murray, Charles. 2015. *By the People: Rebuilding Liberty without Permission.* New York: Crown Forum.

National Center for Charitable Statistics. 2013. "Quick Facts about Nonprofits." Available here: http://nccs.urban.org/data-statistics/quick-facts-about-nonprofits.

New York Global City Partners. 2014. "Best Practice: National Salt Reduction Initiative." Available here: www.nyc.gov/html/ia/gprb/downloads/pdf/NYC_Health_Salt.pdf.

New York Times. 1881. "A Test Bicycle Case." July 15. Available here: https://t.co/yS8zLaxk4i.

———. 1987. "The Right Minimum Wage: $0.00." Unsigned editorial, January 14. Available here: http://www.nytimes.com/1987/01/14/opinion/the-right-minimum-wage-0.00.html.

Nock, Albert Jay. (1924) 1991. "On Doing the Right Thing." In *The State of the Union: Essays in Social Criticism,* ed. Charles H. Hamilton, 317–25. Indianapolis: Liberty Fund.

———. (1935) 1994. *Our Enemy, the State.* San Francisco: Fox & Wilkes.

Nordhaus, William D. 1996. "Do Real Output and Real Wage Measures Capture Reality? The History of Lighting Suggests Not." In *The Economics of New Goods,* ed. Timothy F. Breshnahan and Robert J. Gordon, 29–70. Chicago: University of Chicago Press.

North, Douglass C. 1982. *Structure and Change in Economic History.* New York: Cambridge University Press.

———. 1990. *Institutions, Institutional Change and Economic Performance.* New York: Cambridge University Press.

North, Douglass C., John Joseph Wallis, and Barry R. Weingast. 2009. *Violence and Social Orders: A Conceptual Framework for Interpreting Recorded Human History.* New York: Cambridge University Press.

Nussbaum, Martha. 2013. *Creating Capabilities: The Human Development Approach.* Cambridge, MA: Belknap Press of Harvard University Press.

Olson, Mancur. 1965. *The Logic of Collective Action: Public Goods and the Theory of Groups.* Cambridge, MA: Harvard University Press.

Oman, Nathan B. 2016. *The Dignity of Commerce: Markets and the Moral Foundations of Contract Law.* Chicago: University of Chicago Press.

Ormerod, Paul. 2005. *Why Most Things Fail: Evolution, Extinction and Economics.* Hoboken, NJ: Wiley & Sons.

Ortiz-Ospina, Esteban, and Max Roser. 2016. "Trust." OurWorldInData.org. Available here: https://ourworldindata.org/trust.

Ostrom, Elinor. 1990. *Governing the Commons: The Evolution of Institutions for Collective Action.* New York: Cambridge University Press.

———. 2005. *Understanding Institutional Diversity.* Princeton, NJ: Princeton University Press.

Otteson, James R. 2000. "Limits on Our Obligation to Give." *Public Affairs Quarterly* 14, 3: 183–203.

———. 2002. *Adam Smith's Marketplace of Life.* New York: Cambridge University Press.

———. 2006. *Actual Ethics.* New York: Cambridge University Press.

———. 2010. "Adam Smith and the Great Mind Fallacy." *Social Philosophy and Policy* 27, 1: 276–304.

———. 2012. "The Inhuman Alienation of Capitalism." *Society* 49: 139–43.

———. 2013. *Adam Smith.* London: Bloomsbury Academic.

———. 2014. *The End of Socialism.* New York: Cambridge University Press.

———. 2017. "The Misuse of Egalitarianism in Society." *Independent Review* 22, 1: 37–47.

Oxfam. n.d. "There Is Enough Food to Feed the World." London. Available here: https://www.oxfam.ca/there-enough-food-feed-world.

Paganelli, Maria Pia. 2006. "Why Decentralized Systems?" *Adam Smith Review* 2: 203–8.

Parker, Clifton B. 2015. "Sports Stadiums Do Not Generate Significant Local Economic Growth, Stanford Expert Says." *Stanford News.* July 30. Available here: http://news.stanford.edu/2015/07/30/stadium-economics-noll-073015/.

Pennington, Mark. 2011. *Robust Political Economy: Classical Liberalism and the Future of Public Policy.* Cheltenham, UK: Edward Elgar.

Phelps, Edmund. 2013. *Mass Flourishing: How Grassroots Innovation Created Jobs, Challenge, and Change.* Princeton, NJ: Princeton University Press.

Piketty, Thomas. 2014. *Capital in the Twenty-First Century.* Cambridge, MA: Harvard Belknap.

Pinker, Steven. 2002. *The Blank Slate: The Modern Denial of Human Nature.* New York: Penguin.

———. 2011. *The Better Angels of Our Nature: Why Violence Has Declined.* New York: Viking.

———. 2018. *Enlightenment Now: The Case for Reason, Science, Humanism, and Progress.* New York: Viking.

Pittsburgh Gazette Times. 1907. "The Automobile Terror." August 21. Available here: https://news.google.com/newspapers?nid=1126&dat=19070821&id=c3tRAAAAIBAJ&sjid=jmcDAAAAIBAJ&pg=2240,5193612&hl=en.

Plato. 1992. *Republic.* Trans. G. M. A. Grube. Revised by C. D. C. Reeve. Indianapolis: Hackett.

Popper, Karl R. 1976. "The Logic of the Social Sciences." In Theodor W. Adorno et al., *The Positivist Dispute in German Sociology.* New York: Harper Torchbooks.

Powell, Benjamin. 2014. *Out of Poverty: Sweatshops in the Global Economy.* New York: Cambridge University Press.

Powell, Benjamin, and Matt Zwolinski. 2012. "The Ethical and Economic Case against Sweatshop Labor: A Critical Assessment." *Journal of Business Ethics* 107, 4: 449–72.

Primeaux, Patrick, and John A. Stieber. 1995. *Profit Maximization: The Ethical Mandate of Business.* Washington, DC: Austin & Winfield.

Psychology Today. n.d. "Psychopathy." Available here: https://www.psychologytoday.com/basics/psychopathy.

Rakowski, Eric. 1991. *Equal Justice.* New York: Oxford Clarendon Press.

Ramachandran, Vilayanur. 2003. *The Emerging Mind.* London: Profile Books.

Rawls, John. 1971. *A Theory of Justice.* Cambridge, MA: Harvard University Press.

Reeves, Richard V. 2017. *Dream Hoarders: How the American Upper Middle Class Is Leaving Everyone Else in the Dust, Why That Is a Problem, and What to Do about It.* New York: Brookings Institution.

Ridley, Matt. 2011. *The Rational Optimist: How Prosperity Evolves.* New York: Harper Perennial.

———. 2016. *The Evolution of Everything: How Ideas Emerge.* New York: Harper Perennial.

Rilke, Rainer Maria. 1907. "The Panther." Available here: https://en.wikipedia.org/wiki/The_Panther_(poem).

Rizzo, Mario. 2007. "Should Policies Nudge People? An Exchange with Richard Thaler on Libertarian Paternalism." May 25. New York University. Available here: https://works.bepress.com/mario_rizzo/16/.

Rose, David C. 2000. "Teams, Firms and the Evolution of Profit Seeking Behavior." *Journal of Bioeconomics* 2: 25–39.

———. 2011. *The Moral Foundation of Economic Behavior.* New York: Oxford University Press.

———. 2019. *Why Culture Matters Most.* New York: Oxford University Press.

Rosenberg, Nathan, and L. E. Birdzell Jr. 1987. *How the West Grew Rich: The Economic Transformation of the Industrial World.* New York: Basic Books.

Rosling, Hans, Ola Rosling, and Anna Rosling Rönnlund. 2018. *Factfulness: Ten Reasons We're Wrong about the World—and Why Things Are Better than You Think.* New York: Flatiron Books.

Rousseau, Jean-Jacques. (1755) 1992. *Discourse on the Origin of Inequality.* Trans. Donald A. Cress. Indianapolis: Hackett.

Rummel, R. J. 1997. *Death by Government.* New York: Routledge.

Russell, Daniel C. 2009. *Practical Intelligence and the Virtues.* New York: Oxford University Press.

———. 2012. *Happiness for Humans.* New York: Oxford University Press.

Sandel, Michael J. 2012. *What Money Can't Buy: The Moral Limits of Markets.* New York: Farrar, Straus and Giroux.

Satz, Debra. 2010. *Why Some Things Should Not Be for Sale: The Moral Limits of Markets.* New York: Oxford University Press.

Schabas, Margaret. 2005. *The Natural Origins of Economics.* Chicago: University of Chicago Press.

Scheidel, Walter. 2017. *The Great Leveler: Violence and the History of Inequality from the Stone Age to the Twenty-First Century.* Princeton, NJ: Princeton University Press.

Schelling, Thomas. 1978. *Micromotives and Macrobehavior.* New York: Norton.

Schmidtz, David. 2011a. "Nonideal Theory: What It Is and What It Needs to Be." *Ethics* 121, 4: 772–96.

———. 2011b. "The Institution of Property." In *Person, Polis, Planet: Essays in Applied Philosophy.* New York: Oxford University Press.

Schor, Juliet B. 1999. "Towards a New Politics of Consumption." In *The Consumer Society Reader,* ed. Juliet B. Schor and Douglas B. Holt. New York: New Press.

———. 2004. *Born to Buy.* New York: Scribner.

Schumpeter, Joseph A. 1942. *Capitalism, Socialism, and Democracy.* New York: Harper Perennial.

Schwartz, Barry. 2016. *The Paradox of Choice: Why More Is Less.* Rev. ed. New York: HarperCollins.

Schwartz, Yardena. 2016. "In New Palestinian City, Few Residents and Charges of Collusion with Israel." *Times of Israel.* January 24, Available here: https://www.timesofisrael.com/in-new-palestinian-city-few-residents-and-charges-of-collusion-with-israel/.

Scott, James C. 2009. *The Art of Not Being Governed: An Anarchist History of Upland Southeast Asia.* New Haven: Yale University Press.

Seabright, Paul. 2010. *The Company of Strangers: A Natural History of Economic Life*. Rev. ed. Princeton, NJ: Princeton University Press.

Sen, Amartya. 1995. *Inequality Reexamined*. Cambridge, MA: Harvard University Press.

———. 2000. *Development as Freedom*. New York: Anchor.

Sernovitz, Gary. 2016. *The Green and the Black: The Complete Story of the Shale Revolution, the Fight over Fracking, and the Future of Energy*. New York: St. Martin's.

Shapiro, Daniel. 2007. *Is the Welfare State Justified?* New York: Cambridge University Press.

Sheffield, Rachel, and Robert Rector. 2014. "The War on Poverty after 50 Years." Washington, DC: Heritage Foundation. Available here: http://www.heritage.org/poverty-and-inequality/report/the-war-poverty-after-50-years.

Shlaes, Amity. 2008. *The Forgotten Man: A New History of the Great Depression*. New York: Harper Perennial.

———. 2014. *Coolidge*. New York: Harper Perennial.

Silverglate, Harvey A. 2011. *Three Felonies a Day: How the Feds Target the Innocent*. New York: Encounter Books.

Simon, Julian L. 1998. *The Ultimate Resource 2*. Princeton, NJ: Princeton University Press.

Simpson, Brian P. 2005. *Markets Don't Fail!* Lanham, MD: Lexington.

Singer, Peter. 2009. *The Life You Can Save: How to Do Your Part to End World Poverty*. New York: Random House.

Skidelsky, Robert, and Edward Skidelsky. 2012. *How Much Is Enough? Money and the Good Life*. New York: Other Press.

Smiles, Samuel. (1859) 1996. *Self-Help: With Illustrations of Conduct and Perseverance*. London: Institute for Economic Affairs.

Smith, Adam. (1759) 1982. *The Theory of Moral Sentiments*. Ed. D. D. Raphael and A. L. Macfie. Indianapolis: Liberty Fund.

———. (1776) 1981. *An Inquiry into the Nature and Causes of the Wealth of Nations*. Ed. R. H. Campbell and A. S. Skinner. Indianapolis: Liberty Fund.

———. 1982. *Essays on Philosophical Subjects*. Ed. W. P. D. Wightman. Indianapolis: Liberty Fund.

Smith, Hedrick. 2013. *Who Stole the American Dream?* New York: Random House.

Sober, Elliott, and David Sloan Wilson. 1998. *Unto Others: The Evolution and Psychology of Unselfish Behavior*. Cambridge, MA: Harvard University Press.

Somin, Ilya. 2016. *Democracy and Political Ignorance: Why Smaller Government Is Smarter*. 2nd ed. Stanford, CA: Stanford University Press.

Spitz, Vivien. 2005. *Doctors from Hell: The Horrific Account of Nazi Experiments on Humans*. New York: Sentient Publications.

Spokane Spokesman-Review. 1936. "Purity of Electrons Violated by Radio?" November 4. Available here: https://news.google.com/newspapers?nid=1314&dat=19361104&id=H8pYAAAAIBAJ&sjid=ruMDAAAAIBAJ&pg=6121,1613560&hl=en.

Spooner, Lysander. (1875) 2013. *Vices Are Not Crimes: A Vindication of Moral Liberty*. Indianapolis: Liberty Fund. Available here: http://oll.libertyfund.org/titles/spooner-boll-24-vices-are-not-crimes.

Stark, Andrew. 1993. "What's the Matter with Business Ethics?" *Harvard Business Review*. May–June. Available here: https://hbr.org/1993/05/whats-the-matter-with-business-ethics.

Stevenson, Betsey, and Justin Wolfers. 2013. "Subjective Well-Being and Income: Is There Any Evidence of Satiation?" April 29. Brookings Institution. Available here: https://www.brookings.edu/research/subjective-well%E2%80%90being-and-income-is-there-any-evidence-of-satiation/.

Stigler, George J. 1971. "The Theory of Economic Regulation." *Bell Journal of Economics and Management Science* 2, 1: 3–21.

Stringham, Edward Peter. 2015. *Private Governance: Creating Order in Economic and Social Life*. New York: Oxford University Press.

Sumner, William Graham. (1883) 1992. "The Forgotten Man." In *On Liberty, Society, and Politics: The Essential Essays of William Graham Sumner*. Robert C. Bannister, ed. Indianapolis: Liberty Fund. Available here: http://oll.libertyfund.org/titles/sumner-the-forgotten-man-and-other-essays-corrected-edition.

Sznycer, Daniel, Maria Florencia Lopez Seal, Aaron Sell, Julian Lim, Roni Porat, Shaul Shalvi, Eran Halperin, Leda Cosmides, and John Tooby. 2017. "Support for Redistribution Is Shaped by Compassion, Envy, and Self-Interest, but Not a Taste for Fairness." *Proceedings of the National Academy of Sciences of the United States of America* 114, 31: 8420–25.

Taleb, Nassim Nicholas. 2012. *Antifragile: Things That Gain from Disorder.* New York: Random House.

Taylor, James Stacey. 2017. "How Not to Argue for Markets (or, Why the Argument from Mutually Beneficial Exchange Fails)." *Journal of Social Philosophy* 48, 2: 165–79.

Taylor, Robert S. 2017. *Exit Left: Markets and Mobility in Republican Thought.* New York: Oxford University Press.

Tetlock, Philip E. 2006. *Expert Political Judgment: How Good Is It? How Can We Know?* Princeton, NJ: Princeton University Press.

Thaler, Richard H. 2015. *Misbehaving: The Making of Behavioral Economics.* New York: Norton.

Thaler, Richard H., and Cass R. Sunstein. 2009. *Nudge: Improving Decisions about Health, Wealth, and Happiness.* New York: Penguin.

Tomasello, Michael. 2016. *A Natural History of Human Morality.* Cambridge, MA: Harvard University Press.

Tomasi, John. 2012. *Free Market Fairness.* Princeton, NJ: Princeton University Press.

Tupy, Marian L. 2017. "Things Are Looking Up by Any Measure." HumanProgress.org. Available here: https://humanprogress.org/article.php?p=774.

Tweedie, Neil. 2013. "Bill Gates Interview: 'I Have No Use for Money. This Is God's Work.'" *The Telegraph.* January 18. Available here: https://www.telegraph.co.uk/technology/bill-gates/9812672/Bill-Gates-interview-I-have-no-use-for-money.-This-is-Gods-work.html.

Ubel, Peter A. 2006. *You're Stronger than You Think: Tapping into the Secrets of Emotionally Resilient People.* New York: McGraw-Hill.

———. 2009. *Free Market Madness: Why Human Nature Is at Odds with Economics—and Why It Matters.* Cambridge, MA: Harvard Business Review Press.

US Census Bureau. 2015. "21.3 Percent of U.S. Population Participates in Government Assistance Programs Each Month." Available here: https://www.census.gov/newsroom/press-releases/2015/cb15-97.html.

US Environmental Protection Agency. n.d. "EPA's Budget and Spending." Available here: https://www.epa.gov/planandbudget/budget.

Van der Vossen, Bas. 2015. "In Defense of the Ivory Tower: Why Philosophers Should Stay Out of Politics." *Philosophical Psychology* 28: 1045–63.

Vedder, Richard, and Wendell Cox. 2006. *The Wal-Mart Revolution: How Big-Box Stores Benefit Consumers, Workers, and the Economy.* Washington, DC: AEI Press.

Voltaire. (1764) 1901. *The Philosophical Dictionary.* In *The Works of Voltaire,* vol. 6, trans. William F. Fleming. Available here: http://oll.libertyfund.org/titles/voltaire-the-works-of-voltaire-vol-vi-philosophical-dictionary-part-4#lf0060-06_head_189.

Vonnegut, Kurt. (1961) 1998. "Harrison Bergeron." In *Welcome to the Monkey House.* New York: Dial Press.

Wagner, Eric. 2013. "Five Reasons 8 out of 10 Businesses Fail." *Forbes Magazine.* Available here: https://www.forbes.com/sites/ericwagner/2013/09/12/five-reasons-8-out-of-10-businesses-fail/#4c373d676978.

Warsaw Stock Exchange. 2010. "Respect Index." Available here: http://www.odpowiedzialni.gpw.pl/csr_indices_worldwide.

Washington, George. 1796. "Farewell Address." Available here: http://avalon.law.yale.edu/18th_century/washing.asp.

WebMD. n.d. "Estimated Calorie Requirements." Available here: http://www.webmd.com/diet/features/estimated-calorie-requirement.

Whaples, Robert, ed. 2017. *Pope Francis and the Caring Society.* Oakland, CA: Independent Institute.

White, Mark D. 2013. *The Manipulation of Choice: Ethics and Libertarian Paternalism.* New York: Palgrave Macmillan.

———. 2017. *The Decline of the Individual: Reconciling Autonomy with Community.* New York: Palgrave Macmillan.

White, Matthew. 2011. *The Great Big Book of Horrible Things: The Definitive Chronicle of History's 100 Worst Atrocities.* New York: Norton.

Wilkinson, Will. 2016. "The Great Enrichment and Social Justice." Washington, DC: Niskanen Center. Available here: https://niskanencenter.org/blog/the-great-enrichment-and-social-justice/.

World Bank. n.d. "Fertility Rates, Total (Births per Woman)." Available here: http://data.world-bank.org/indicator/SP.DYN.TFRT.IN.

Worstall, Tim. 2017. "Congratulations to Bolivarian Socialism—Venezuela Declares Humanitarian Crisis." *Forbes.* Available here: https://www.forbes.com/sites/timworstall/2017/03/25/congratulations-to-bolivarian-socialism-venezuela-declares-humanitarian-crisis/#dbdce7c7a835.

Wydick, Bruce, Elizabeth Katz, Flor Calvo, Felipe Gutierrez, and Brendan Janet. 2016. "Shoeing the Children: The Impact of the TOMS Shoe Donation Program in Rural El Salvador." World Bank Policy Research Working Paper No. 7822.

Yunus, Muhammad. 2017. *A World of Three Zeros: The New Economics of Zero Poverty, Zero Unemployment, and Zero Net Carbon Emissions.* New York: Public Affairs.

Zak, Paul J. 2012. *The Moral Molecule: The Source of Love and Prosperity.* New York: Dutton.

———. 2014. "Why Your Brain Loves Good Storytelling." *Harvard Business Review.* October 28. Available here: https://hbr.org/2014/10/why-your-brain-loves-good-storytelling.

———. 2017. *Trust Factor: The Science of Creating High-Performance Companies.* New York: American Management Association.

Zwolinski, Matt. 2007. "Sweatshops, Choice, and Exploitation." *Business Ethics Quarterly* 17, 4: 689–727.

———. 2008. "The Ethics of Price Gouging." *Business Ethics Quarterly* 18, 3: 347–78.

INDEX

9 780190 914219